What and where was 'Green Beach'?
Why did one man land there in Canadian
Army uniform when he was neither a
Canadian nor a soldier, under security
conditions so strict that no one was told
his name?

'Green Beach' was the code name for
Pourville, a small seaside town near Dieppe
where, on 19 August 1942, Canadian and
British troops landed in Operation Jubilee,
an essential rehearsal for the D-Day
landings two years later.

Jubilee Force, six thousand strong, had
been set sixteen special objectives;
target 13 was to discover the importance
and accuracy of a German radar station
on the cliff-top just outside the town.
The man in Canadian uniform was a
British radar expert who had volunteered
for this assignment: Jack Maurice
Nissenthall, an RAF flight sergeant from
Bow, in East London.

What happened to him and his bodyguard
in Jubilee's fearful nine hours of fighting
on the sun-burned beaches is one of
the war's strangest episodes, a story of
heroism and ironic humour; one man's
determination to pay a debt of honour to
the country which had given his parents
a home.

GREEN BEACH

James Leasor

CORGI BOOKS
A DIVISION OF TRANSWORLD PUBLISHERS LTD

GREEN BEACH
A CORGI BOOK 0 552 10188 5

Originally published in Great Britain by
William Heinemann Ltd.

PRINTING HISTORY
Heinemann edition published 1975
Corgi edition published 1976

Corgi Books are published by Transworld Publishers Ltd.,
Century House, 61-63 Uxbridge Road,
Ealing, London, W5 5SA
Printed and bound in Canada by
Universal Printers Ltd., Winnipeg, Manitoba

To CHARLES PICK

─ONE─

By the Spring of 1942, the third year of the Second World War, the flood of Axis victories had reached high-tide, and Allied successes could be counted on the fingers of a man who had no hands.

The Nazi empire stretched triumphantly from the French Atlantic coast to the Black Sea, from Arctic to Mediterranean, embracing more than 400,000,000 people. Switzerland was the only remaining European sovereign state between Spain and the Ukraine. In North Africa, the desert lay littered with the detritus of British defeats; that June, Tobruk had surrendered with 33,000 men, including all their arms and stores, to a German force roughly half the size.

In the Far East, a similar calendar of disaster had followed Japan's shattering assault on Singapore, Pearl Harbor, and Hong Kong. In March, Japanese forces landed in New Guinea; then Bataan surrendered and all resistance ceased in Burma. Within days, Japanese bombers raided Calcutta, while her navy bombarded Colombo and threatened the South African coast. Such was the decimation of Allied power in the East that two British and three Dutch submarines faced the impossible task of patrolling the whole Indian Ocean, more than 28,000,000 square miles of disputed sea. In May, Japanese troops crossed India's Eastern frontier, bringing the new fear that they might eventually link up in the Middle East with their German and Italian Axis partners and seize Egypt and Persia.

In Russia, the Germans had reached the outskirts of Moscow, and the Russians admitted casualties of at least

5,000,000 killed or wounded. By July, when Sevastopol and Rostov fell, Nazi Germany occupied half of Russia's mining resources, and her troops stood poised to seize the gigantic Caucasus oil fields. Forty-eight million Russian people were already under Nazi jurisdiction.

The Western Allies were limited by meagre and stretched resources, and by distance, in what aid they could give to Russia. The Royal Navy ran convoys of supplies to Murmansk at enormous cost in casualties; of thirty-five ships comprising convoy PQ17 in July, only twelve reached their destination. And in the Atlantic, German U-Boats were destroying Allied ships faster than replacements could be built. During the first six months of 1942, 989 vessels went down—almost the total tonnage lost during the whole of 1941. So, after nearly three years of war, the only major Allied victories had been won in the Battle of Britain in 1940, and in the snows around Moscow in the following year.

In May 1942, Stalin used his envoy Molotov to warn President Roosevelt that if Hitler threw in more troops against his forces, then the Red Army might not be able to hold out. The threat was clear: events might force Stalin to seek a separate peace with Germany, as Lenin had done in 1917.

'On the other hand,' added Molotov, 'if Great Britain and the United States . . . were to create a new front to draw off forty German divisions, the results could be very different.'[1]

No one would dispute this, but the Western Allies simply did not command enough ships, tanks, planes or even sufficient amphibious strategic skill to mount a serious invasion of *Festung Europa*. Their forces were already fighting in the Western Desert, on the India-Burma border, and in the South Pacific; in Europe they had to rely on bombing raids to relieve German pressure on Russia. But even the effectiveness of these raids was now in doubt.

In the Autumn of 1941, Lord Cherwell (formerly Professor Frederick Lindemann), Churchill's personal scientific adviser,

[1] *The Second World War*, Vol IV by Winston S. Churchill (Cassell).

calculated that only a quarter of the bombs dropped had landed within five miles of their target. Over the Ruhr, Germany's industrial heartland, only one in ten was even as close as this.

The RAF's Bomber Command losses were rapidly approaching bomber production, about 200 a month, and American aircraft allotted to Britain were being divided between Coastal Command and Russia. Bombers were so few that when Bomber Command mounted its 1,000 bomber raid on Cologne in May, Coastal Command and training units were combed to scratch together enough planes.

Alongside this open war of advance and retreat, of planes and ships and tanks and men, another secret war, totally beyond public knowledge or belief, but equally fierce and possibly even more important, was also being waged. This was a war fought in laboratories and radio testing stations, in unlikely factories and guarded, lonely outposts—the war of radar. Its aims were to give early warning of enemy attack, how best to guide planes to their targets, how to seek out intruders from a night or foggy sky. Its troops were scientists, civilians and men and women in uniform.

Whoever won this secret war would also win the open war, and Britain's position was desperate. Convoys, which were her vital source of all supplies, from food to petrol, had to be protected. Next, some means had to be found to diminish the losses to her own bombing aircraft, and at the same time to allow Bomber Command to deliver punishing blows to an Axis that every week seemed to grow stronger and more successful.

Radar was of the utmost importance in these three basic objectives for survival and victory. Any chance, however slim, however dangerous, of discovering exactly how far advanced the enemy might be in the principles of jamming the beams to render the stations useless or adapting them in other ways, must be taken. No opportunity could be lost or allowed to pass by; it would never come again.

Germany and Britain and the United States had experimented with radar since the 1930s. In October 1934, a German scientist, Dr Rudolf Kühnold, was given a government grant equivalent to £11,500 to develop a simple transmitter he had designed. In that same year the RAF staged a mock air attack on London in which only two out of every five attackers were intercepted. To increase this proportion called for a day-and-night standing patrol of defending fighters in the sky, or an extremely efficient early warning system.

On Romney Marsh in Kent, an acoustic wall, 25 feet high and 200 feet long, had been built and embedded with microphones in the hope that they could 'hear' planes from fifteen miles away—in any case twenty miles less than the minimum safe warning distance to allow fighters to be airborne. This instrument could not calculate the height or numbers of approaching aircraft, and all readings could be rendered useless by sounds such as bird song. Once, the driver of a horse-drawn milk float had to remove his vehicle because the clatter of churns interfered with the apparatus.

Such primitive equipment was useless for practical defence purposes, and in a letter to *The Times*, Frederick Lindemann, at that time Professor of Experimental Philosophy at Oxford, criticized the defeatist official attitude to the problem, and urged that 'the whole weight and influence of the Government should be thrown into the scale to endeavour to find a solution'.

Lindemann, a rich bachelor, was a close personal friend of Winston Churchill, who, out of office, was campaigning energetically, but with little success, for improved air defence. Lindemann's criticisms—and similar suggestions from other eminent scientists—finally moved the Government to set up a Committee for the Scientific Survey of Air Defence, under the chairmanship of Sir Henry Tizard, a distinguished scientist with personal flying experience in the First War.

Various proposals, including so-called death-rays, were discussed, but no solution was forthcoming. Then Robert Watson-Watt, a scientist at the Radio Research Station in Slough, working on means of providing advance warnings of thunderstorms, informed the Committee that when an aircraft passed overhead during his experiments, his equipment recorded a 'reflection' from its fuselage. Watson-Watt believed that it should be possible to control and calibrate these readings to provide details of the height, speed, direction —even the numbers—of approaching aircraft. He was encouraged to do further work in this direction, and in February 1935 Watson-Watt was able to 'bounce' a radio signal from an RAF Heyford bomber flying eight miles away at an altitude of 6,000 feet. He was given a grant of £10,000 for more experiments, and, to keep expenses low, he and his team moved to an existing research establishment at Orfordness, on the east coast, where civil airliners flying overhead could provide him with regular 'targets' at no cost to the British Treasury and taxpayer.

By June of that year, Watson-Watt's team could pick up an aircraft seventeen miles away; in July they extended this to forty miles. By August, their equipment showed separate planes flying in formation, and operators could calculate their direction. In the same month, the Germans had a test set working aboard a ship capable of revealing another vessel five miles away, and a coastline from twelve miles.

The British scientists moved to larger premises centred on the manor house at Bawdsey in Suffolk, and a chain of aerials and radio-location stations was sited along the south and east coasts. For security reasons, the description of Radio Direction Finding (RDF) was used to explain these tall latticed masts, but the initials actually stood for Range and Direction Finding. The American reversible word RADAR, Radio Direction and Ranging, came later.

Nazi Germany, fearing no aggression from any other country, developed new radar equipment that would help guide their bombers on to distant targets. The British, realizing how vulnerable their island was to attack, concentrated their activities on building a radar defence system. When war broke out in 1939, both countries were advanced in their own special fields. Neither side realized the extent of the other's progress in radar, and assumed that they did not possess it; or, if they did, then only in a simple and relatively ineffective form.

In November 1939, the British Naval Attaché in Oslo received an anonymous letter which quite literally changed the whole course of this secret war. The writer declared that if the British genuinely wanted to know the extent of German scientific progress relating to the war then the preamble to BBC German broadcasts should be altered in a certain way.

This strange document was passed to Dr Reginald Jones who, as a student, had worked under Lord Cherwell at Oxford and was then in Air Intelligence.

Dr Jones arranged for the broadcast to be altered, and shortly afterwards a parcel was left anonymously at the Embassy in Oslo, and forwarded on to him. It contained astonishing information about rockets, rocket engines, glider bombs and other research being carried out at Peenemünde on an island in the Baltic. Details were also given of magnetic torpedoes, and methods used by German aircrews to calculate their position by means of special radio transmissions. And there was mention of a radar station that had detected RAF bombers from a distance of seventy-five miles.

Dr Jones checked all he could with other sources of information and found it to be accurate. So, against considerable scepticism from the Admiralty, he decided to treat the information seriously, and by the early summer of 1940 he was able to prove that while British bombers were still navigating largely by compass and the stars, German bombers were guided to their targets by radio beams and were advised by radio when to release their bombs.

Despite this proof, many British authorities were reluctant to accept the uncomfortable fact that the German radar system could possibly be as far advanced as their own.

Teams of British scientists meanwhile worked desperately to produce a radar with an extremely narrow beam not yards, not feet or inches, but only centimetres wide. This would have enormous advantages. The sets would possess vastly increased precision, and, instead of using aerial masts between 250 and 350 feet high, they would only need very small aerials—for radar aerials employed carefully spaced metal rods each exactly half the length of the waves they transmitted.

German scientists, who had also been seeking the same ultimate accuracy, abandoned further serious research after Hitler decreed in 1940 that since the war was as good as won, work in this extremely costly, complex and frustrating centimetre or microwave field was unnecessary, and so would cease. The British persevered out of desperation, the threat of German invasion adding urgency to their efforts, and in February of that same year, Professor J. T. Randall and Dr H. A. H. Boot, two scientists working in Birmingham University laboratories, devised a valve known as the cavity magnetron.

The magnetron was in appearance a circular piece of metal, the size of a telephone earpiece, with eight holes punched around a centre cavity and edged with fins to dissipate the terrific heat it generated. Its unique ability to transmit micro-waves at very high power enabled radar equipment to be built that was infinitely more powerful and accurate than anything previously designed—and far smaller. Radar sets could now be built into planes—to 'see' other aircraft or targets on the ground. The cavity magnetron with its vital applications gave Britain a big lead in radar, and in 1940, when Britain stood alone, Churchill used this priceless knowledge as a lever to persuade the United States, then still neutral, to help with their vast production potential.

American scientists were at first sceptical about the high claims made for the cavity magnetron, but its fantastic performance impressed them so deeply that they immediately recommended total co-operation with British scientists. James Phinney Baxter III, the official American scientific historian, later described it as 'the most valuable cargo ever brought to our shores', and 'the single most important item in reverse lease-lend'. Obviously, no inkling of the cavity magnetron could be allowed to reach Germany, for on the briefest description, their scientists would be able to design and build one—with calamitous results for the Allies.

In July 1940, six months after the invention of the cavity magnetron, Dr Jones received an abstract of a confidential Luftwaffe report describing how German fighters had been able to intercept British reconnaissance planes through the *Freya-Meldung*—the Freya warning.

Was Freya the code word for a secret radar?

The same source later reported that a Freya was in use at Lannion, on the north coast of Brittany, guarded by a ring of anti-aircraft guns. Dr Jones researched the meaning of the name Freya. She was the German goddess of beauty, love and fertility, who had been unfaithful to her husband in order to gain a precious necklace. Heimdal, the sentry of the gods, protected this necklace for her—and *Heimdal could see for one hundred miles by day or night*. Might this not also describe a radar that could locate aircraft from a similar distance? The reference to seventy-five miles in the Oslo report came immediately to mind.

Aerial photographs did not produce any satisfactory pictures of such a radar, but agents reported that two Würzburg sets, precise but short-range instruments named after the old Bavarian university town, and already known to Dr Jones, were being moved to Bulgaria, with a Freya, for coastal defence. This suggested that the two types of set might be used in conjunction; that the Freya could cover a radius of around sixty miles and the Würzburg, about twenty-three. Gradually, a mosaic picture of German radar was built up. Throughout 1941, information on Freya stations came in regularly. By the end of the year, twenty-seven were believed to be in action along the Atlantic coast between Bodö and Bordeaux. Aerial photographs of Bruneval, on the north coast of France between Le Havre and Dieppe, showed a track trodden along the cliff from known Freya aerials towards a black dot—believed to be a Würzburg—between the headquarters building and the cliff. It was decided to raid Bruneval, dismantle this Würzburg equipment and bring it back for examination.

Lord Louis Mountbatten, at that time Adviser to Combined Operations, and within weeks due to become Chief of Combined Operations, decided on a brilliant scheme which proved totally successful. An experienced RAF radar technician, Flight Sergeant C. W. H. Cox, was dropped with paratroops to dismantle the equipment. Commandos assaulted the German garrison from the beach while Cox, working furiously in darkness inside the radar station, sawed and cut and eventually pulled vital parts of equipment from their mountings. These were then wheeled down to the beach on a specially designed trolley, and transferred to Royal Naval landing craft which took off the paratroops, the Commandos and Flight Sergeant Cox. The whole scheme worked perfectly, an excellent example of co-operation between the three services, an operation in which their talents, skills and courage were completely combined.

Dr Jones now calculated that the Freya picked up the planes, maybe as far as one hundred miles away, and fed them into the jaws of the Würzburg, which passed on the information to fighter aircraft controllers. Once the German early warning system was known, its success in seeking out bombers from the night sky could be weakened or totally nullified by jamming—a technique producing a mass of meaningless flickering dots on the operators' screens. But Britain, as a small island, was much more vulnerable to jamming should the Germans retaliate.

Lord Cherwell and Sir Charles Portal, the Chief of the Air Staff, were reluctant to jam German radar until an antidote had been developed against possible German retaliation. Bomber Command and the Deputy Chief of Air Staff, Air Vice-Marshal Sir Norman Bottomley, and Dr Jones urged its immediate use. Beset by such distinguished opposing opinions, the War Cabinet decided to delay a decision. In the meantime, it was absolutely vital to learn everything possible about German radar installations—and especially if they were equipped with sophisticated anti-jamming devices.

In 1941, listening posts on Beachy Head opposite Dieppe received signals quite definitely emanating from a new and higher-powered Freya. By calculating the source of the beam, and by air reconnaissance, the station was located on a clifftop, between Dieppe and the village of Pourville two miles to the west.

The total success of the Bruneval raid had posed an unexpected problem for others who sought to learn more secrets from German radar stations by raiding them and bringing back equipment. The Germans had increased the defences of all their stations against any further attacks. They had ringed them with wire, which incidentally made them easier to locate in aerial photograph. The wire prevented rabbits eating grass within the entanglements, which showed up more clearly in these pictures.

Surprise and brilliant planning had secured success at Bruneval. Neither of these qualities would be sufficient for any further attack to learn the secrets of other radar stations by direct reconnaissance, yet it was essential that these secrets should be uncovered. British Intelligence knew that Germany possessed several radar systems working on different frequencies. The Würzburg and Mannheims were on 600 Megahertz, the Seetakt on 375 MHZ and the Freya on 125 MHZ.

Britain was already developing a secret stand-by system, AMES (Air Ministry Experimental Station) Type 11, working on the known German wavelengths, so that should Germany jam British radar, this could immediately come into operation. Clearly the Germans would never diminish their own defences by interfering with their own wavebands.

Could Germany possess another secret radar chain, working possibly in the 250 MHZ band and hitherto unknown, that could instantly be brought into action if the existing Freya early warning system were jammed?

There was no evidence that such a radar existed, although there was abundant evidence of the other types. Nevertheless, if the Freya stations were jammed, and a completely unexpected precision early warning radar on this frequency came into action, British scientists would have shown their hand to no avail.

Early tests showed that the Freya of that period was a relatively precise early warning instrument, but its plotting accuracy left something to be desired. It lacked the ability to calculate the height of aircraft and had no equivalent of the British PPI—Planned Position Indicator—which could record the position of incoming planes.

16

If the Freya and the Würzburg were to work successfully together, the Würzburg would have to recognize almost immediately any target that the Freya disclosed. Yet the wide beam of the original Freya would not allow this close co-operation because, under long-range conditions, their plots might have an error of between ten and twenty miles. It was thus crucial to examine the Freya as well as the Würzburg, and to find out whether it had been significantly modified since the Allies had first discovered its existence. Only then could the best means of neutralizing it be agreed, and a definite answer provided to nagging fears about a third radar system.

The nearest Freya was still the station built on the cliff west of Dieppe, and only sixty-seven miles from the English south coast. It was imperative that a radar expert examined this apparatus closely—but how?

Only an experienced scientist could tell instantly whether it was fitted with anti-jamming equipment, and, if so, how effective this could be. Only he could calculate the accuracy of the set and report the extent and importance of any modifications.

If any Commando raid or similar landing on this coast were planned, then one of its top priorities must be to escort such a radar expert to the Freya, in the hope that he would return with answers to these vital questions.

During these months the public in the United States and Britain, under adroit local Communist Party pressure, and knowing nothing of the intricacies and logistics of invasion but genuinely eager to help Russia, vociferously continued to demand a Second Front—now. President Roosevelt told Molotov: 'We expect the formation of a Second Front this year.' But how was this to be achieved?

The last large Allied sea-borne invasion, at Gallipoli in the 1914–1918 war, had been a fiasco. Another similar disaster was unthinkable; there had already been too many defeats and debacles elsewhere. American and British planners therefore considered, and then discarded, a number of possibilities within the limited means the Allies then possessed.

In March 1942, Churchill appointed Lord Mountbatten Chief of Combined Operations, and with the First Sea Lord, the Chief of the Imperial General Staff and the Chief of the Air Staff, he was also a member of the Chiefs of Staff Committee. Mountbatten's particular brief from the Prime Minister was to devise techniques for amphibious landings, to design whatever special vessels and vehicles, appurtenances and appliances might be needed for the invasion, and to see that they were produced in sufficient numbers, and to train soldiers, sailors and airmen to work together as an integrated team in Combined Operations.

While he prepared long-term plans for the main invasion with General Sir Bernard Paget, the Commander-in-Chief of British Home Forces, he also organized Commando raids in order to perfect the techniques of landing on enemy occupied coasts, to give positive evidence to the people of occupied Europe that they had cause to hope for eventual liberation, and to force the Nazis to maintain more troops in Western France than they wished to do, in view of the heavy demand for reinforcements on the Russian front. Not until the early summer of 1942 did Mountbatten have sufficient landing craft and other vessels to transport a division for a simultaneous assault. Then it was important to try out these craft under active service conditions, to discover at first hand the worst that could happen when a flotilla of landing craft approached an enemy-held coast in the dark.

In March, Mountbatten had conceived a daring raid on St Nazaire, to destroy the huge dock—the only one along the whole Atlantic coast capable of repairing the mighty German battleship *Tirpitz*, then lying at Trondheim. This raid was successful; the dock was blown up so effectively that it could not be used again throughout the war, and the *Tirpitz* never ventured out into the Atlantic. Surely a rather more ambitious raid on the French coast could be attempted with equal prospects of triumph—both political and military?

The target would have to be within reach of British fighter cover, and it should be a major port. Cherbourg and Le Havre were too large and too heavily defended. Long-range guns at

Boulogne could command all approaches for a twenty-five mile radius. Caen was too far inland, and Fécamp was too small. Finally, the choice fell on Dieppe, once the greatest port in France, from which, in 1066, a Norman fleet had set out to invade England.

Mountbatten therefore instructed his staff to draw up a plan for a raid on Dieppe, specifically avoiding a frontal assault. The beach was covered with shingle and had a very steep incline from the sea, with a sheer wall at the top which could prove difficult for tanks to surmount. Mountbatten's plan therefore called for one battalion of infantry and one battalion of Churchill tanks to land at Quiberville, six miles west of Dieppe, where the beach was more suitable for tracked vehicles.

They would have two objectives: the local Luftwaffe airfield, and the high cliffs west of Dieppe, from which guns could command the town. At the same time, two other battalions would land at Pourville, two miles from Dieppe, still on the west side, and two more battalions would land at Puys, a mile east of Dieppe, leaving two battalions still at sea as a reserve force to be deployed if necessary.

Lord Mountbatten discussed this project with the Chiefs of Staff, and obtained the Prime Minister's enthusiastic approval. Field-Marshal Sir Alan Brooke, Chief of the Imperial General Staff, was adamant that the Home Forces should deal with planning involving the Army, for the number of troops involved would obviously be far greater than the relatively few Commandos whose previous raids had been planned by Combined Operations.

Mountbatten had intended to use the Royal Marine Division and Commandos, who were well trained for such an assignment. But this raid presented an ideal opportunity to involve a model, tight-knit volunteer army, which for two years had been training continuously in Southern England and was ardent for action: the Second Canadian Division.

Their leaders knew what was planned and personally urged the Chief of the Imperial General Staff to use their troops for this landing. Mountbatten did not wish to do so; he had used

Royal Marines and Commandos with great success at St Nazaire and on other raids before, and knew exactly what they could achieve. The Canadians were magnificent troops, no doubt, but they had not yet been in serious action, and a raid like this was not the occasion to test their mettle.

Since they had arrived in Britain in 1940, some Canadian units had taken part in minor operations, but nothing that had been really worthy of them. They had sailed from Canada to help frustrate a German invasion of Britain that had not taken place. Now they had been away from home for nearly two years, and some felt that they might as well have remained in Canada.

So, after consultation with the Allies, it was agreed that the Canadians would form the main contingent for an attack on Dieppe to take place after a tremendous aerial bombardment, under a protective umbrella of fighters, and with strong airborne and naval support.

The Canadians in Britain served under General Bernard Montgomery in South Eastern Command. General Sir Bernard Paget, the Commander-in-Chief of British Home Forces, therefore delegated to Montgomery and the Canadian senior officers the responsibility for the plan involving the land forces. These Army planners did not agree with Combined Operations' plan on the grounds that Quiberville was six miles from Dieppe, and separated from it by two rivers. If the Germans blew either or both bridges, the tanks could not reach Dieppe. They therefore insisted that tanks must land much nearer the harbour, involving a frontal assault on Dieppe.

Late in April, Lord Mountbatten called a meeting to discuss the two plans. He was still very strongly against a frontal attack, but the Army maintained that heavy bombing of defences immediately before the landing craft came in, with low-flying aerial attacks afterwards, would neutralize the risks. Since Sir Alan Brooke had given authority to the Home Forces to mount their plan, Mountbatten had to agree with this majority proposal.

In June, he flew to Washington on the Prime Minister's

instructions to discuss future overall strategy with President Roosevelt and the United States Joint Chiefs of Staff. While he was away, the Force Commanders met, with General Montgomery taking the chair, and decided to dispense with the intense bombing preliminary to the raid. The Military Force Commander, Major-General John Hamilton Roberts, a Canadian professional soldier who had served in the Canadian army since 1914, feared that bombing would choke Dieppe's narrow streets with rubble and so prevent the tanks from using them. The Air Force Commander, Air Vice-Marshal Sir Trafford Leigh-Mallory, thought that preliminary bombing would only alert the enemy, and the bombers could be put to better use in diversionary attacks.

When Mountbatten returned from Washington, he learned of this decision and voiced his doubts to Sir Alan Brooke, who insisted that the Army Commanders must be allowed to do things their way. On June 30, the Prime Minister held a final discussion on the Dieppe raid, which was then timed to take place around July 5, when tides and moon would be favourable.

Lord Mountbatten explained to Churchill the important part that Captain Hughes-Hallett, his Chief Naval Planner, had taken in drawing up plans for the raid, and Churchill immediately asked Hughes-Hallett whether he could guarantee success. Before Hughes-Hallett could answer, Sir Alan Brooke interrupted.

'If he, or anyone else could guarantee success, there would indeed be no object in doing the operation. It is just because no one has the slightest idea what the outcome will be that the operation is necessary,' he said. Churchill replied that this was not a moment at which he wanted to be taught by adversity.

'In that case,' Brooke replied, 'you must abandon the idea of invading France, because no responsible general will be associated with any planning for invasion until we have an operation at least the size of the Dieppe raid behind us to study and base our plans upon.'

The Chief of the Imperial General Staff made it clear that

if there was no raid, there could be no Second Front. On this basis, Churchill agreed that the operation must go forward. Mountbatten still remained extremely critical of a frontal assault without maximum aerial bombardment, and to compensate for the lack of preliminary bombing, he asked the First Sea Lord to provide heavy support from battleships or cruisers. This was refused on the grounds that heavy naval gunfire would merely increase the debris in the streets which the Army so specifically wished to avoid.

So authority was given for the raid to go on. Its code name, Rutter, chosen simply because it was next on a list of code names, meant a mercenary horse-soldier. This was ironic, for the Canadians were all volunteers, with not a horse among them.

They were given sixteen objectives: to destroy enemy defences around Dieppe; to attack the airfield at St Aubin some miles inland; to blow up power stations and petrol dumps, docks and rail-heads; to remove secret documents from local German divisional headquarters, and papers from several officers' messes; to bring back invasion barges moored in Dieppe harbour; to capture German soldiers and release certain Frenchmen held captive in a Dieppe prison.

They were also to escort a radar expert to the Freya radar station outside Pourville. This was Target Thirteen, and could only be assigned to a man without superstition, for it called for unusual qualities and a special kind of courage.

First, this unknown scientist must be fit enough to take part in an opposed landing at dawn, then climb the cliffs under ferocious defensive fire and reach this station where defences had been heavily increased since the raid on Bruneval. Next, he needed such a wide knowledge of radar that he would know instantly how to gauge the set's performance and capabilities. But anyone qualified to cope with this unprecedented situation would presumably know so much about British radar secrets that he could not possibly be captured. The printed orders issued to senior officers detailing the South Saskatchewan Regiment, due to land at Pourville (code name Green

Beach), to guard him, therefore added laconically: '*S.Sask. R, to provide adequate protection, as RDF expert must under no circumstances fall into enemy hands.*'

What this meant in simple terms was surely that if they could not bring this specialist back alive, then his escort must ensure he stayed there—dead. This, at least, was how the orders were immediately translated. But what kind of scientist would volunteer for such a mission on these grim uncompromising terms?

In Edwardian days, the house outside Leighton Buzzard in Bedfordshire had been considered one of the most attractive in the area. On summer afternoons, there would be tea and croquet on the barbered lawns, and muted laughter from women playing tennis in voluminous skirts. The long drive had been raked regularly every morning then, and tame peacocks spread their iridescent plumage to the admiration of the guests.

In the twenties, the house had still boasted a butler, a housekeeper, two maids and three gardeners. This staff diminished in the thirties to a living-in maid, a good daily and a man who 'did' the garden on three days a week. Now, the lawns and shrubberies were overgrown. Flowerbeds teemed with insolent weeds. Fifteen-hundredweight RAF trucks in drab blue paint waited in rows on the cracked, oil-stained tennis courts.

This house formed part of the headquarters of Sixty Group, the heart of the RAF's radar establishment. In what had formerly been a guest bedroom, with chintz curtains to match the wallpaper, metal filing cabinets now stood on bare floorboards, and a middle-aged RAF officer, his uniform unbuttoned, pipe in hand, was speaking to a colleague in the Air Ministry in London over a scrambler telephone.

'He'll only have minutes to do his stuff, and remember, he's got to climb that cliff about 300 feet up before he can even start.'

'I know all that,' said the voice impatiently at the other end of the line. 'All *you* have to do is to give us a name.'

'What about Flight Sergeant Cox? He did the Bruneval job very successfully.'

'Surely enough is enough? We'll put his name forward, but let me have another name, too.'

'Hold on.'

The officer was opening a file as he spoke, thumbing through typed sheets of confidential records. It was irrelevant to him whether the man selected was married with children, or single with old parents—or was it? Suddenly, he felt uneasy as he picked over the pages, for he guessed that the man he chose was already as good as dead. He could easily give his colleague in London one name and let another stay, and no one would ever know; only *he* would know. His pipe had gone out; he did not rekindle it.

'You still with me?' asked the voice irritably at the other end of the line.

'Still here. We've looked over a lot of possibilities, but there's one chap who seems to fit the bill absolutely. He's already volunteered to Squadron Leader Keir of 78 Wing Headquarters at Ashburton for any dangerous operation involving radar, so that gives him a head start. He seems mad keen, is fit as a PTI[1] and absolutely first-class technically. Suggested all kinds of mods we've used in circuits, and so on. Number is 916592. Name of Jack Maurice Nissenthall. Flight Sergeant.'

'Where is he now?'

'GCI station, Hope Cove, in Devon.'

'Thanks. He won't be there tomorrow.'

A knock at the door; an orderly carried in a cup of tea and put it down on his desk. The middle-aged officer nodded his thanks, and walked to the window and stood looking out over the rolling parkland, above the weathercock on the stable, the unpainted garage doors, the tufted grass sprouting in the cracked yard. He felt a totally unusual distaste for himself and for his job. Why did *he* have to be the one to select a man for a task like this?

[1] Physical Training Instructor.

On paper, the candidate's qualifications seemed ideal. He had worked in radio and TV since his teens in the EMI factory at Hayes, and then in London. He had taken an advanced course in these subjects at the Regent Street Polytechnic at a time when TV was widely considered to be only a passing craze. He was so enthusiastic about radar that he had even worked without pay at week-ends in the experimental radar station at Bawdsey. He had volunteered for aircrew when war was declared, but because of his knowledge and background, he had been posted to RAF Yatesbury to assist in setting up the first top secret RDF school. Subsequently he had served on radar stations as far apart as the north of Scotland and South Devon. He had once volunteered for Commando training, simply out of enthusiasm, willingly foregoing leave to spend the time instead at a special Army training camp in Scotland.

He was unmarried, tough, fit and right on top of his job—to the extent that the regular modifications and improvements he suggested for radar equipment and techniques were invariably incorporated. He was undoubtedly the best man for the task. Yet, in other ways, some would consider him a most unlikely choice. He was the son of a Jewish tailor who had emigrated to England from Poland. He had been born a Cockney in the East End of London, and he was still only twenty-four.

A squad of young RAF men came marching smartly up the drive. Not many of them would be more than twenty-four, thought the middle-aged officer reflectively. And he wondered what chance his nominee would have of reaching his twenty-fifth birthday.

Jack Nissenthall was washing, stripped to the waist, in a bucket of cold water outside his mobile ops room at Hope Cove, in South Devon, when he heard the roar of approaching aircraft. This was nothing new, for four squadrons of Spitfires were stationed nearby. But suddenly the ground trembled with the thump, thump of bombs exploding. Jack wiped soap from his eyes and peered up at the sky. All around, trucks and trailers were parked under brown-and-green camouflage nets, while above him, four German Focke-Wulf 190s were already turning for another low-level run over the station. Jack leapt sideways beneath the nearest vehicle as they dived, spraying the hedges with bullets. Then they were away, the noise of their engines diminishing down the sky as they flew south across the Channel. On every side, men were shouting orders, cursing, calling to each other. Jack's Orderly Room Sergeant, Bill Powell, formerly a policeman in Shanghai, who viewed all human behaviour with the cynical approach of one who has exposed too many of its secrets, crossed over to him.

'You all right, Flight?' he asked Jack.

'Just.'

'Lucky for you, then, mate. Your air raid shelter was a flaming petrol bowser! Hardly the place I'd choose. We've got a movement order for you. You're being posted to Air Ministry Unit, RAF Long Cross. With effect from today.'

Long Cross was the name of a small camp near Egham in Surrey, to which RAF men with special qualifications or technical knowledge were sometimes posted to await further orders.

A shave, then into his number one uniform, with his overnight kit packed, and Jack was on the train to Egham. He was tallish and very slim, with unusually fair hair. He spoke with a slight Cockney accent, and had a way of moving his hands expressively as he talked. His hands were strong, like a surgeon's, and he possessed a remarkable patience with temperamental electrical apparatus which he did not always bestow on temperamental people.

As he sat in the empty compartment, he wondered what awaited him at Long Cross. Sometimes he was posted briefly to other radar stations around the coast to carry out tests or modifications; no doubt this was a similar job. He smiled inwardly as he recalled the last such trip he had made. A Beaufighter pilot had landed late one night on the runway behind his station and asked to speak to him privately.

'You've a bloody fine radar beacon here,' he told Jack. 'I

can pick it up eighty miles out to sea. The one at my station, Predannock, barely reaches twenty-five miles.'

'That's a problem for your own radar man, then,' Jack replied.

'We haven't got one,' the pilot explained. 'Only an electrician. He does his best, but that's no help to us. We have to fly for our full endurance miles out to sea, and time and again we only scrape home by the skin of our teeth with a smell of petrol in our tanks. If we can't get that beacon working better, some of us are going to end up in the drink. Could you fly up with me and have a gander at it?'

Jack suggested the pilot tried the 'correct channels'—making a complaint to Wing, and asking for a radar mechanic to examine the set. The pilot shook his head.

'By the time they get weaving, the war will be over.'

So finally Jack agreed to help him—on the strict promise that he could be back in time to go on duty at 1800 hours on the following evening.

They set off next morning in the Beaufighter and Jack found that the problem lay with the radar aerial and its mode of connection. He had brought his own home-made test equipment, and carefully turned the transmitter/receiver combination. Now he needed to test the beacon by flying around it, but before he could do so the squadron was briefed to go on an immediate emergency shipping escort operation.

'Don't worry, Flight,' the pilot assured him. 'You fly with me as observer and then we can test the beacon on the way home.'

So Jack borrowed some warm flying clothes and they took off into the clouds. After an hour's flying and still in thick cloud, they had not sighted any of their comrades, but the pilot assured him that soon they would. A further half an hour passed and still nothing. Then Jack caught a glimpse of two single-engined fighters disappearing into cloud too far ahead to identify them, and reported this to the pilot.

'You must be mistaken,' he replied. 'We're too far south over the sea for any single-engined planes.'

Then they both saw what seemed to be other Beaufighters

27

ahead of them and, far beneath, toy ships turning in a white wash. The pilot nosed down towards the Beaufighters and then turned away, laughing over the intercom.

'What's up?' Jack asked him.

'You'll be interested to hear we almost joined the Luftwaffe! Those planes in front of us aren't Beaus—they're JU 88s.'

The ships steamed steadily towards England with their Beaufighters behind them, and with the JU 88s higher up behind them. And far above them all, the two single-engined planes that Jack had spotted—Focke-Wulf 190s. Jack expected the enemy aircraft to attack at any moment, but they all flew on peacefully; maybe they had also mistaken the RAF plane for one of their own.

'This must be the only time the Luftwaffe have escorted Royal Navy ships back to base,' the pilot assured him as they landed at Hope Cove. Once was enough, Jack thought now, watching the patchwork fields flash past the windows of his train. . . .

Over the past year, he had built up one of Britain's most successful night fighter stations from literally nothing more than a map reference, in the middle of a field of cows. This station, near Hope Cove, specialized in ground controlled interception—GCI—by which operators in the radar station gave navigational instructions to the pilots that guided them on to the enemy. The operators could 'see' both the RAF planes and the bombers on their radar screens—and so could control the night fighters by giving them the course, position, height and speed necessary to intercept the intruders.

Jack's interest in radio and TV circuitry went back to his boyhood. Anything involving 'electronics' was not work but an absorbing, unending pleasure. During his two years in the RAF he had suggested so many valuable modifications to radar equipment that his friends had nicknamed him 'The GCI King'.

A few hours later, at Long Cross, he received orders to present himself at the Air Ministry in London to Air Commodore Victor Tait, the RAF's Director of Radar.

Victor Tait was a big bluff Canadian of forty-nine, who had been an ice-hockey player of Olympic standard. He held a Bachelor of Science degree from the University of Manitoba, and after joining the Canadian Army in the First World War, had transferred to the Royal Flying Corps, specializing in wireless and signals duties. In 1919, he accepted a permanent commission in the RAF, and in a varied career had once been seconded to command the Egyptian Air Force.

His office overlooked Whitehall; a high ceilinged room with big windows, rather a change from the mobile ops room in the back of a Crossley truck with which Jack was more familiar. The windows were criss-crossed with sticky tape against bomb blast, and through them Jack could see two grey barrage balloons, part of the city's air defences, turn their huge elephant ears in the summer sky.

'I understand,' said Tait, 'that you have put your name down for any special operation involving radar.'

Jack nodded. 'That's right, sir.'

This was not quite what he had expected to discuss—but then Tait would not have asked to see him simply to chew the fat about vetting some distant radar station. Jack listened attentively as the air commodore continued.

'Even if the odds might be weighed against you coming through safely?'

'Air-crew accept that risk every day and night, sir.'

'Quite so. Well, we require a volunteer with a very specialized knowledge of radar to take part in a raid on the French coast that's now being planned.'

'You mean like Flight Sergeant Cox at Bruneval?'

'Something similar. But instead of being mounted *specifically* to deal with a German station, the present task will only be one part of a much larger operation. If you volunteered, while you would, of course, be given a team of soldiers to help you carry out your task, you will appreciate that your knowledge of our radar is far too valuable to be compromised. Their orders would therefore have to be that, because you do know so much, you could not be allowed to fall alive into enemy hands.'

Nissenthall sat in silence. He had guessed the reason for this terrible condition—his involvement with centimetre radar and the cavity magnetron. He fully understood its crucial importance to the Allies and accepted the fact that its existence could not under any circumstances be revealed to the enemy.

'This raid has the highest importance,' Tait went on, 'and we expect the fighting will be very fierce. Which is why we need a volunteer who is extremely fit physically and top of the form in his job—not always an easy combination to find. But Sixty Group have submitted your name, and you seem well qualified. Of course, in view of the hazardous nature of the operation we can only accept a volunteer. I'm sorry I can't tell you more about it.'

The Air Commodore glanced down briefly at Jack's service record that lay on the desk in front of him, and then looked up at him.

'I am not asking for a definite answer now,' he said. 'Think about it tonight, and report to me here tomorrow morning at eleven o'clock with your decision. And if you change your mind meanwhile, I will quite understand.'

'Very good, sir.'

Jack saluted and made his way out of the office. He was puzzled. Had Air Commodore Tait suddenly read something in his papers that he had not seen before—and this had made him decide to offer Jack the chance of changing his mind? The fact that Jack was Jewish would no doubt be noted in his personal file among all the other details of age, height, date of enlistment and various postings. He wondered whether Tait had seen this for the first time, and so was understandably hesitant about sending a Jew on a special mission to occupied France?

Still thinking about this, Jack went downstairs to the security office near the entrance, where three middle-aged officers from the Army, Navy and Air Force, unfit for more active service, sat behind a long table covered by a grey blanket. He had to leave a form with them which he had signed when he entered the building, giving his name, rank and service number, and the officer he wished to see. As Jack saluted, a telephone on the table rang and he heard an ADC telling the RAF officer that Jack would return on the following morning, and meanwhile would require a twenty-four hour ration card. The officer turned to his colleagues.

'Flight sergeant's reporting back tomorrow about eleven,' he explained. 'Some special job.'

The Army captain grunted. Jack waited while his name, rank and service number were copied on to a ration card, then he saluted and turned to leave. As he reached the door, he heard him remark grumpily to his colleagues: 'You'd think they could find someone better than a *Jew* for a special job, wouldn't you, whatever it is?"

Jack felt sick, as though someone had punched him in the stomach. He balled his fists instinctively and rose on tiptoe, and then he relaxed, trembling with suppressed rage. Only the knowledge that he would face a certain court-martial stopped him from turning round and striking the officer who had insulted him. If he was court-martialled, he would clearly be found guilty, especially with two witnesses, to what they would consider an inexplicable and totally unprovoked attack. If that happened, he would miss this raid—but why the hell should he care about that? If these people thought so little of him, why should he risk his life for them? But, of course, it wasn't just for them, and if this argument was carried further, why should anyone risk anything for anyone else? And the captain's view was only his own; it was the first time Jack had heard anyone in any service refer to him slightingly because he was Jewish.

He hesitated for a moment, and then walked out of the building, past the brick bomb-blast wall outside and the protective piles of whitewashed sandbags around the door, pondering the irony of his situation. One moment, an officer asked him to volunteer for a mission so delicate that he must agree to be killed rather than captured—and at the same time, another sneered at him because he was a Jew! As he walked, he remembered words that he had so often heard at evening service every Friday when he would go to the synagogue with his father: 'May it be thy will, O Lord, my God, and God of my fathers, to deliver me this day, and every day, from arrogant men and from arrogance, from a bad man, from a bad companion and from a bad neighbour, and from any mishap, and from the adversary that destroyeth . . .'

He felt comforted by the ancient prayer of his people, and determined to prove to his own satisfaction that Tait could not find anyone better than a Jew for his special mission; and presumably he could not, otherwise Jack would not have been asked.

Jack walked along Whitehall, past the grey metal emergency water tanks set up to supply fire engines after incendiary raids, hardly noticing the sandbagged doorways, and the familiar posters: Is your journey really necessary?

He crossed Trafalgar Square, where newly-arrived American soldiers were photographing English girls with Veronica Lake hair-styles as they fed fluttering pigeons, and went on up Charing Cross Road and into Leicester Square. There he sat down thankfully on a bench in the sun. He felt tired. He had been on night duty for a week and had missed a day's sleep in coming to London. As soon as he arrived at Waterloo he had telephoned his mother at her home in Ealing, and explained that he was unexpectedly in London and would be home for the night. She was delighted, and told him that his girl-friend, Adeline Bernard—known to all the family as Dell —had just called to say she had been given tickets for the new Greer Garson film, *Mrs Miniver*, at the Empire cinema in Leicester Square. They had arranged to meet in the foyer, so it was not worth Jack going back to Ealing; he could sit in the Square until they arrived.

Dell was a pretty, dark-haired vivacious girl with a great sense of fun. Like Jack, she was keen on outdoor sports, especially swimming and netball. She had gone to school in the East End of London only half a mile away from where he had been brought up, and then had qualified as a short-hand typist. Her first job had been at the Ministry of Production in the Strand as secretary to the regional director; then she had moved to Mrs Churchill's Aid-to-Russia Fund in Carlton House Terrace, a few doors from the Foreign Secretary's official house.

Jack had known her for some years, but although they shared so many interests, they had not become engaged. The war had made the future too uncertain. They were close, of course, and when Jack had been stationed in Scotland, and found it impossible to telephone her because lines were busy, he would sometimes quite unofficially give his emergency code word 'Priority Urgent' to the operator so that a line could be made available. Dell, like his mother, knew he was engaged on some unusual work, but the rule of secrecy about radar was so strict that neither had any idea whatever of the real nature and importance of his duties.

What would Dell or his mother think if they knew he had agreed impulsively to go on some overseas raid about which he had been told nothing except that he could not be taken prisoner? They would say he was mad. And perhaps they would be right. Surely it was to safeguard such spontaneous decisions that the unwritten rule in all three services should be obeyed: never volunteer for *anything*?

As so often when he had a problem to face, a decision to make, Jack found himself wondering what his father would have done, what advice he would have given him. For although his father had been dead for two years, he recalled him as one of the main influences on his life.

Jack's father had been a remarkable man—cheerful, resourceful, almost fanatically patriotic—and, as he described himself, in the old-fashioned way, an 'anti-Bolshevik'. He was one of seven brothers and two sisters born in Poland, where he had worked as a young man in the family timber mill in the forest outside Vilna. They had been a tough, healthy crowd, who spent a considerable amount of their time in the saddle. Horses were their life and their off-duty enjoyment, and when winter snow halted tree-felling, he and his brothers prepared the horses they had bred during the rest of the year for the long trip across the frozen Vistula; for Jack's grandfather had an agreement with the German military authorities on the far bank to supply stallions to the German army.

As a boy, Jack had often sat on his father's knee, close up to a roaring fire in their house in Cottage Road, Bow, while he told him stories of that time in his thick accent. They would all look forward to the journey, camping each night in the silent snow, until they delivered the horses to their new masters, and then they invariably enjoyed a friendly riding contest and a boisterous party with the Kaiser's cavalrymen before they returned. He was a wise, kindly man who never tired of answering Jack's constant stream of questions.

Jack's father and his younger brother Max had come to England in the early years of the century to escape the pogroms in Poland, and he had set up as a tailor in the East End of London. His business had prospered and, while he never forgot the country of his birth, he constantly acknowledged his great debt to England, the country that had given him freedom and a chance to succeed.

One of Jack's earliest memories was being lectured on the merits of the wonderful country in which he had been fortunate enough to be born. Another vital memory was holding hands with his elder sister, Marie, waving a small Union Jack, and marching with a long stream of children to celebrate Empire Day, in what seemed to be an enormous playground in Malmesbury Road School in Bow. This ceremony, where the senior boys and girls lined up to play 'Rule, Britannia', always ended with the whole school singing 'Land of Hope and Glory', and made an indelible impression on his mind. Jack's father wisely did not neglect to point out another side to life in Britain in the 1920s. He explained the reasons behind the General Strike, and took his son to see troops in the streets and volunteers driving the open-topped, solid-tyred 'buses.

If his father were still alive, Jack was convinced he would have only one word of advice to give him about his mission: 'Go!'

Jack's own boyhood heroes had been aviators like Captain Albert Ball, VC, the First World War fighter pilot. Jack had made model aeroplanes as soon as he could use a pair of scissors, and had collected every book about gallantry in the First War that he could borrow or buy. He kept them all in a little collection of his own, opposite the familiar piano in their sub-basement lounge.

During that war, his elder uncle Michael had been wounded and trapped for forty-eight hours in a dug-out in Flanders, and Jack would continually quiz him about this experience. His younger uncle, Lew—who Jack greatly resembled in outlook—had joined up when he was only fourteen, and his mother wrote in despair to Lloyd George, the Prime Minister, asking for her son to be released. As soon as Lew was returned home, he immediately ran away to join the Royal Army Medical Corps. He was wounded and came back to England, and then crossed to France for the third time to serve until the end of the war in the Welsh Regiment. Jack's first ambition as a boy was to emulate the example of these uncles—and of his father, who had also served in the infantry —and fight for England should the opportunity ever arise. Now it had unexpectedly presented itself, and the advice of his two uncles would have been the same as his father's: 'Go!'

Air Commodore Tait had been right in his remarks about Jack's physical fitness. As a boy, he was told he suffered from asthma—although he never felt ill—and for a time he lived at Whitstable, on the Kent coast, often racing barefoot over fields and dyke and the shingle beaches. When he returned to London, Jack found he could out-distance his school friends with practically no effort, and every summer at the school sports he took prizes for the 100 yard sprint and the hurdles. Here he was coached by the sports master, Mr Markham, an ex-Olympic hurdler.

His science master, Mr A. H. Raines, had a flair for communicating his own enthusiasm for his subject, and soon infected Jack with an interest in electrical gadgets. Jack had built a one-valve radio set on his own, and Mr Raines patiently showed him how to improve its performance; and then, under his guidance, he went on to construct receivers with two, three and four valves, and a magnificent range for their day. They wound coils by hand, and chokes on a gramophone turntable. The maths master also took an interest in Jack's progress and together these two dedicated East End teachers guided him into a love of science. They readily coached him in maths and physics, and since the school possessed a complete engineering shop including drills, lathes, a forge and milling machines, Jack was able to learn more about the practical side of radio construction. Here, a German metalwork master helped by teaching him how to devise wireless components, then to draw them and finally to make them.

Jack left school in his teens and went into the radio industry, joining EMI at their factory in Hayes, Middlesex. In the evenings, at Regent Street Polytechnic, he studied subjects such as wideband technology and cathode ray tube technique, which fitted perfectly into the allied science of RDF. He could not have had a more useful grounding in the art. Television was in its infancy, of course, but he was immediately impressed by the vast potential of vision allied to sound, and in a short time he was earning several pounds a week. Older and more experienced radio technicians still believed that TV was simply a fad that must soon fade. Jack did not hold this view, and so came to deal more and more with TV problems.

An RAF technical officer visited the EMI factory, seeking volunteer technicians willing to work at week-ends on new radio projects. Jack and a few friends accepted this offer and drove out in an old Fiat car belonging to one of them across the empty flat countryside of East Anglia to Bawdsey, Britain's pioneer radar experimental station. Here, against the unlikely background of a country manor, with hot-houses filled with peaches and nectarines, Jack worked with Robert Watson-Watt and other scientists on experiments which would soon revolutionize the arts of navigation, flight and war, and save their country from defeat. Because money for early radar experiments was always short, volunteers like Jack were first vetted for security and then they spent regular week-ends without pay, working purely for the excitement of being so closely involved with revolutionary scientific techniques. During these week-ends at Bawdsey, Jack's natural climbing ability was given full rein. He would shin up the wooden aerial masts, 240 feet high, to operate relays and 'make off' cables, regardless of howling gales blowing in from the North Sea.

Now, sitting in the sun, remembering all these events, Jack felt as though every individual strand of his life—his eagerness to emulate his patriotic uncles, his knowledge of radar, his physical fitness—were now to be drawn together for a grand purpose. It was as though all that had gone before was but a preparation for what he had now been asked to do.

At eleven o'clock next morning, Jack was back in the Air Commodore's office.

'I've thought it over, sir,' he reported. 'I'd still like to go.'

He did not add that he had suddenly walked out of the cinema where he had gone with Dell and his mother on the previous evening. One scene in the film showed a rescue fleet of small civilian motor boats and launches leaving for Dunkirk to pick up the retreating British Army in 1940. A naval officer warned of the grave dangers ahead. If anyone wished to turn back, he should do so now. Not a man moved. This parallel with Jack's own predicament proved too much for him, and he left his seat and stumbled outside, to wander about aimlessly until his nerves relaxed. He had been offered the chance to withdraw and, like the characters in the film, he had refused. There had been some difficult explaining to do when he eventually got back to Ealing, for neither Dell nor his mother had the slightest idea of the mental anguish he was enduring.

Tait said, 'Right. There's nothing more I can say at this moment, except to wish you good luck. You'll report to me personally on your return. Now I want you to go across to King Charles Street to see the Intelligence people. They're expecting you.'

Jack said goodbye, saluted and left the room.

For a moment, Tait stood behind his desk. No doubt, young men all over the world were at that hour going unknowingly in different ways to their deaths. But somehow the odds did not seem so highly stacked against them; they only had to face the guns of the enemy, not of their own side. Tait picked up the green scrambler telephone and dialled a number. The buzzer rang in a small office on the far side of St James's Park, in the fourth floor of a nondescript nine-storey block, No. 54 Broadway Buildings, the headquarters of MI6, the British Secret Intelligence Service.

This particular office had pale grey walls papered with maps which were spattered with coloured pins. Its minimal furniture included a Civil Service issue kneehole mahogany desk, and green metal filing cabinets with combination locks and toughened steel bars padlocked vertically across them. It was one of three offices in different parts of London used by Dr Reginald Jones.

'We've got our volunteer for Rutter,' Tait told him. 'He's on his way to the IO[1] now. Then he'll take a look at what Cox brought back, and get some practice in dismantling it.'

'I had Cox here as a possible candidate,' Jones replied. 'But I told him he'd already done his whack. Let's hope the new volunteer can do as good a job—and also come back alive.'

The RAF Intelligence Officer was a wing commander in his early forties. An Army colonel shared his office. Both nodded to Jack as he entered and saluted.

'I've had a rail warrant made out for you to Malvern, and then you will report back to Hope Cove until we send for you,' said the wing commander. 'Tell people on your station that you will probably be going off shortly on another refresher course. We'll brief you fully next time round. Now—any questions?'

Jack had many, but he saved them until he reached Malvern, the new home of the Telecommunications Research Establishment, TRE, the heart and nerve centre of radar research and development in Britain. A few weeks earlier, TRE had requisitioned Malvern College, a boys' boarding school in Worcestershire. They had moved precipitately from

[1] Intelligence Officer.

Swanage on the south coast, after rumours—later found to be false—that German paratroops planned to attack them in retaliation for the Bruneval raid. The college had been taken over a week before the start of the summer term, and now was packed with scientists and equipment. Metal reflectors for centimetre radar were installed in the windows looking out over the Vale of Evesham. Other equipment was erected on the playing fields. Classrooms and dormitories had become laboratories; the school library was a drawing office and the gymnasium a storehouse.

At Malvern Jack discussed the assignment at length with a senior scientist, Mr D. H. Preist, one of the handful of men who had pioneered British radar. He was also aware that Preist, although a civilian, had been specially commissioned as a flight lieutenant in the RAF, so that he could accompany Flight Sergeant Cox on the Bruneval raid. He had travelled in a special craft so that he could instantly evaluate the equipment brought out of the radar station. Preist had also volunteered to go on the Dieppe raid, but he was not allowed to do so—and he strongly envied Jack his chance of action.

Both men agreed that the essential need was to evaluate the Freya's performance in case special equipment would need to be designed and manufactured in order to jam it. All that could be learned about any anti-jamming gear the station contained, plus the speed, accuracy, range and capabilities of the apparatus, would be of the utmost value. Jack studied Intelligence material that had already been collected on the Freya, and on the basis of this he decided how best he should tackle the problem. He committed the relevant details to memory, and then was driven to the station to catch a train back to Hope Cove.

The beautiful Cottage Hotel overlooking the sea had been requisitioned to accommodate the radar team, and Jack occupied what in peacetime had been called 'The Blue Room'. Everything in this magnificent suite was blue: the curtains, the blankets, even a blue tiled bathroom with a sunken bath.

Lying in the bath that night, with the prospect of a dinner in the mess where routine service rations would be augmented by lobster and crayfish caught by spare-time RAF fishermen, and by illegal cream in his coffee afterwards, Jack contrasted the present apparent luxury with the sombre prospect ahead.

There seemed something almost Biblical in eating so well before leaving for such a dangerous trip. It reminded him of the Rabbi's story of the fatted calf, and the sacrificial lamb. The irony of the situation was overwhelming, and he burst out laughing. Here he was, in luxury. Where would he be when the firing started?

—TWO—

Captain Murray Osten removed the half-smoked cigarette from his mouth and placed it carefully on the sea-wall. Then he picked up the Thompson submachine-gun, blew invisible dust from its barrel, pulled back the actuator handle and took careful aim. Gently, he squeezed the trigger.

Reeking cartridge cases sprayed across the pebbles. The fifty empty beer bottles, so carefully set up on the wall, each exactly one foot apart, disintegrated in a glittering spray of green and brown glass splinters. The air was suddenly sharp with the smell of burned cordite. Osten handed the Tommygun back to the sergeant, and picked up his cigarette. He was a lean man, all muscle and sinew, who moved with the deceptive slowness of the very tall.

'Beat that if you can,' he said cheerfully.

'Sure will,' replied the sergeant. 'Set up some more goddam bottles, Les.'

A corporal began to unload a beer crate of empties, while Osten stood watching, arms folded. His saturnine face concealed a cheerful spirit; and he had every right to feel pleased with himself, for he had just taken over command of 'A' Company, the South Saskatchewan Regiment, in the Second Canadian Division. The previous OC, Major Jack Mather, had broken a leg on a practice assault landing only a short time before, and he was still in hospital. Murray Osten would therefore lead the company in action—and any day now.

His father was a grain buyer in Oxbow, who appreciated the value of a good education and had paid for his son to stay on for an extra year at High School. When Murray left, he took a number of jobs. Like most of his contemporaries, he served in a drug store, worked in a creamery and on farms, and had a spell cutting trees on contract. His liking for an outdoor life showed in his tough muscular frame. Murray had held a commission in the Canadian Militia, roughly the equivalent of the British Territorial Army, and now here he was, still in his early twenties, a captain commanding a company of men, many older than himself, roughly 4,500 miles east of Oxbow, in the grounds of Norris Castle on the Isle of Wight.

The sergeant pushed the broken bottles off the concrete ledge with the Tommy-gun butt and clipped in a new magazine. He and Osten spoke to each other easily and as equals, disregarding the difference in their rank. This was one of several refreshing singularities of service with the Canadian Army, that showed itself in other characteristic ways. Once, in Weyburn, Saskatchewan, when a fellow officer, Captain N. A. Adams, was carrying out the Saturday morning barracks inspection, he saw a trodden-out cigarette, and coldly asked the soldier nearest to it, Pte Bill White: 'Is this your cigarette butt on the floor?'

'Go ahead,' replied White generously. 'You saw it first!'

When another soldier, 'Frenchie' Chamberlain, was up before the CO, then Lieutenant-Colonel J. W. Wright, on a charge of fighting, the colonel said to him in a puzzled voice: 'You admit breaking a bottle of beer over Corporal Roberts' head, and then you have the audacity to stand there and say it was an *accident*?'

'That's right, sir,' Chamberlain agreed. 'I didn't mean to *break* it!'

This droll attitude extended to all ranks. When General Montgomery watched the Regiment give an impressive demonstration of Commando-style training in Sussex just before they crossed to the Isle of Wight to prepare for Rutter, he noticed that one officer's jaws were constantly moving, and asked his CO what he was chewing. The colonel admitted that the officer was chewing gum, and he added seriously that all Canadian and American athletes regularly chewed gum, since it was so good for their wind and general stamina. General Montgomery was extremely impressed at this information, which he assumed was genuine, and gave his opinion that it would therefore be admirable if *every* soldier chewed gum.

The South Saskatchewan Regiment—known colloquially as the SSR (and sometimes by nicknames such as Sirloin Steak Rustlers) contained a cross-section of their particular community. In its ranks were business men, lawyers and cat-skinners; bank clerks, trappers, truck drivers and, most of all, sod-busters—the slang name for prairie farmers. These men had driven or ridden or hitched rides to enlist at recruiting centres in Regina or Weyburn, from their homes in towns and villages with what to English ears seemed most unlikely names: Humming Bird and Swift Current; Medicine Hat and Red Deer. They had left farmhouses in the Lost Horse Hills or around Old Wives Lake, offices in Golden Spike, lumbermills in Moose Jaw. They were more fiercely individualistic than the British—how else could they explain the reason for unusually broad streets in their home towns, except that the pioneers refused to travel in each other's dust, but must ride several abreast?

But one intention had united them all: the wish to fight in a war thousands of miles away, for a little country that the vast majority had never visited, but to which they still felt bound by umbilical cords of language or tradition or other shared affinities. They had joined for reasons as far apart as the towns and villages of their birth and upbringing, and as varied as their family roots in Scotland or Poland or England or France. Some men of Indian blood—Mètis—readily admitted that they relished the prospect of adventure and battle in preference to fishing or logging or trapping. Others joined because they were out of work, and they seized the opportunity of learning the trade of war, and maybe a whole new career in the Army.

Some enlisted to escape from pressing family ties, and as many for exactly the opposite reason: because they hoped to be united or reunited with other members of their families when they reached Britain. Those with Irish, Scottish and English blood or relations looked forward to visiting places about which they had only heard from relatives. A number had, of course, been members of the peacetime Militia, and this was the challenge for which years of training and annual camps had been but a long preparation. This was their hour, and they were proud that they were ready when it struck.

Following more than a year's training in Canada, the South Saskatchewan Regiment had sailed for England in December 1940, aboard a filthy ship that had put into Halifax, Nova Scotia, from carrying internees to the British West Indies. The Dutch captain admitted he could not control some of his supernumerary crew, who were renegades, and warned the SSR's commanding officer that if the ship were torpedoed, these men could seize the lifeboats and leave the troops to go down with the ship. So the colonel detailed 100 SSRs to keep watch day and night in a lounge on 'A' Deck, with rifles and Bren-guns at the ready—just in case. Rarely had a ship ferried troops so far under such conditions—and for what result? To train along the English south coast for eighteen months—or to train forever?

It was difficult for people in England, who believed that ten miles was a long distance between one town and another, to appreciate what space meant to these men from the prairies. It was equally difficult for the Canadian to explain to them how free a man could feel on a vast plain with nothing but a waving sea of wheat as far as his eyes could see, where a farm might be larger than two or three English counties put together. The prairie landscape to which they were accustomed was not broken and bisected by buildings, but stretched flat as a table, with hazy horizons pierced at most by one or two distant grain elevators. Here and there, clapboard farmhouses, their walls painted in oddly bright colours, yellow or blue or green, added vivid sparks of colour to an apparently endless land.

Men who grew up against this vast emptiness, with harsh winters and hot summers, were not like men raised in a kinder climate, in towns and cities, where people lived crowded together. They spoke slowly; they possessed a different kind of pride, and a toughness all their own. They did not necessarily respect a man simply because he wore stripes on his arms or pips or crowns on his shoulders; they respected army rank only when the man who held it showed himself worthy of their regard. Life had been rough on the prairies in the 1930s, and this had hardened them and fostered its own special discipline, that could not always be translated into strict military terms of polished cap-badges and smart salutes.

Before Murray Osten took over 'A' Company, he had been in charge of regimental transport and would allow the sergeant major the use of a motor-cycle on Sundays to enjoy a run through the countryside—a rare privilege in wartime England when no petrol was available for what was officially described as 'pleasure motoring'. But when Osten felt that the sergeant major was being too strict on his men he did not conceal his displeasure.

'See here, you son-of-a-bitch,' he told him shortly, 'if you don't stop putting my fellows on charges, you won't get the motor-cycle again.'

This was accepted as it was intended, as a discussion between equals, for men in the South Saskatchewan Regiment enjoyed the rare feeling of belonging not just to a regional unit or a county regiment, but to a company of friends. Many brothers and other relatives had joined up to serve together. Major Mather had two brothers with him; Frank, the Company Sergeant Major of 'B' Company, and Ted, a private with Battalion Headquarters. Roughly one-third of the regiment had even attended the same school, Weyburn Collegiate Institute, where their teacher had been a stockily built émigré Englishman, Claude Orme, who now commanded 'C' Company.

In 1922, shortly after he graduated as a Bachelor of Science from London University, Orme had read a newspaper advertisement appealing for 50,000 harvesters in Winnipeg. The fare was £12, so he and his elder brother, a First World War POW, borrowed this sum from an obliging aunt and sailed to

45

Canada together. After the harvest, they discovered they liked the country too much to leave it. Claude Orme settled in Weyburn where he taught science. He was a born teacher, and his enthusiasm and dedication were deeply appreciated by two generations of pupils. He still kept his English accent, and grew to be highly regarded throughout Saskatchewan.

One former pupil who had joined the Regiment told Claude Orme that he had first discussed his intention with his mother. His father had been killed in the First War, and so she was understandably dubious about her only son volunteering for the Army; but when he explained that Claude Orme would be his officer, she cheered up considerably.

'If Mr Orme is in the Regiment, then that's okay by me,' she said immediately. 'You can go along, too.'

These shared experiences and common background strengthened the spirit of the Regiment, so that, for many men, soldiering with the SSRs became simply an extension of peacetime associations, if in different clothes and a different country.

A corporal approached the group on the promenade.

'Captain Osten, sir,' he said. 'CO would like to see you.'

Osten flicked his cigarette butt over the shingle and followed him up the path. As he walked, he heard the sharp metallic chatter of the Tommy-gun behind him and the tinkle of breaking glass. In a few days now they would be firing at live targets across the Channel. Rumour was busy about the imminence of action.

Murray Osten walked through the gardens toward the castle. The roses were in full bloom, and their scent lay sweet as syrup on the air; some quality in Isle of Wight soil encourages roses. War could be a world away, he thought.

The room in Norris Castle that the SSR Commanding Officer, Lieutenant-Colonel Charles Cecil Ingersoll Merritt, occupied as his office, also seemed unwarlike with the faded trappings of Victorian and Edwardian elegance; its ceiling was still divided into small blue sections edged with gilt. The castle was not so old as it appeared, for the nineteenth-century architect, James Wyatt, who designed it, had been much in demand for his Gothic creations, and deliberately stained the stones he used to give the impression of vast age— an effect strengthened by the thick ivy trained across the walls. Queen Victoria had visited Norris as a girl, and was so impressed that she later decided to buy the neighbouring 5,000-acre estate and build a palace near it for herself, Osborne House, which eventually became her favourite residence.

Colonel Cecil Merritt, known to his friends as Cec (pronounced Ceese) was standing, hands behind his back, looking out of the window across the sloping lawn, covered now with khaki bell-tents. A soldier in shirt-sleeves was scrubbing a webbing belt at the mouth of one of them, and whistling. Beyond the tents and through the trees, sea-water glittered like green glass. How different the scene was from his home near Vancouver! The hills across the bay would be wreathed in cloud, with thick firs darkening the lower slopes, and white sails moving on the cobalt sea. He wondered what his wife and small daughter were doing, and when he would next see them.

Merritt was a big man, dark-haired and broad-shouldered, a natural leader. In his early twenties he had been a considerable footballer, and was a popular member of Vancouver Athletic Club. He graduated from the Royal Military College, Kingston, Ontario, and after being articled for three years in a law firm, he had taken his finals and practised successfully at the Bar. He spoke in a deep, sonorous voice, as though measuring out every word; and when he had spoken and given his opinion, his was generally the last word. He was thirty-two, and had taken command of the battalion that April. He turned as Murray Osten entered.

'Shut the door, Murray,' he said. 'I have a job for you. Division's just been on. Fellow's coming down from London to join us for the party. RDF expert. Radio beams and so on. Very hush-hush. He will be attached to "A" Company when we go across the Channel because the RDF station he wants to look at is in your area. I told Jack Mather about this earlier on, but he's in hospital, so I'm repeating it to you.'

'Very good, sir.'

'First, you'll have to detail some men to stay with him. They must give him cover up to the RDF station.'

Merritt paused for a moment; he might have been finishing a final speech for the defence.

'Now here's the other side, Murray. Sounds a bit stupid to me. But this fellow's not to be captured.'

'We'll sure give him all the cover we can, sir.'

'I know that. But if he is wounded and can't make it out, or if he is about to be captured, you will have to deal with him. He's a real back-room boy, who knows too much to be taken prisoner. Is that clear?'

'Yes, sir, but . . .'

'No buts. I'm going to put this out of my mind and leave you to get on with it. Right?'

'Right, sir.'

Osten saluted and walked out, a bit bewildered, into the sunshine and the fragrance of roses. Behind him, Merritt wondered about the orders he had just passed on, half hoping that Murray Osten would not take them too seriously.

So many things about the Army, which initially seemed of the utmost importance, proved in fact to be of little consequence. An example had occurred a few weeks earlier when his regiment had taken over Norris Castle from the Welsh Guards, under conditions of total security. Two days later, he was summoned to Divisional Headquarters, where a staff colonel presented him coldly with a letter addressed, against all orders, to Lieutenant-Colonel Merritt, OCSSR, Norris Castle, Isle of Wight, Hants.

This was a fearful breach of security, but Merritt simply said: 'Well, open the darned thing. I don't know anything about it.'

The colonel did so—and found that the envelope contained a note from the outgoing CO who explained that he had unfortunately left his dog behind at Norris Castle—and would Colonel Merritt please forward it to him at his present station?

Maybe this extraordinary instruction about the RDF expert was simply another example of priorities he found difficult to reconcile?

Regiments and units were billeted across the island in houses or under canvas. They included the Queen's Own Cameron Highlanders of Canada; the Royal Hamilton Light Infantry; the Essex Scottish; the Fusiliers Mont-Royal; the 14th Canadian Army Tank Regiment (Calgary Regiment) and the Royal Regiment of Canada; the Black Watch (Royal Highland Regiment) of Canada; the Calgary Highlanders; the Toronto Scottish Regiment, plus detachments of Canadian Signals, Engineers, Artillery, Service, Medical, Ordnance, Provost and Intelligence Corps. All were accommodated in what was literally a moated fortress containing, in round figures, 5,000 Canadians, 4,000 sailors, 1,000 British Commandos, a detachment of the United States Rangers, who would form a token presence on the raid, with RAF men, glider pilots, paratroops, signals teams and demolition experts of various kinds and nationalities.

The formation of the First United States Ranger Battalion, later to become a famous fighting force, had been proposed by the Senior American Observer at Combined Operations Headquarters, General L. K. Truscott, who had persuaded his superiors that the United States should adopt British Commando training for at least one of their own units. This had been agreed, and volunteers were called for from American divisions newly arrived in Northern Ireland. The US Ranger Battalion was commanded by Major William O. Darby, who had selected fifty representatives—forty-four enlisted men and six officers—to join the raid.

Civilians already living on the Isle of Wight were allowed to remain in their houses, but no one could cross over from the mainland without identity papers, which were specifically issued for the journey. Equally, no service men or women were allowed to leave the island without special permission from a senior officer.

Since their arrival, the troops had undergone intensive training, wading ashore from landing craft, running through fields of live mines, and scaling nearly perpendicular cliffs, using tubular telescopic ladders and special ropes. Tank crews had practised coming ashore in water-proofed tanks from landing craft to manoeuvre on beaches chosen because the shingle was the same size as shingle at Dieppe. Two full-scale night assault landings had also been carried out along the Dorset coast.

The first was a fiasco, with inexperienced naval crews putting troops ashore at the wrong places, and some craft actually colliding in the water. Lord Louis Mountbatten heard of this on his return from Washington, and demanded a second one, which was more expert, but still not as smooth as he had hoped. But then some mistakes were inevitable; to minimize them was the reason for these rehearsals, and now everyone was in a state of tense readiness for real action. They knew that there would only be several periods during the summer when tide and moon would be right for a landing on the French coast. The first of these, for which meteorological experts also forecast good weather, was the night of July 4.

In the last week of June, nearly 300 officers from all the regiments in the Second Canadian Division were summoned to Osborne House for a special and secret briefing. The photographic Central Interpretation Unit had built a ten-foot-long scale model of Dieppe and the cliffs for several miles on either side, based on aerial photographs taken from low-flying reconnaissance planes in the preceding weeks. Officers crowded round to examine the beautifully-made toy; shops, the casino on the beach, the Vieux Château, the tobacco factory; the hotels, and the harbour. Conversation died as General Roberts faced the officers.

'Gentlemen,' he began, 'we have waited for over two years to engage the enemy. The time has now come for a party. This scale model is the target. You will now be briefed on the intentions of the assault. I must emphasize the need for complete security. Other ranks will not be told until they are aboard their ships.'

Colonel Merritt had a word with his Regimental Sergeant Major, Roger Strumm, another prairie man who had served in the Canadian army in the First World War and then had worked in the Post Office. He had joined the Militia in 1920, and was renowned for his tremendous voice and his faith in the overwhelming value of discipline, a belief which not every soldier in his regiment shared to the same extent.

The regimental sergeant major of an infantry battalion is the link between the commanding officer and other senior warrant officers and sergeants. He would therefore need to know something about this RDF expert who was due to arrive. Colonel Merritt pointed out discreetly that this unknown expert was too valuable to be allowed to fall into German hands. He therefore suggested to the RSM that some reliable older soldier in the regiment should be his escort while he was on the Isle of Wight to show him how the South Saskatchewan Regiment worked. He would then have the opportunity of gaining confidence in their ability to protect him.

Roger Strumm suggested Sergeant Blackwell, the signals sergeant. Signals involved radio, which would surely give Blackwell something in common with the RDF expert.

Sergeant Amaranth Anthony James Blackwell, otherwise known by his nickname, 'Newt', or simply 'Blacky', according to the degree and length of friendship, sat in a mess-tent, writing a letter home to his wife. He was a quiet man of medium height, with hair cut very short, light on his feet, wearing the red and blue Distinguished Conduct Medal, awarded in the First War. He had been named Amaranth after a brother of that name who had died a week before Blackwell was born. He would often say that his mother was the only person who ever called him Amaranth. She had also told him that it meant an unfading flower. Now in his forties, but tough as a whip, Blacky felt he had lived up to the adjective.

As a boy in Grimwold, Manitoba, he had spent many happy hours in puddles and ponds trying to catch frogs and newts—hence his nickname of Newt among those who knew him then. He was older than most men in the regiment, and some of his experiences had written their story on his face. He had served with the Signals in France in the First World War, and afterwards joined the Canadian Pacific Railway. In the mid-thirties' depression he was laid off when he was earning 200 dollars a month, and the only job he could find was as a farm worker in a remote part of the prairies.

The thirties were hard times for Canadian farmers as well as for their labourers, and the farmer who offered Blackwell work gave him no wages, only food for himself and his wife. And because he knew no one else who would better this basic offer, Blacky had been forced to accept. As soon as possible, he moved to another farm for a few dollars a week, and then he found work with a grain buyer in Porcupine Plain. Farmers would bring along their grain in wagons and trucks, and he would grade it as first, second or third quality. Gradually, his salary climbed back to 200 dollars a month, and life seemed settled at last. Then, in early 1939, a grain disease, known locally as smut, ruined crops for miles around, and the superintendent called Blackwell into his office.

'We're paying you 200 bucks a month,' he said. 'And I can get a guy to do your job for 60. But since you're here, Blacky, I am offering you the chance to stay on for that amount.'

'Nothing doing,' Blackwell told him simply. This reply had not been unexpected, and they parted amicably. But once more, Blackwell and his wife were homeless and jobless. They moved into her mother's home, where they would not have to pay rent.

'What are you going to do now?' his wife asked him, for jobs were few, and young single men would work for less money than men with wives or families to support.

'I'm going to join the Army, that's what,' Blackwell replied.

'Don't be silly,' she told him. But Blackwell was not being silly, he was being serious; at least he would be employed. So he hitched a ride to Regina, and went into the recruiting office. The first person he was to see was Murray Osten. Blackwell explained he had served in the Signals during the First World War.

'Fine,' Osten told him enthusiastically. 'In Weyburn we've got a signals platoon of thirty boys, many of whom don't know a dot from a dash. I'll have the doctor look you over.'

Blackwell would often tell younger soldiers what happened next. He claimed that the doctor gave him a shot in the arm —and when he woke up he was in the Army. He drilled for sometime in civilian clothes, for no uniforms were available, but when Blackwell was issued with his uniform, he sewed on his DCM ribbon. Strumm recognized the decoration, and immediately Blackwell was promoted to corporal. The two men respected each other: shared memories of another war long ago and hard years in between were a strong bond.

'We've got a stranger coming,' Strumm began now. 'A scientist—RDF expert. And when we go abroad we are taking him to do a special job. He'll be attached to "A" Company. Meanwhile, we have to look after him here and show him how to do things. I want you to stay close to him, Blacky. He may be an odd-ball, long hair, absent-minded professor type of guy. Okay?'

'Okay,' agreed Blackwell, and went back to his letter.

He was too good a soldier to waste time asking any awkward questions; and too old a soldier to expect any answers.

Murray Osten lit a cigarette, blew smoke in the air, and wondered how he should set about finding men who would risk their lives to protect a total stranger—and then agree to kill him if his capture seemed imminent. There seemed no other certain way to make sure this RDF expert was not captured, and yet was it not possible that the two qualities required in such men—protectiveness and aggression—might somehow cancel themselves out? However, no amount of thinking round the problem would solve it; he would have to tackle it head on.

He walked across to the mess and had a word with the adjutant, Lieutenant George Bruce Buchanan, generally known as 'Buck', and told him of his predicament. Buck was one of the older men in the regiment; he was all of twenty-nine, while many of the other lads had joined straight from school or off the farm. His father had been Fire Chief in Medicine Hat, Alberta, and Buck had also worked as a fireman. Because of his age, some of the boys called him 'Dad'.

Buck did not seem surprised at what Osten had to say, so he guessed that the adjutant had already heard about the RDF expert; adjutants were well placed to hear more than most other officers. But he was surprised when Buchanan began to laugh.

'What's so funny?' he asked him.

'I think it's a kind of joke, because some of these fellows have never shot more than a buck rabbit before. And their first bit of blood-letting may be to put a bullet through one of their own guys!'

'There has to be a first time,' retorted Osten. 'And maybe it will never happen.'

If he could find two good sharpshooters and give them, say, four men each to help this RDF expert, he might be on the way to something. Or, better still, why not select the two leaders and then let the RDF character choose the men he felt would be most useful when he arrived? He saw a possible choice almost immediately: Graham Mavor, the mess corporal.

Mavor was in his early twenties, fair-haired, of average height, fit and quick-witted. Before he joined the regiment, he had worked in a bank, and the battalion used his considerable financial ability by making him the officers' mess corporal, where one of his duties was to look after the accounts. It was a regimental rule that all officers should pay their drink bills by the seventh of every month following the four weeks to which the bills referred. But not all officers could afford to comply with this requirement, for sometimes thirsts proved bigger than pockets. This was where Mavor's fiscal ingenuity proved useful. Young officers would explain to him their temporary inability to settle up, and he would reply sympathetically: 'That's all right. Those guys at Brigade don't know anything about arithmetic.'

And he would then obligingly proceed to juggle figures from one column to another until the following month, when the officers concerned always settled. Like many men with a head for practical finance, Mavor was an independent character. He had already been promoted from private to corporal and then demoted from corporal to lance-corporal to private several times for differences of opinion with his superiors. A corporal who had worked in the mines before the war once put Mavor on a charge because he said he had been abusive to him when ordered out of bed.

'Go to hell,' he had told the corporal. 'It's five o'clock in the morning, and I'm no goddam coal-miner!'

Now Osten took Mavor on one side and told him about the unusual job he had in mind for him. Mavor nodded gravely. Whatever he thought, nothing registered on his face; he might have been back in the bank explaining to a new customer why he could not see the manager without an appointment.

'What does this RDF guy look like?' he asked.

'Don't know yet. He's not arrived. I'll introduce you then.'

'Very good. Oh, and while we're talking, sir, I wonder if I could have something towards your last month's mess bill . . .?'

One of the best shots in the regiment—some thought *the* best—was another corporal, not in 'A' Company, Corporal Les ('Muggsy') Thrussell, of No. 7 Platoon. A few discreet words with the officer commanding that platoon, and Thrussell was transferred as a private to 'A' Company. There was no vacancy for a corporal, but temporary demotion worried Thrussell no more than it worried Mavor. He was equally independent.

'You want my hooks, you have 'em,' he said simply. Rank meant nothing to him; what mattered was the man who carried the rank, and what was especially important to Thrussell as a soldier was that particular man's ability to shoot straight and fast and accurately. For however good he might be, he would find it about impossible to beat Les Thrussell as a shot. That was certain.

Thrussell had the slow speech and calm outlook of someone who had grown up in the country. His blue eyes were clear and always appeared fixed on some distant target, scanning the horizon; shooting had been his hobby and his passion from boyhood. Thrussell's father had emigrated to Canada from England in 1914—arriving on August 4, the day the First

World War began. He volunteered immediately, and after the war had joined the Provincial Police, a force which was later incorporated into the Mounties. As a boy in England, he had sung regularly in the choir of a church at Chalk Farm in north-west London, and Les Thrussell had paid a visit to this church during one of his leaves, hoping to find someone who remembered his father. But the area was run-down and shabby; houses had been bombed and broken windows were boarded up. No one seemed to have lived there before the war. Like most sentimental journeys, this had been unsuccessful. He was sorry, for he had grown up very close to his father; he would like to have met someone who knew him when he was young.

Les Thrussell was born in Fillmore, Southern Saskatchewan, and even as a child he had been fascinated by firearms. One of his earliest treats was to fire his father's revolver, and the heavy feel of the cold, blue metal, with its distinctive smell of gun oil and cordite as it leaped in his two hands, fired his own imagination. Once he used all his father's .45 rounds shooting gophers, and all the .303 ammunition as well, so that when his father had to turn out unexpectedly for a shooting practice, he found to his considerable surprise he had no ammunition left. By the time Les Thrussell was fourteen, he was in the Militia, marking targets at rifle meets. He was soon such a good shot that a rifle in his hands became not just a separate instrument of steel and wood, but an extension of his own arm, his own mind and eye. He was a born marksman, and as such ideal for this assignment; moreover, Muggsy Thrussell would never panic. Indeed, Osten could not remember when anything had ever disturbed Thrussell's calm or his cool.

Now that two leaders had been chosen, the rest would be up to the RDF expert. Idly, Osten wondered—as Merritt had wondered—as Strumm wondered—as Mavor and Thrussell also wondered—just what sort of man would arrive. What kind of character would not only attempt a hazardous task but feel so strongly about it that he would agree to the unheard of conditions that his own comrades could shoot him if he failed—or, even worse, if he fell in succeeding?

THREE

For a few days after Jack's return to Hope Cove, he slipped back into the familiar routine of running a night fighter ground control station. Then one morning, after he had been on duty all night, his Orderly Room Sergeant, Bill Powell, came to see him.

'What's the matter?' Jack asked, as Powell stood surveying him quizzically from the doorway.

'You should tell *me*, Jack,' Powell replied with mock gravity. 'Humber Snipe staff car has just arrived. Driver says he's orders to collect you. I don't know what it's all about, Jack, boy, but we've never had a summons like this before. What have you done wrong?'

For a moment, Jack did not connect the car's arrival with his new assignment.

'He's got no Air Ministry experimental station permit to come into the station, so he's waiting at the guard-room,' Powell went on, watching Jack's face for his reaction. 'Says he's got to take you up to London.'

'London?' Jack repeated. Instantly, he knew what this meant, and it was difficult to keep excitement out of his voice.

'It's that new posting,' he explained as casually as he could. 'Tied up with my last trip to Long Cross. I'll only be away for a few days.'

'Oh,' said Powell, in a disappointed voice. Frequently Jack was called away to visit other radar stations; there was nothing scandalous or exciting here.

Jack walked over to the guard-room, saw the driver and told him to follow his own Bedford fifteen-hundredweight truck, which he drove back to the Cottage Hotel through narrow lanes where green summer hedges leaned out at each other across the banks. He stopped for a moment when the road came within sight of the sea, surveying the hotel, the sandy cove, the sweep of beach, and the green sea merging into a summer sky. Never had the view looked so lovely, and as he let it soak into his tired mind, he realized why it appeared so overwhelmingly beautiful. Subconsciously, he knew that this could be the last time he saw it.

He drove on to the hotel, checked there were no messages for him, and ordered tea for the driver. Then he went to his room, and crammed his pyjamas, toothbrush, razor, a change of underwear and socks into his RAF small pack.

On his return from Malvern, he had collected his own personal wireless testing equipment in a similar blue pack, and included his most precious professional possession—a small avometer that his father had given to him on his thirteenth birthday. He hoped that this link with his boyhood might be a lucky talisman. At the least, some momento from his father was going into action with him.

Then, feeling that this might be the last opportunity he would have to enjoy the luxurious facilities of the hotel, he ran a bath, and lay in the hot, steamy water, completely relaxed. Well, he thought philosophically, if he didn't come back, he had thoroughly enjoyed his stay here. Hope Cove was now a highly successful operational station, the centre of a whole defence complex. If he achieved nothing more, he had achieved that.

Jack dressed, and went down to the mess in the bar, which had been made from the timbers of a four-masted schooner, the *Herzogin Cecile*, which had gone aground off Hope Cove before the war and had broken up. He ate breakfast, picked up both his packs and went out to the staff car.

He had already written two letters, one to Dell and the other to his mother, and had put them in a drawer in his room. There was no risk they would be posted in his absence, for no one knew they were there. But if he did not come back, his belongings would be collected—as he had so often helped in the melancholy task of collecting the belongings of aircrew who had not returned from a raid—and then they would be discovered and forwarded.

He had not told his mother or Dell any details of his mission, of course; only that it had been secret and highly important, and he was thinking of them as he left to join the unit to which he would be attached. He had added a few words from the Jewish prayer used before leaving on a journey: 'O deliver us from every enemy, ambush and hurt by the way, and from all afflictions that visit and trouble the world. Send a blessing upon the work of our hands.'

That was the important thing; the work of his hands. On this raid, his efforts might quite literally alter a whole aspect of the air war, for he believed that what he discovered might influence the decision to jam German radar, with all the infinity of benefits that could flow from this move. To jam or not to jam, Jack and other experts knew, could be a pivotal decision and would have to be resolved soon.

They drove in silence through empty roads towards London. All road signs had been taken down two years previously, when the threat of a German invasion was strong, and even the names of towns on advertisements had been painted out or crudely obliterated with tar. The driver took him to the Intelligence offices in King Charles Street, Whitehall.

'First of all,' the wing commander told Jack, 'we want any papers and letters you may have with you. Then we're going to issue you with an Army private's uniform. Let's see your identity discs, too.'

Jack unbuttoned his collar, and pulled the string with its two maroon fibre identity discs over his neck. Each was stamped with his name, his service number, the letters RAF and J for his religion. The object of having two discs was for identification after death; theoretically, one disc would be removed for records purposes and the other left on the corpse.

The wing commander glanced sharply at Jack, who read his thoughts in his eyes. Jack must be mad to land in occupied France wearing identity discs that branded him as a Jew, when he could quite easily be supplied with discs that would record his religion as C of E for Church of England, or RC for Roman Catholic, or anything else.

But the reason why Jack chose to sail labelled as a Jew was personal and private. He had no wish to explain the remark he had overheard about a Jew's suitability for the task. And what the hell did it matter that he *was* marked as a Jew? If the Germans ever discovered this, then presumably he would already be dead and beyond all interrogation, all torture? The wing commander had apparently forgotten this basic fact. Jack had not. He would live or die with the mark of the religion into which he had been born. The thought brought him a peculiar feeling of comfort.

Jack emptied his pockets. A cinema ticket; a letter from Dell; his paybook, a comb, a notebook, two stubs of pencil. He placed them on the desk. The wing commander opened a drawer, pulled out a large envelope, put the ticket, the letter, the notebook and paybook inside, sealed it up, scribbled his signature over the flap and on the outside wrote: 'Personal Effects 916592 Flight Sergeant Nissenthall, J. M.' He pushed the comb and pencils across the desk towards Jack.

'How will I get the other stuff back?' Jack asked him.

'When you return, you'll report here. We'll keep them for you.'

'And—if I don't return?'

'They'll be sent to your next of kin, your mother. We have details in your file already. Now, we have something to help you in a positive way. An escape kit. Officially known as Special Ration Pack, evaders, for the use of.'

He opened another drawer and pulled out a small box, the shape and size of a tin of twenty-five De Reszke Minor cigarettes. The lid was sealed with a strip of waterproof sticky tape. These kits, Jack knew, were issued to air crew to help them survive and find their way to friendly or neutral territory should they be shot down over Germany or occupied France. The wing commander tore away the tape and opened the lid, pointing out the contents: a tube of cream, twelve Horlicks tablets, a needle and thread, a small bar of chocolate, and two pills in transparent wrapping on which was printed *'Important: only one to be taken in twenty-four hours'*.

'Oh, and here's an extra pill. Just for you.'

The wing commander took a small green capsule in an individual wrapper and dropped it inside the open tin.

'Don't take this one unless you have to,' he said casually. 'It doesn't taste nice and it's fatal in a few seconds. Now go into the next room,'—he nodded towards a door—'and change into your Army uniform. Put this kit in your field-dressing pocket.'

Jack went into the adjoining room. A private's battledress with boots, webbing belt and gaiters, was hanging from a hook behind the door. He changed into it, buttoned the tin box into the pleated pocket on his right thigh and returned. The wing commander had been joined by an Army colonel. They both looked Jack carefully up and down.

'Well,' the RAF officer said at last. 'You may not *be* a soldier, but from a distance you look like one. Now you've got to act like one.'

He turned to the colonel.

'What do you say?'

'Hm. He'll pass. Doesn't look like a Brylcreem[1] boy, anyhow. That's the main thing.'

Jack smiled.

'Now we have to deliver you to the Isle of Wight. You'll have an escort in case anything happens on the way.'

'Like what?' Jack asked innocently.

'Like some inquisitive MP[2] asking to see your paybook when you haven't got one,' replied the colonel. 'He might not appreciate the aptness of the Spanish proverb: "*No son soldados todos los que van a la guerra*—All are not soldiers who go to the wars".'

'Or, if he asked for your number, he might wonder why you've an RAF number and not an Army one, when you're in Army uniform,' said the wing commander.

---

[1] Brylcreem boy. Army slang for RAF men, because a well-known advertisement for Brylcreem showed a perfectly groomed airman.
[2] Military Policeman.

'Couldn't you give me an Army number then, just for this job?'

'Not possible, not in the time. Flight Sergeant Cox didn't get an Army number either.'

'But you must have known about this for weeks,' protested Jack. 'What if the Jerries find out I'm RAF and not Army? They must know the difference between service numbers, surely?'

'Well, you won't be able to tell them, will you?'

The three men looked at each other, suddenly embarrassed. Death was something to deal with at second-hand. You cloaked it in seemingly light-hearted euphemisms: you bought it; you had your chips; your number came up; your name was on it; you went for a Burton. Death was rarely mentioned directly, and never to a man so clearly almost certain to die. The wing commander cleared his throat, as though physically dismissing such unpleasant thoughts from his mind.

'Right,' he went on briskly. 'You will report to the Commanding Officer, South Saskatchewan Regiment, on the Isle of Wight. You are to be attached to the Canadians for the trip. What I am telling you now is for your ears only. Officers of the Second Canadian Division know the target already, but other ranks will not be told until they are actually in the ships, ready to sail. It's Dieppe. Your target is the radar station at Caude-Côte about two miles west of Dieppe, on top of the cliffs, just outside the village of Pourville. We want you to take a look at that station.'

He took a key from the desk, unlocked a safe, spun an inner combination lock and brought out a rolled-up map and two enlargements of aerial photographs. Then he spread the map on his desk, weighting one side of it with the telephone, the other with an ink-stand.

'You'll be landed here, west of the River Scie—it's more like a stream than a river. Jerry is in these houses on the far side. You won't have to pass them, for they're probably a couple of hundred yards from the river, maybe a bit less. You'll have full support from the Canadians to get up the hill and approach the station. There's a road here that runs behind it and on to Dieppe. If you have surprise—and you almost certainly will have, because you'll be landing just before dawn—you should be able to use the road. Then—it's up to you.'

Jack picked up the two photographs. The wing commander handed him a magnifying glass. The radar station was on top of a cliff; he could see rolls of barbed wire circling its perimeter, like the coils of a guardian serpent.

'That wire makes it easier to identify from the air, but it won't make things any easier for you.'

Jack nodded, and moved the glass slowly across the glossy print. The area around the station appeared much lighter than the grass down near the main cluster of houses; all shrubs and bushes had been cut down for a distance of about forty yards around it.

After the Bruneval raid, the Germans had carefully shaved away every bush that could provide the slightest protection to raiders in any attack. Jack handed back the photographs in silence. He knew now what the target looked like from the air; his problems would begin when he saw it at ground level.

'Any questions?' the wing commander asked him.

'Yes, sir. One.'

Jack was still carrying his two RAF small packs. They were blue, but if he really were a soldier, they would be khaki.

'What about these packs, sir?' he asked.

'You'd better get them changed on the Isle of Wight. The quartermaster there will fix you up. Sorry we can't help you here. Now, we have an officer waiting to escort you. He'll see you don't talk to anyone on the journey—or let anyone talk to you. It's a little early for Cowes Week, but—good luck. We look forward to seeing you when you return.'

The wing commander pressed a bell-push on his desk. An Army lieutenant came into the room. He wore battledress with a web belt, a .38 Smith and Wesson revolver in a web holster. He had no regimental insignia, no divisional signs or regimental name on his shoulders; not even the coloured shoulder flash to distinguish the arm of the service to which he belonged. He was as anonymous and nondescript as Jack.

They made fit companions; an anonymous officer and an anonymous other rank.

'I've got the rail warrant,' he said. 'Nothing else you need?'

'Nothing at all,' said Jack.

They went out down the stairs into the street. An Austin ten horse-power car with dull khaki paintwork waited outside with a driver. They drove in silence along Whitehall and over the bridge to Waterloo. Familiar posters added reality to what seemed an unreal situation: 'Ten minutes to wait—so mine's a Minor'; 'Uniform Opinion—leave it to Austin Reed'; 'Did you Maclean your teeth today?'

The officer led the way to Platform Seven where a train was already waiting. Everything had been well timed; no hanging about, no queueing for tickets. Within minutes they were on their way, trundling through the shabby, sooty, bombed streets of South London. Weeds and flowers that had not bloomed in the capital for a century now blossomed bravely in the early July sun. Gradually, houses gave place to allotments, and then they were in the country. Old cars and farm carts and ancient pieces of farm machinery still littered the fields, relics from the invasion scare of 1940, when locals had dragged them out to stop enemy planes from landing and to hinder parachutists.

The lieutenant produced two newspapers from his briefcase and handed one to Jack. It was only a folded sheet with four sides, because of the paper shortage. He skimmed the depressing war news from North Africa and Russia, then turned to other items. In India, Gandhi was threatening what he called 'open rebellion' against Britain. In England, the British middleweight champion, Jock McAvoy, was ready to fight Freddie Mills, the light heavyweight champion. The maximum charge for a restaurant meal had been fixed at five shillings a few weeks before, but this was held to make little difference, as people seldom spent so much on a meal. One reporter had found that for this price, so long as a customer spent a pound on a carafe of *vin rosé*, a Jermyn Street restaurant would serve *hors d'oeuvres* or crab salad, with a choice of salmon, trout, lobster, roast lamb and a dessert. Jack scanned the advertisements, finding reassurance in their familiarity. Bournville Cocoa, fivepence per half pound ('Still less than pre-war prices.') . . . Piccadilly cigarettes, ten for ninepence ('For pocket and palate.') . . . A Coronet box camera for ten shillings and sixpence. Another advertisement instantly took him back to pre-war days: 'Treasure your Hercules cycle . . .'

In the thirties, Jack had frequently crossed to the Isle of Wight with two friends who were keen cyclists. He particularly remembered their last visit, lying on the beach at Ventnor, watching a Walrus flying-boat thrash noisily above them, while another smaller RAF plane made mock attacks on it. His friends had been scornful about such aerial war games.

'Who do you think would ever attack England?' one asked him. Less than a year later, they all had the answer. Now Jack and his friends would enjoy no more holidays together. One had been killed at Dunkirk, and the other had gone down in the *Rawalpindi*. Of that cheerful trio, Jack was the only survivor. How long ago their trip seemed now, not in years but in experience! And how innocent he and his friends must have been then, throwing themselves on the empty beach, swimming through the sparkling sea, thankful that for two weeks they could forget the other fifty weeks of the year, running after buses, and travelling in stuffy tube trains!

He called other cycling trips with those two friends, or on his own. Quite regularly he would ride to the south coast on Friday evening after work, spend Saturday and Sunday camping in a field near the sea, cooking sausages, bacon and eggs in the open air, drinking Camp coffee and washing in a canvas bucket, and then he would cycle home on Sunday night to be ready for work at half past eight on Monday morning.

The economic depression that had darkened their youth, like a long grey storm cloud, had brightened by the late 1930s. There were music-halls to visit: Jessie Matthews, Lupino Lane, Billie Bennett to applaud. There were radio shows so popular that they rushed home early to hear them: Monday Night at Eight, Bandwagon, Billy Cotton's Band

Show. Life had been good then, and looking back at it now from the edge of this new departure, the sense of danger, of time rushing out like a tide, accentuated the safety and pleasantness of the past.

There had been some worries, of course, but they had appeared small and far away. Hitler had proved in Guernica how effective air-raids could be; Mussolini had suppressed the Abyssinians with gas and fighter-planes, but these things were happening in foreign countries. All kinds of idiotic things happened in foreign countries that could never affect the island race.

Well, now they had been affected. Now Jack was going to a foreign country himself, and under conditions of travel that neither his friends nor he would ever have imagined. They would have thought he was crazy; and probably he was. He smiled to himself, wishing he could hear their comments.

The train drew into Southampton station, and Jack and the lieutenant crossed the docks to the ferry. The military sergeant on duty at the gangway saluted the officer, glanced at Jack, and made an entry in his book as they went aboard. As the ferry headed south across the Solent, Jack felt excited in being at sea, even for so short a voyage; it was almost like visiting another country. The fresh salt air in his face acted as a tonic. A Jeep waited for them on the quay at Ryde. They drove past the narrow gauge railway, peculiar to the island, that enhanced the illusion of being abroad, and then into the grounds of Norris Castle. An orderly came down the front steps and saluted as they stopped.

'Colonel Merritt,' said the lieutenant briefly. 'Field Security.'

'This way, sir.'

They followed him into the hall, the studs in their boots echoing on the floor. The orderly knocked on a door and went in. Then he came out, and held open the door for them. Merritt was sitting at his desk, and stood up as they entered. The lieutenant saluted, and Jack, as the junior in rank, stood to attention.

'I've brought you one RDF expert, sir,' the lieutenant explained.

'Right,' replied Merritt. 'We'll take care of him. What do we call you?' he asked Jack, holding out his hand.

'He is under orders not to divulge his name, sir,' the lieutenant said quickly.

'You'd better call me Jack, sir.'

'Right—Jack,' said the colonel. 'Glad to meet you.'

He nodded dismissal to the lieutenant, who saluted smartly. The door closed quietly behind him, and Jack and the colonel were alone.

'You'll settle down here,' said Merritt in a friendly way. 'The RSM will detail someone to help you find your way round. I expect you'll want to take part in some training—get to know how we work, eh?'

'Thank you, sir.'

Merritt spoke briefly into his telephone. Sergeant Blackwell appeared.

'Here's the RDF expert,' the colonel explained. 'Known as Jack.'

'Very good, sir,' said Blackwell. 'Follow me—Jack.'

They went out into the garden.

'I was in the Signals in the First War,' Blackwell explained, 'so I know something about wireless. Anything I can do to help. . . . Meantime, you'll be wanting to know where your quarters are. I'll take your gear.'

He carried Jack's two RAF small packs up the wide curved staircase, and opened the door of a room on the landing. Jack saw a bed ready made up with white sheets, an old-fashioned washbasin with nickel-plated taps and a big mirror above it.

'Where will you eat?' Blackwell asked him.

'I don't mind. Anywhere not too conspicuous.'

'I could fix it to have your meals up here, if you want?'

'I'll have my first meal up here, and then find my feet.'

'Right,' said Blackwell. 'Now, you'd better meet Captain Murray Osten, "A" Company commander. They've the job of giving you support up to this RDF station.'

'What do I call you, Sergeant?'

'Newt is one nickname I've got,' Blackwell admitted. 'Blacky's another.'

'I don't go much on Newt,' said Jack. 'It's generally something to get pissed as. You're Blacky.'

Jack met Murray Osten in 'A' Company office.

'So you're the guy we've got to look after, right to the bitter end?' said Osten.

'That's it.'

'I understand you want some guys to help you with whatever you've got to do? How many are you thinking of?'

'Possibly six or seven. If we get into the RDF station, we may want to carry some equipment away. It will be heavy and probably fragile. The valves—tubes to you—could be as big as a Chinese vase, and about as delicate.'

'Right,' said Osten. 'We'll parade the company. Then you can choose them yourself. We've already selected two leaders for you. Both crack shots.'

The two men stood looking at each other for a moment as the full significance of the last three words sank in. Then Osten said awkwardly: 'Come into the mess, Jack, I'll stand you a drink.'

Next morning, Jack read Company Orders pinned on the notice board outside the CO's office. They contained news of promotions, postings, and particulars of daily training. In the 'A' Company detail was the line: 'RDF expert will attend'. As he turned away, Blacky came up to introduce a man about his own age. He wore a crown and laurel wreath on his sleeve; he was 'A' Company's sergeant major, Ed Dunkerley. They shook hands. Dunkerley was wiry, slightly built, with a bright, quick, keen look about him, not at all Jack's idea of the traditional type of sergeant major.

'I've read about you in Orders,' Dunkerley told him. His Canadian accent was not so pronounced as Blacky's; there was even a trace of Lancashire about it. Jack remarked on this, and Dunkerley explained that he had been born at Lees, near Oldham. Before the war, he had farmed in Carlyle, about seventy-five miles east of Weyburn. Ed Dunkerley had two children, a son and a daughter; the boy had been born only a few weeks before the CSM had sailed for England.

'Can't say much about myself except I'm Cockney and single, and have no children—so far as I know,' Jack told him.

'It's sure a wise child who knows his own father,' declared Blacky gravely.

Dunkerley said: 'We've got two leaders—"Muggsy" Thrussell—who's temporarily come down to private especially for this job—and Corporal Graham Mavor. Then there's Charlie Sawden, who's also a good marksman. He'll probably be on it. How do we introduce you?'

'As Jack. As an RDF man. And one other thing. You've just told me the names of three men who'll be with me. Please don't tell me any more. I don't want to know their real names, any more than I'd want them to know mine. No names, no pack drill, right? Then they'll know nothing about me, and I'll know nothing much about them. That way none of us will have anything to forget.'

Jack waited until the parade had fallen in, and then walked down the three platoons that formed the company. As he nodded briefly when he passed men he thought suitable, the order was given: 'Fall out at the side of the parade ground.'

Soon, ten men—Thrussell, Mavor and Sawden, with seven others—stood in a little group. Jack crossed over to them. They eyed him warily, puzzled how someone in the uniform of a British Army private, without any badges or markings, should be afforded this sort of treatment. What the hell was it in aid of? Jack explained as much as he could.

'Maybe we'll get inside the RDF station,' he went on, 'and if so, I'll need you to help carry back any bits and pieces I can dismantle. You don't know who I am, and I'm not going to tell you. I've only heard three of your names—Graham Mavor and Les Thrussell and Charlie Sawden. I will try to forget them, and I don't want to know who anyone else is. Nothing personal, but it will be safer that way all round if anything goes wrong. If the Jerries ever discover we're trying to do more than simply attack their RDF station, they'll go mad to find out who is involved—and why, and what it is we're after. So if any of you are unfortunate enough to be taken prisoner, forget all about me and the RDF station.'

'But what if *you* are captured?' one soldier asked Jack.

'I won't be.'

'How not?'

'I'll explain later,' interrupted Mavor quickly. 'Just listen to the guy. What he says goes. He makes sense. And he knows too much to be captured by the Heinies.'

'This on the level, Blacky?' asked a tall man, chewing a wad of gum.

'Sure is,' replied Blacky. 'This guy's a British scientist. That much I can say.'

'What do we call you then, buster?'

The Canadian who asked the question had very dark skin and high cheekbones. He pushed the gum from one side of his mouth to the other as he spoke. Jack guessed that he probably had Indian blood, which would make him the first part-Indian Jack had seen, except on a cinema screen. He suddenly felt parochial. These soldiers had come all the way from Canada, and so far he hadn't even been on a day trip to France. Well, this outing would at least change that.

'Jack,' he said. 'Call me that.'

'I don't want to know your real goddam name,' went on the dark-skinned man, 'any more than you want to know mine. But Jack's a fairly common name. I'll not forget it any road. But you sound like a Spook to me.'

He took out a packet of cigarettes, and did not offer them around. He lit one and drew heavily on it. The tips of his fingers were brown with nicotine. His voice sounded rough and gravelly.

'I'll call you Smokey,' said Jack. 'You look as though you get through forty a day.'

'Sixty,' corrected the man next in line. 'Like me.'

Jack turned to him. He was the soldier who had asked about Jack being taken prisoner. A man as tall as Smokey, broad-shouldered, but with a more friendly face; a farmer's face, Jack thought.

70

'You're Lofty?' he asked, searching for a nickname by which he could remember him.

'Nope,' said the man. 'Sounds like something out of Snow White and the Seven goddam Dwarfs.'

'You're the tallest dwarf I've ever seen—Lofty,' said Jack. A third man held out his hand.

'I come from Quebec,' he said in a slight French accent.

'Then you were a long way from home in Saskatchewan?'

'Maybe in miles,' the French Canadian agreed. 'But they're not a bad bunch—for sod-busters.'

'You're Frenchie, then,' said Jack. 'Okay?'

'Sure. But there's another guy in the regiment already called Frenchie—Frenchie Chamberlain.'

'I'll not confuse you. Must be a lot of other people called Jack, too.'

'Sure are, but you're the only *Limey* Jack. The only Spook.'

The next man in line had reddish hair and a way of laying his head on its side as he talked.

'I tell you, Jack,' he said, nodding towards Frenchie, 'he only joined up by mistake. Came over to Regina for some twenty-first birthday party. This guy was joining up, and Frenchie got pissed and when he came to he found he'd enlisted as well.'

'You should be useful to us in France,' said Jack. 'Speaking the lingo.'

'No problem,' said Frenchie. '*Pas de problème.*'

Jack faced the man with reddish hair.

'I'd better call you Red, because of your hair.'

'There's already a sergeant who's "Red"—Sergeant Ralph Neil of the Carrier Platoon.'

'I won't let that worry me.'

The next man had a hard-lined face as though it had been carved from a tree by a hatchet. His hands were the strongest Jack had ever seen.

'What did you do before the war?' Jack asked him, out of genuine interest.

'Tree felling. Contract work. Logging. A good life. And a good bunch of buddies to work with.'

'I can imagine,' agreed Jack. 'I don't know your name, but I'm going to call you Buddy—or Bud.'

The next man in line was slightly taller than Jack. The sun glinted metallically on his peculiarly fair hair, and Jack nick-named him Silver. Then there was Charlie Sawden, a trapper from Consul in Saskatchewan, in his twenties, a slim, taciturn man, who gravely shook Jack's hand. There was something about his quietness that Jack found impressive; Charlie Sawden was the sort of man it would be good to have on his side in a tough situation. But then they all were; after all, that was why he was selecting them.

The last man was younger than the rest. He explained that he had been a student, and had interrupted his training as a teacher to join up. His cheerful smiling face made him seem younger than he must have been. His grin reminded Jack of a character, Sunny Jim, who was used for advertising a brand of breakfast cereal; his face appeared on every packet.

'I'll call you Jim,' said Jack.

'He's always got some goddam quotation for every situation,' said Silver, with grudging admiration.

'That's the value of education,' retorted Jim. 'You may not know much yourself, but you sure know where to find it.'

'Jim don't need to go looking for it no place,' said Lofty drily. 'He's got it here. He's gonna marry a Limey girl.'

After these introductions Blackwell took Jack along to the stores to be issued with a revolver.

'You'd better have a rifle, too,' Blackwell added.

Quartermaster Sergeant Frederick Webb issued Jack with a .38 Smith and Wesson and a Lee-Enfield rifle, letting them go with the evident reluctance of his kind.

'I'd like a khaki small pack, too,' Jack told him.

'Sorry. Out of those,' Webb replied cheerfully. 'You can indent for one when the new lot come in, if you like.'

'When's that due?'

'Maybe a week. Ten days.'

'You haven't *anything* I could scrounge before then?'

'Sorry, buster, no can do.'

'We're on a forced march this morning,' Blackwell

explained as they walked back to the castle. 'Along with the Rangers.'

'Rangers?' Jack was puzzled. This sounded like a Girl Guide troop.

'Americans. They've been up with us at the Commando Training Centre at Achnacarry Castle in the Highlands. And you know something? We were the first non-Scottish soldiers to use that castle and its land in 200 years.'

'How did they take that?' Jack asked him.

'Oh, they didn't mind. After all, it's not as if we're goddam English!'

Later that afternoon, Jack wandered off on his own through the grounds to the sea. His thoughts kept returning to his last visit to the island before the war. He felt closer to his friends now than he had felt at any time since then. He followed a path that led across lawns and between trees. Some slight noise, the feeling he was not alone, made him pause. Feet ahead of him, a blade quivered in a sapling barely an inch wide. What the hell? he thought.

Then twigs crashed behind him and the tall, dark-skinned Canadian he called Smokey came past. He pulled the blade out of the wood, wiped it on the back of his hand.

'You aiming at me?' asked Jack.

Smokey shook his head.

'Nope. If I'd been aiming at you, Spook, I'd have got you.'

'You're pretty expert with that thing, then?'

'Uh huh.'

'Let's see you use it again.'

'Why?'

'No reason,' admitted Jack. 'But bet you a pint you couldn't hit that stick over there.'

He nodded towards a small branch that had fallen from a tree about thirty feet away.

'I only drink shorts,' said Smokey.

'Okay, then. If they've any whisky in the local.'

'Rum,' said Smokey. 'That's my juice.'

'Right. Rum.'

73

Smokey held the knife by the tip of its blade between his right thumb and forefinger, the handle resting against his wrist. Then his hand moved with shimmering speed. The twig splintered and the knife handle was trembling on its long blade above the grass.

'That's a large rum you owe me.'

'Fair enough. When did you learn to throw so well?'

'Not much else doing where I come from. So I learned some old Indian tricks,' said Smokey. 'Like making fire from sticks. Tracking. Knife throwing.'

'Could be helpful in a tight place.'

'To whom?' asked Smokey. 'Don't forget that drink, Spook.'

He walked back towards the castle, wiping the blade of his knife against his right trouser-leg. Jack walked on, and saw that half a dozen other Canadians were already standing in a group near the sea-wall. He recognized the men he called Lofty and Red. Lofty waved to him.

'We've been having a bit of target practice,' he explained. 'Know how to use a Sten or a Tommy-gun?'

Jack nodded.

'Even a rifle and bayonet,' he said. Stationed on a radar station at Rosehearty, north of Aberdeen, he had spent hours off duty with an old soldier in the Gordon Highlanders, who had been in the station guard. Archie Forbes-Smith had taught him how to handle a rifle and bayonet. He had learned the footwork, the follow-through; how to use the butt as a club; how to parry with the bayonet. None of the other technicians could understand why Jack grew so interested. It was simply that he genuinely enjoyed acquiring any new military skill.

'We aim at bottles. Empty ones,' Lofty went on.

Half a dozen beer bottles stood on the stone sea-wall, about a foot apart.

'Which one do you want me to take out?'

'Third from left,' said Jack.

'Right.'

Lofty raised the Tommy-gun, pushed over the lever to single shots, took aim and fired. The third bottle disintegrated.

'You make it look easy,' said Jack.

'Should do,' admitted Lofty. 'Worked in a fairground once. With a friend who was a pro boxer who'd take on anyone from the crowd at five dollars a round.'

'Did he always win?'

'Sure. Had to. It was his living. Weighted gloves helped.'

'What did you do?'

'Set up the ring for him. Looked after the rifles in the shooting gallery.'

Jack remembered regular travelling fairs at Blackheath and Hampstead Heath; thundering steam organs; plunging, prancing, painted wooden horses on the roundabouts; the chatter of air-rifles aimed at ping-pong balls in water jets or ringed targets.

'And you made a living at it?'

'Of a kind. Goddam barrels were all bent or the sights leaned on. Now you have a go, Spook.'

Lofty handed the Tommy-gun to Jack. He tossed it in his hands to grow accustomed to the feel and weight, then took aim and squeezed the trigger. Another bottle disintegrated. Jack handed the gun back to Lofty.

'You've got a good eye,' said Lofty, in a surprised voice.

'Two good eyes,' grinned Jack. 'Tell me, what made you join up?'

'Fair went broke. Every sideshow split up. People went every which way. You know? I wanted a living. And I could shoot good.'

'So you took the oddest job of all—a soldier.'

'Not so odd as your job, Spook. Whatever it is.'

'Well, hope you don't miss over on the other side.'

'You betcha I won't,' Lofty assured him.

Their eyes met for a second, then both men turned away, each suddenly embarrassed by the unintended inference.

On the following day, orders came to fall in for a practice night landing, code named Klondyke I, involving two passenger vessels, *Princess Beatrix* and *Invicta*, which, in peacetime, had been used by the Southern Railway to carry passengers on their Golden Arrow service across the Channel. Now both were festooned with landing craft suspended from huge davits on either side. The SSRs filed aboard, grumbling good-naturedly at the serious loss of a night's drinking time. Around them in the harbour lay a flotilla of destroyers, gun-boats and tank-landing craft.

Jack was pleasantly surprised to find he had a small single cabin in *Invicta*. He was separated from his bodyguard, and had indeed seen so little of them apart from Lofty and Smokey that he hoped he would recognize them again. Part of the difficulty lay in the fact that he did not know their real names. It was one thing to call a friend by a nickname, and quite another to remember false names you had invented for seven strangers. Several times, he addressed a Canadian as Bud or Silver and met with a blank stare of incomprehension.

A Tannoy announcement cut into his thoughts. The commanding officers spoke to their men: this was not just another practice; this was war. They were to sail through the night and land in France before dawn. For a moment there was silence, then the Canadians began to cheer. Soon the decks trembled with men stamping their boots in delight at the prospect of early action. They were briefly silent, as General Roberts, who was to command the landing, came aboard to address them.

'At last you are going to meet the enemy,' he announced. 'This evening, we are to sail for France and the target is the port of Dieppe. This is the operation you have been trained for, so at dawn tomorrow come off these boats running, and don't stop until you reach your objectives! And good luck to you all.'

Lord Louis Mountbatten also came aboard both ships and addressed the regiments in turn. They cheered him wildly. General Eisenhower then visited the US Rangers, to give them his best wishes for what he said would be an historic voyage. Under the command of Captain Roy Murray, they would be the first American troops to land in Europe since the Great War, a quarter of a century previously. Eisenhower described them simply and accurately as 'the first of thousands'. Colonel Merritt then briefed his company commanders on their special tasks.

When the briefing was over, Jack walked along the deck to his cabin. On the way he saw Lofty and Silver, but when he called to them, they turned away. Then he saw Bud, and he was sure Smokey was with him, but other soldiers came between them, and when he looked again they had also gone. Mavor came up the companionway, nodded briefly and went into the mess deck. Some of Jack's exhilaration at the prospect of imminent action began to evaporate.

He leaned on the rail, watching the activity on the shore, feeling as he had done on his first day at school, only much more deeply, that he was somehow alone, an outcast. He felt isolated from the others by reason of conditions he had accepted, but worse, he was psychologically an odd man out. The Canadians to whom he had been so briefly introduced on the Isle of Wight were already checking over their Stens and Brens and rifles. Their business was the business of war; to kill quickly and live to kill again. They had nothing in common with him, except they were on the same side and wore army uniform. They were tougher, rougher, brought up in a big country of harsh extremes. Jack was of a quieter more reflective countenance, an East End Jew, absorbed with the mysteries of radar and 'electrics'. His companions knew nothing about radar. To them 'electrics' meant a dynamo on a windmill behind some prairie shack, or the sparking plugs in their Chevy pick-up truck. The army food tended to divide them also. At Norris Castle, Jack ate his cheese and eggs, but left the ham. Even service slang separated them. They talked of screwing; he talked of horizontal PT.

He realized now, for the first time, how he was completely and absolutely alone; a crowd could never be company. Despite the easy bonhomie on the Isle of Wight, and the Canadians' apparent acceptance of him, he was still a stranger, a Spook; a man without a name or background; a volunteer forced on other volunteers against their wish; an unwanted passenger to soldiers about to go into battle.

77

He walked on to his cabin, and was early in bed. Tomorrow, they would see action.

In fact, tomorrow, they saw the same view of the Isle of Wight coast; and the day after, and the day after that *and* the one following.

All the time the weather stayed cloudy and the overcast sky made it impossible for paratroops to land with precision. Each day the cramped quarters of the ship became more irksome, and Jack was fortunate in having a cabin. He found some books and magazines in a cupboard and spent most of the time reading. On the fourth morning, four German planes flew in very low and bombed two of the ships carrying the Royal Regiment of Canada. Fortunately their bombs went right through both vessels before they exploded beneath their keels. Only four Canadians were injured. The rest disembarked and all marched back to their billets. On the way, a despatch rider handed their colonel a message. The raid was off. A sense of almost unbearable disappointment gripped everyone; of futile anger against the weather, of wild reaction after the prospect of action.

'Where does this leave you?' Blacky asked Jack. He intended retiring to Hope Cove, but when he felt in his trouser-pocket he found he had not enough money to pay for a snack on the way.

'I hate to ask this, Blacky,' he said, 'but I'm completely broke. I didn't think we'd need money in France so I spent all I had with me. Could you possibly lend me a quid?'

'No,' replied Blacky firmly, 'I'll lend you two.'

'I'll pay you back,' Jack assured him.

'When?'

'Bet you we'll be on this do again next month.'

'You're on,' said Blacky, and handed him two pound notes. Jack returned his rifle and revolver to the quartermaster's store. He was given a rail warrant, and within hours was back in the Blue Room at the Cottage Hotel, Hope Cove. Nothing seemed to have changed. As he sank gratefully into the sunken bath, he felt he might never have been away.

—FOUR—

Paul Brunet's flower shop stood on the north side of the Rue de la Barre, the main street in the centre of Dieppe that runs roughly parallel to the sea. The buildings are old and grey, and when the sun strikes at a certain angle, they seem to lean together. Brunet, a slimly-built, active man of forty-three, was making up the last of several wreaths in the back of the shop. Like all florists, he calculated the seasons of the year by flowers as much as by the calendar: daffodils in March; roses in June; stocks in July and dahlias in August. The roses were at their best, and he was adding some white and pink stocks to the white roses in the final wreath.

As Brunet worked deftly, winding thin wire around the long-stemmed roses, so fresh that they still had beads of moisture on their petals, he thought about his ancestors, who for five generations, father to son, father to son, had run the Brunet market-garden from 1760. How would they have coped with the strange flowers he sometimes had to use these days! Before the war, train-loads of spring and early summer blossoms for sprays, wreaths and bouquets arrived regularly in Dieppe from the South of France. Now, apart from what flowers he could grow himself in his greenhouse and market-garden at Les Vertus, a few miles inland from Dieppe, he had to make do with wild flowers picked in banks and hedges.

The sun, magnified by the plate-glass window, shone brightly into the shop; the air felt heavy with the scent of many blooms, and for the moment, thoughts of war seemed far away. Paul Brunet was an old soldier, who had joined up as a boy in the 129th French Infantry in the First War, and despite his age, had volunteered again in 1939. He had driven lorries, transporting shells and guns through Belgium, but for the past two years he had been back in the flower shop where he had worked in peacetime, for the war had ended for France in 1940.

He was now a member of the local 'Passive Defence Force', formed to help in air raids and other emergencies. He had no uniform, but on duty generally wore an old French army helmet, camouflaged in the German fashion, which hung on a peg in the back of his shop. Otherwise, his business was much the same as it had been in peacetime; only his customers, of course, were different. Instead of flowers for weddings, for anniversaries and funerals in Dieppe and the surrounding area, the majority of Paul Brunet's orders now were for wreaths in memory of young men—mostly German sailors. The German Army in France had suffered few casualties since 1940, apart from road accidents or through carelessness on firing ranges, but the Navy was regularly in action off the coast.

A German naval officer would come into Brunet's shop, bow to him with grave, rather distant courtesy, and then say, 'Monsieur Brunet, you must make five wreaths for us. Your best flowers, please. For an officer and four other ranks. They will be collected tomorrow at 0900 hours.'

Or maybe it would be an order for seven wreaths, or ten or twelve, for German sailors killed in clashes between their patrol boats and British motor torpedo boats out in the Channel. No matter what flowers Brunet used, each wreath was always bound with a bow of bright red ribbon, in such a way that its two long ends hung down. The German authorities had issued him with a generous supply of this special ribbon, and also a carton of two kinds of gummed paper labels. One was cut in the shape of the Iron Cross, to be attached to the left ribbon; the other, the Swastika, was fixed on the right. No cards with names or service numbers were ever asked for; the dead stayed discreetly anonymous.

Dieppe was a prohibited area, known as a Red Zone, and because even Frenchmen with business in the town needed a special pass which would be examined by a French gendarme at the police station, and sometimes by a German officer on duty with him, many people had moved out into the countryside. Monsieur Brunet still lived in a flat above the shop, but when he went to visit friends with his wife, they would invariably ask him: 'And how many wreaths have you made *this* week?'

He would tell them, and at once they would know how many German sailors had been killed. These small sea-battles occurred nearly every week, making the night sky flicker and rumble with distant shell-fire. In the harbour next morning, Brunet would see a patrol boat with mast slashed or funnel carried away, and more bodies lying under blankets on stretchers along the quay.

His present order was for six wreaths. In the past two or three weeks there had been nearly as many German casualties as during the previous three months. During daylight, too, there had been much more activity in the air. With a sudden roar of engines, RAF planes would swoop in so low over the cliffs that their slipstream flattened the long grass. Then they would fly around the harbour, above the cafés by the station, where some signs were still written in English—a reminder of pre-war days and the week-enders' Newhaven-to-Dieppe trips —and back north, over the Channel, sowing white vapour trails in the blue summer sky. Paul Brunet and other ex-soldiers guessed that some must be reconnaissance planes, for they had no guns, and what use was a fighter plane without guns—unless it carried cameras?

As an ex-soldier, too, Brunet appreciated the army aphorism that time spent in reconnaissance is seldom wasted. Surely the British would not be wasting time and petrol sending in so many inquisitive planes or patrol boats unless they planned to use the information they collected? He was convinced that this meant that there must be at least the hope of a raid or a landing soon, or maybe even the long-expected liberation.

The little bell above the front door tinkled on its curved flat spring. A German naval orderly entered and looked enquiringly at him. Paul Brunet's thoughts returned to the present.

'Ah, monsieur. Your flowers. They are ready,' he murmured, handing them across the glass-topped counter.

The success of any night landing during the summer along the north coast of France depended not only on the skill and bravery of those who attacked and those who defended, but also on three other essential elements: tide, weather and moon. For no matter how warm the summer, or how smooth the sea, each month had only three or four days when tides and moon were right for this purpose. And if the weather then should be wrong, the whole enterprise would have to be postponed.

Field-Marshal Gerd von Rundstedt, the German Commander-in-Chief in the West, responsible for the defence of France, was as aware of this as the planners in Combined Operations. He had accordingly made his own list of possible dates for such an enterprise. Von Rundstedt was a careful methodical man of sixty-six, a professional soldier for half a century, who could proudly trace his family back to 1109—with a soldier in nearly every generation. As a child, von Rundstedt had been brought up by an English nurse, and he spoke English well. Because he was an officer in the old tradition, he was no favourite of Hitler, and as early as 1934, he had clashed with Captain Ernst Röhm, the homosexual who had been one of Hitler's earliest associates, and who had helped the Führer in his schemes to seize power. Röhm, heavily involved with the *Sturm Abteilung*, the Brown Shirts, tried to corrupt the regular German army with his political ideas. There were many clashes between soldiers and SA men, and the inflammable situation only cooled when Hitler ended Röhm's aspirations to power by having him murdered.

Von Rundstedt had hated these earlier years of crude Party intrigues, and had offered his resignation, first to President Hindenburg and then to Hitler, the old Chancellor's successor. It was finally accepted in 1938, but he was recalled in the following year to be Commander-in-Chief of an army group during the Polish campaign. Because of von Rundstedt's refusal to become involved with Nazi politics, he was—

despite his seniority—never on Hitler's staff as a member of the HQ *Wehrmacht* (OKW) or the Headquarters staff of the Army (OKH). This meant that he inevitably had to receive supreme directives from above, and could not always give the orders that, with his ability and experience, he knew were correct.

In 1941, he had commanded an army group on the Russian front, and in March 1942, was appointed Commander-in-Chief of the West. His headquarters were in a hutted encampment in a wood near Amiens, but he lived in a villa at St Germain, outside Paris. During the summer, when the weather was fine, he and his Chief of Staff and adjutant maintained the pleasant English custom of taking afternoon tea in the garden at half past four.

The German troops most likely to be involved in throwing back any Allied landing under Field-Marshal von Rundstedt's overall control belonged to 15th Army, which was in charge of defences along the North Sea and Channel coasts from Ostend to Normandy. Their commander was Colonel-General Curt Haase, a man of sixty-one, with his headquarters at Tourcoing, inland from Boulogne. The 15th Army consisted of seventeen divisions, divided into three corps. The 81st Corps was responsible for the area from Caen to Dieppe, and was commanded by General Adolf Kuntzen, nine years Haase's junior, with headquarters in Canteleu, a suburb of Rouen.

The troops concerned directly with the defence of Dieppe within this Corps were the 302nd Infantry Division, whose commander, Major-General Konrad Haase, shared the same name as his army commander, but was no relation; he had been born in Dresden, and his army commander came from Honnef on the Rhine. His headquarters was established in Envermeu, a small town built around a crossroads, on the Route Nationale 320, about ten miles inland from Dieppe.

The Dieppe garrison only totalled about 1,500 men of the 571st Infantry Regiment under the command of Lieutenant-Colonel Hermann Bartelt. He kept two battalions, with his regimental headquarters, in Dieppe; a third was stationed to the west of the port, and a fourth to the east. The fifth was in reserve at Ouville-la-Rivière, five miles from the coast. This reserve force was a mobile column equipped with cycles.

Much further inland, and centred on Amiens, the 10th Panzer Division waited in readiness under its commander, Lieutenant-General Wolfgang Fischer. This division had originally been formed in April 1939, and had fought through the Polish campaign and surged west towards Amiens, eventually capturing Calais. It had been posted to the Russian front, and in April 1942 was withdrawn from Smolensk, after it had been severely mauled in heavy fighting. The division's transport had been driven for months under exceptionally harsh weather conditions, and many vehicles were running on almost bald tyres; others lacked spare wheels. Petrol was generally so short that new drivers lacked experience in convoys, and the standard of vehicle maintenance was poor, due to a shortage of spares.

Further inland still, at Vernon, the SS Adolt Hitler Brigade was stationed under its commander, Sepp Dietrich. Like the 10th Panzer Division, this brigade had also fought in Poland and through France, and had only returned in early July from the Donets Basin on the Russian front. But among the other generals, who were professional soldiers from families with military traditions, Dietrich occupied a uniquely powerful political position, for he had been one of the earliest Nazis, and was still among the most vociferous and influential Party members. In 1934, the year after Hitler seized power, Dietrich had commanded Hitler's SS bodyguard, and in this capacity he had personally directed Röhm's liquidation and those of some other early associates of the Führer, whose energy and popularity had inevitably made them expendable. Sepp Dietrich was a big, tough, rough man who enjoyed the trade of war. His complaint this spring was that France seemed to be at peace.

The success of the British Commando raid in Bruneval in February had caused concern to the German High Command, and when this was followed by the equally successful raid on St Nazaire, the result was a further increase in German concern and preparedness. The Bruneval raid had shown the vulnerability of lonely radar stations along the coast, so all such radar stations were given extra guards and surrounded by barbed wire defences and machine-gun posts. Bushes, small trees, and even long grass were also cut down around each isolated station to deny cover to any attackers.

On March 23, Hitler issued his 40th Directive of the War, which was headed:

> Ref. Competence of Commanders in coastal areas.
> General Considerations:
> The coastline of Europe will, in the coming months, be exposed to the danger of an enemy landing in force.
> The time and place of the landing operations will not be dictated to the enemy by operational considerations alone. Failure in other theatres of war, obligations to allies, and political considerations may persuade him to take decisions which appear unlikely from a purely military point of view. Even enemy landings with limited objectives can interfere seriously with our own plans if they result in the enemy gaining any kind of foothold on the coast. . . .
> Enemy forces which have landed must be destroyed or thrown back into the sea by immediate counter-attack. All personnel bearing arms — irrespective to which branch of the Armed Forces or to which non-service organization they may belong — will be employed for this. . . .

On July 9, Hitler issued a further directive to his three fighting services, urging them to reinforce the Western Defences. In this, he said:

> Our great and rapid victories may face Great Britain with the alternative of launching a full-scale invasion with the object of opening a Second Front, or of seeing Russia obliterated as a military factor. It is therefore highly probable that an enemy landing will take place shortly in the area of C-in-C, West.

General Haase immediately ordered extensive landing exercises on Puys, Dieppe and Pourville beaches. Fatigue parties uncoiled rolls of barbed wire over sea-walls and promenades, and built brick walls across gulleys leading up from beaches to deny them to tanks. Rows of wood and metal stakes were driven into fields and concrete cubes dumped along main roads, ready to block them. The whole coast bristled with artillery emplacements, shielded by concrete walls impregnaable to all known shells.

Miles of cliff face overlooking the Channel were diligently tunnelled out, and stacked with ammunition and food to make artillery crews independent for a minimum of forty-eight hours' siege. Special guns were installed on wheels and rails so they could be run forward to cave-mouths to fire, and then drawn back for protection. Six-foot deep trenches lined with concrete linked many defence posts, so that, in the event of one gun jamming or being hit, the crew could move in safety to another. Individual weapon pits were dug for snipers who were issued with special smokeless cartridges, so that their positions would not be given away by muzzle flash and smoke from their rifles.

Engineers and forced labourers of the Todt Organization, including many French and Belgian workers employed on this urgent strengthening of what Hitler called the Atlantic Wall, were billeted at strategic points around the French coast, so they could be rushed to wherever they might be needed. They occupied a large hostel in Pourville, where they had sited weapon pits and pill-boxes with concrete walls three feet thick; their senior operatives lived nearby in the Hôtel de la Terrasse.

Throughout the spring and early summer, German Military Intelligence—the *Abwehr*—attempted to form some mosaic of Allied intentions from such isolated facts as they could glean. The Intelligence Officer of the 302nd Infantry Division reported that on May 20 a message had been found in a small hole dug beneath the drive of a house in Criel-Plage near Dieppe. This claimed that several British agents were due to arrive by parachute within the following week. In June, a sailor aboard a neutral ship calling at Portsmouth, willingly described concentrations of landing craft and barges along the English south coast. A third indication of possible Allied intentions followed the success of the *Abwehr* in breaking certain British radio codes between London and French Resistance groups. This feat led eventually to a loft of homing pigeons in the garden of a house outside Dieppe. These pigeons had originally belonged to a French pigeon-fancier who escaped to England after the fall of France, with several cages of his birds. British Intelligence employed them to carry messages, largely as confirmation of earlier radio signals made under bad transmission conditions. A French Resistance courier collected these messages and was followed. Unsuspectingly, he led the Germans to an SOE radio operator, who was persuaded to work for the Germans—just as German radio operators captured in Britain were similarly made to see that their only hope of survival lay in co-operation. As a result, the *Abwehr* deliberately and systematically fed false information to British Intelligence, along with some true but unimportant facts. One consequence was the British and Canadian planners underestimated the strength of German defences around Dieppe.

On July 20, Colonel-General Haase, as 15th Army Commander, issued a special Order of the Day, in which he urged extra vigilance over three remaining periods of that summer when he considered that moon and tides would be right for an enemy landing. These were from July 27 to August 3; from August 10 to 19; and from August 25 to September 1.

The walls of the orderly officer's workroom in Field-Marshal von Rundstedt's headquarters were papered with maps. Some showed the French Atlantic coast, with the disposition of German defences, but two other maps were consulted more often by young officers on the staff; these were large scale plans of Paris streets. Everyone who went on leave to Paris was asked to chart his experiences on one or both of them. Blue-headed drawing pins indicated the position of restaurants that they considered worth a visit. Red drawing pins marked the location of other, more lascivious pleasures. Von Rundstedt, entering his room one day, glanced at both maps and remarked drily: 'Here, your red map isn't *nearly* full.'

The three possible periods for the expected enemy landing were ringed in red on a large wall calendar. The first set of dates had already been crossed out. By all accounts, the weather should be better in the middle of August than at the end of the month, when sudden sea mists could shroud the coast and render navigation difficult.

Colonel-General Curt Haase was well aware of his responsibility should any invasion be attempted, for considerable numbers of his troops were relatively new recruits who had never been in action. It was impossible to know how they would acquit themselves in such an emergency, so on August 10 he issued a special Order of the Day, which he hoped would stimulate a sense of mission, patriotism and reponsibility in the minds of all under his command. Copies were pinned on the notice boards of all units.

> The information in our hands makes it clear that the Anglo-Americans will be forced, in spite of themselves, by the wretched predicament of the Russians to undertake some operation in the West in the near future.
> They must do something —
> (a) in order to keep their Russian allies fighting;
> (b) for home front reasons.
> I have repeatedly brought this to the attention of the troops and I ask that my orders on this matter be kept constantly before them so that the idea sinks in thoroughly and they expect henceforward nothing else.
> The troops must grasp the fact that when it happens it will be a very sticky business.
> Bombing and strafing from the air, shelling from the sea, commandos and assault boats, parachutists and air-landing troops, hostile civilians, sabotage and murder — all these they will have to face with steady nerves if they are not to go under.
> On no account must the troops let themselves get rattled. Fear is not to be thought of.
> When the muck begins to fly the troops must wipe their eyes and ears, grip their weapons more firmly and fight as they have never fought before.
>
> ### THEM OR US
>
> must be the watchword for each man.
> The Führer has given the German Armed Forces tasks of every kind in the past and all have been carried out. The task which now confronts us will also be carried out. My men will not prove the worst. I have looked into your eyes. I know that you are German men.

YOU WILL GLADLY DO YOUR SIMPLE DUTY TO THE
DEATH. DO THIS AND YOU WILL REMAIN VICTORI-
OUS. LONG LIVE OUR PEOPLES AND FATHERLAND.
LONG LIVE THE FÜHRER, ADOLF HITLER.

(Signed)   Your Commander,   HAASE
                 Colonel-General

Von Rundstedt personally favoured the night of August
18/19, and said so in a Special Order. The Luftwaffe commander in the Dieppe area did not share the commander-in-
chief's opinion. The weather forecast was cloudy, and it
seemed unlikely that there would be much air activity under
such conditions. Accordingly, he granted many of his pilots
extended leave until noon on August 19. General Haase's
divisional headquarters, however, was manned on a twenty-
four-hour basis by relays of officers in response to von
Rundstedt's Special Order:

> The night 18/19th can be regarded as suitable for enemy raid-
> ing operations. Commanders of coastal defences to maintain
> troops at the Threatened Danger Alert.

Throughout July and August, the public in Britain and the
United States, with no inkling that any raid on France had
even been proposed, continued to clamour for an immediate
Second Front with rallies and meetings, and slogans chalked
on factory walls. Casualties on the Russian Front were still
enormous, and Churchill, due to meet Stalin soon, faced the
disagreeable task of having to inform him that despite Roosevelt's unwise promise to Molotov, there simply could not be
any Second Front in 1942. Now, it seemed that there would
not even be a rehearsal.

Lord Mountbatten discussed the situation with Churchill
and the other Chiefs of Staff. All agreed that unless the Allies
could carry out a successful amphibious landing on the Continent that summer, it would have to be postponed at least
until the following spring, when once again the three essential
factors would be favourable. This, in turn, meant postponing
the real Second Front to some even more indefinite date, with

all the bitterness any further delay would cause between Russia and the West. And the dilemma of the secret war—whether to risk jamming German radar or not—was still as serious as ever, with no firm decision taken either way.

With only a few brief periods remaining when moon and tide would favour an amphibious landing, no other operation of equal size could be mounted for a new target. Mountbatten then made a new proposal which he felt was so daring that he decided it should not be committed to paper, but simply discussed: it was to remount Rutter, the original raid on Dieppe, and carry it out in August.

The Chiefs of Staff and Churchill argued against this suggestion on the grounds of security. Six thousand troops, and probably nearly as many men in the other two services, had been actively concerned with Rutter, and had then dispersed on leave, or to their units. Surely some must have mentioned the abandoned raid to friends or family? Mountbatten replied that although German aircraft had sighted an assembly of ships off the IOW in July and attacked them, they could have no idea why they were there—or what had been their destination. If, by now, they had discovered that a raid had been planned for Dieppe, but later cancelled, they would never seriously consider that the Allies would remount the same operation on the same target.

The original Commander of the Naval Force had taken up a new posting, but Captain Hughes-Hallett, who had been Mountbatten's chief naval planner for Rutter, was available to take his place. General Crerar, who commanded the First Canadian Corps, had taken over General Montgomery's responsibilities. Both these officers approved of Mountbatten's proposal. It was thus decided to go ahead, but instead of using paratroops, they would employ two new infantry landing ships to carry Commandos, who could deal with the batteries at Berneval and Varengeville.

The paratroops were dispensed with because of possible weather difficulties. They would need cloud at a certain height if they were to drop accurately and effectively, and such cloud conditions might not coincide with weather suitable for a sea-borne landing. And instead of leaving from the Isle of Wight again, the ships transporting the Canadians and the Commandos would be dispersed in harbours along the south coast. Thus, even if German reconnaissance planes did succeed in photographing them, no alarm would be caused, for these vessels would not be grouped in significant numbers in any one place. The troops concerned would board them believing they were to make another practice landing on the English south coast. Instead, they would immediately set sail for France. This would prevent any security risk about revealing their destination prior to departure.

Churchill and the Chiefs of Staff agreed to Mountbatten's request not to keep written minutes of all these decisions. Churchill added that on no account should the First Lord of the Admiralty be told beforehand. Indeed, the first news that this gentleman heard of the matter was in a BBC broadcast —while the raid was actually in progress.

On August 10, headquarters, Second Canadian Division, gave orders for tanks to be waterproofed in preparation for 'a Combined Operations' demonstration'. Three days later, they announced three motor transport exercises, code named Ford I, II and III, which were to last for a month, starting on August 15. In fact, Ford I was simply to cover the movement of transport to Southampton, where they would embark for this new raid, code named Jubilee.

The speed and secrecy of this totally unexpected move took at least three SSR officers by complete surprise. On Friday, August 14, Major Claude Orme was ordered to attend a lecture in a village west of Chichester. On arrival, he discovered that this was in fact a briefing for this resuscitated raid on Dieppe, to take place within the following week. He was to be Officer Commanding Troops aboard one of the mother ships, *Invicta*. He met *Invicta*'s captain and they discussed what accommodation the troops would need, but all the time Orme's mind was partly on his own personal arrangements for the following evening. He had planned to go to a concert in London with some friends; now his orders were to stay strictly within the camp confines. So Claude Orme had to telephone his friends, and make up an unconvincing excuse for being unable to join them.

The second officer, Lieutenant Douglas Johnson, who had worked in an audit department of a store with branches in Calgary and Regina before the war, was transport officer with the unit. He had just returned from a course on his motor-cycle, and was still wearing his regulation despatch-rider's boots, with high lace-up sides, when Colonel Merritt happened to see him.

'Doug,' Merritt told him, 'you'd better change those boots.'

'Why?'

'You might have to do some running.'

Puzzled by this remark, Johnson changed his boots and, still on his motor-cycle, accompanied the convoy on its exercise, Ford I. While Johnson had been away on his course, another young officer had taken over his duties. When the convoy reached Southampton docks, and the troops began to embark, Johnson asked Colonel Merritt: 'What am I supposed to do now?'

'Just take the empty transport back.'

'Is that all?'

'This is no exercise, Doug,' said Merritt quietly. 'This is the real thing. Do you want to go?'

'Of course,' replied Johnson instantly.

So Colonel Merritt sent back the replacement officer with the empty trucks, and Johnson joined them, armed only with his revolver, and without any kit whatever. He managed to scrounge a Tommy-gun from someone, and was ready for battle.

The third officer, Lieutenant Leslie England, commanding Special Force, had recently returned from a visit to London, where he had bought himself a fine pair of new boots from Burberrys. They were a most distinctive brown colour, perhaps not entirely military issue, but extremely comfortable and smart. To break them in, he decided to wear them on Ford I. This chance decision was later to save his life.

* * *

Jack had ringed two dates in his diary for quite different reasons. Monday, August 17, was the last of a period of night duty, and on the evening of Tuesday, August 18, he had invited a WAAF sergeant, Mary Conlon, to a station dance.

Monday night had been busy. The weather was good, and the Early Warning radar chain had reported an unidentified aircraft within 120 miles of the coast.

Night fighters were instantly scrambled from Exeter, while attempts were made to identify the aircraft to see whether it was British or not, for every RAF plane carried a secret radar transmitter/receiver, known as IFF, Identification, Friend or Foe. There was no reply, which could mean this plane was hostile.

A circular map of the entire area, with the radar station at its centre, was engraved on a perspex mask that fitted over the radar screen in Jack's ops room. The rotating radar transmission was like a narrow lighthouse beam illuminating the aircraft as a blip on the screen under this mask. This equipment, known as PPI, Plan Position Indicator, showed the exact position of the plane and its course.

The night fighter pilots changed their radio-telephone frequencies when they were airborne and came under Jack's direct control. On his screen he could see exactly where the unidentified aircraft was at that moment, and, by calculating its speed, direction and height, could guide the fighters straight towards it. The Beaufighters were almost on to it when the pilot belatedly gave his identification signal—a lapse that had nearly cost his life.

When there was a kill, excitement in the station was phenomenal. As the pilot administered the *coup-de-grâce*, the operators would see the blip suddenly disappear from the screen as the enemy plane went down out of control. This was always accompanied by excited jubilation from the pilot over the radio-telephone and one of Jack's team would immediately paint up another swastika on the ops room wall. The fact that this was a false alarm brought its own reaction, and Jack felt more than usually tired when he went off duty. He made out a tracing with detailed times of the whole operation, for

Fighter Command and the Operational Research Section. As he climbed thankfully into bed, the telephone rang by his ear; the guard-room corporal reported that a staff car had arrived with orders to take him to Long Cross immediately. Jack guessed the raid must be on again.

Wearily, he pulled on his socks and pants, his blue Air Force shirt, and then he paused. Perhaps he should wear a khaki battledress? Better use his own instead of the outfit from the wing commander, which fitted only where it touched. But the only khaki battledress he possessed had the blue stripes and crown of a flight sergeant and RAF spreadeagle badges at the shoulders. He removed the blade from his Gillette razor, snipped the thread, and ripped off the stripes and badges. Then he put on his boots and gaiters and checked his testing gear including, again, the avometer his father had given him.

Into another pack he put his razor, comb, lather brush, towel, bar of soap in its aluminium case; spare pair of socks and pants, handkerchief, and a metal shaving mirror. Jack then hurried out of his room, carrying his two small packs. Crossing the airfield, he met Mary Conlon and he suddenly and guiltily remembered their date that same evening.

'Where are you off to?' she asked him in surprise.

'An urgent job has suddenly come up. I'm sorry, but I won't be back in time for the dance.'

She only half believed him.

'I suppose you'll be dining and dancing at the Savoy instead?' she said sarcastically.

'Back in a couple of days,' Jack assured her. 'Sorry!'

The driver held open the door of the staff car.

'Where is it this time?' Jack asked him.

'Combined Ops HQ in Richmond Terrace, Flight.'

'I'll sit in the back, then,' said Jack. 'I must get some kip on the journey.'

When Richmond Terrace had been built in the early nine-teenth century, on the ruins of an older structure, Richmond House, the family home of the Dukes of Richmond, it had been described as 'eight residences of the first class, and appropriate domestic and stable offices thereto'. Now one of these residences behind the imposing stone façade with six Ionic columns, housed Combined Operations Headquarters. The driver stopped the car outside and produced his pass for an armed sentry. Jack's paybook was examined, an entry made in a record book at the Security Office, and then he was shown into a room on an upper floor. Sitting at a table were the RAF wing commander and the Army colonel he had seen previously in King Charles Street.

'We'd better check your gear again,' said the wing commander. 'You're wearing your own khaki uniform this time?'

'Yes, sir.'

'Well, you can't wear that RAF cap. Here's the Army cap you had before. And a steel helmet. And identity discs without RAF on them. And your escape kit. Leave your paybook here. No envelopes addressed to you, no letters, tram tickets, cinema tickets? Nothing like that?'

'Nothing at all.'

'The car will take you to Southampton. You will embark this evening. Destination and orders as before. Any questions?'

'Nothing, sir.'

'Good luck, then.'

Jack saluted and went down the stairs into the street. It was still early afternoon. They drove out through West London, down through Staines, on to the Southampton Road. The warmth of the car, and lack of sleep on the previous night, combined to make Jack drowsy. Presently, he slept.

At the same moment, and entirely unknown to Jack, a Canadian army sergeant, Roy Hawkins, was kick-starting his 350 cc BSA motor-cycle outside the headquarters of the Canadian Field Security Section on the edge of East Grinstead, in Sussex, thirty miles away. That morning, Roy Hawkins' commanding officer, Major John Green, who had served with Hawkins' father in the Royal Canadian Mounted Police—the Mounties—had called him into his office.

'The Second Div. is going into action,' he explained. 'It's a chance for you to gain experience in the field, doing a very delicate job.'

Roy Hawkins knew that Major Green was eager to help him gain promotion; Hawkins' name had already been put forward for a commission, and active service would doubtless help his chances.

'You'll report to Southampton Docks by motor-cycle. I'll give you a sealed envelope to show to the provost sergeant to get you aboard the ship, the *Princess Beatrix*. Some British scientist is going ashore with the boys, dressed as a soldier, to crack the secrets of a German RDF station. You have to give him cover, and if things go badly for him, you've got to see he isn't captured. He knows too much.'

'You mean, shoot him, sir?'

'How you carry out your orders is your affair, Hawkins. He either has to come back alive, or he stays there dead.'

'What kit will I need?'

'Battle order and your revolver. Report back here afterwards.'

'How will I recognize this man, sir?'

'Aboard ship, report to the intelligence officer or "A" Company commander—this guy is attached to "A" Company. They'll point him out. Make yourself known. And then stay with him. Good luck.'

'Thank you, sir.'

Hawkins saluted, and walked out of the room. There was one matter he had not thought it politic to mention to the major; his revolver. He had been experiencing some trouble with it, for the firing pin was not operating satisfactorily. To exchange the weapon officially would involve long explanations, delays and form filling, and might even mean that someone else went in his place. There was fortunately, another easier way. . . .

Hawkins cautiously opened the door of the sergeant major's office. The sergeant major was out, but his revolver, in its webbing holster, was hanging on its webbing belt from a hook behind the door. Hawkins unbuckled his own revolver, quickly exchanged it for the sergeant major's, then went on to his own quarters and packed his small kit.

He emptied his pockets of paybook, letters, bus tickets, some pound notes and copper coins. Suddenly, on impulse, he took off his battledress blouse and pulled on a thick grey sweater, buttoning up his blouse on top of it. This sweater had been specially knitted for him by his English fiancée, Rowena. She had impressed on him that she had used eighteen months' precious clothing coupons on the wool, and Roy felt he could not leave this magnificent sweater behind. It was too precious, literally a labour of love; also, it would be useful if the Channel crossing was cold.

Roy had first met Rowena and her mother in a cinema at Epsom one week-end, when he was with a French-Canadian soldier. Rowena's mother was Belgian, and when she heard the French-Canadian speaking French, she had replied in the same language. That conversation led to tea after the film, and tea eventually led to Roy Hawkins becoming engaged to Rowena.

He checked the level in his petrol tank, started the engine and set off, still slightly bemused by the astonishing orders he had been given. Surely this sort of thing was more suitable to a film than to real life? Hawkins was a well-built, slow-speaking man, just twenty-one, who had been born in Regina, Saskatchewan, and moved when he was six to Fort McMurray in Alberta, where his father was stationed. Fort McMurray was originally a Hudson's Bay trading post for trappers, and marked the end of the railway line. It was built on the Athabasca River, which meant, in the Indian dialect, 'Muddy River'. There was no bridge across in those days, so in winter they would build what they called an ice bridge. Waiting until the river froze, they would then pack more and more ice on top of the frozen water. When the ice covering was several feet thick, they could lay logs across it and drive over to the other side. Fort McMurray was a small town, carved out of an infinity of trees, with names Hawkins had known from boyhood: jack-pine, tamarack, birch, spruce, poplar. In winter, these trees would stand white with snow; in summer, miles of different greens would merge around the shores of steel blue lakes linked by rough roads, straight as sword blades. Hawkins had attended St John public school and then worked for an airline as an apprentice engineer. When war broke out, he and four friends walked to the local recruiting office to join up in the Fleet Air Arm or the Navy, which seemed more exciting than the Army. But neither of these services were accepting recruits, so he joined the infantry, and later transferred to Field Security.

At Southampton Docks, two armed naval sentries stopped him. Hawkins showed his Field Security pass, and they waved him on. He puttered along, past the loading sheds, across sunken railway lines, to find a place to park his motor-cycle. Then he turned off the petrol, pulled the machine up on its rear stand and walked towards the ship.

Jack woke up as the car bumped over cobbles at the main entrance of King George V Dock in Southampton. The driver paused briefly to show his pass to the sentry, then drove on. They stopped by the side of a towering grey hull, streaked and scabbed with rust. Jack recognized the *Princess Beatrix*, the sister ship of the *Invicta*, in which he had waited for four days off the Isle of Wight the previous month. The gangway was still down, and the decks were packed with Canadians leaning over the handrails, cheering and whistling, still thinking that this was just another goddam exercise. Some of them shouted and jeered and gave the 'V' sign as Jack's staff car stopped near the gangway. No doubt this was just another stupid senior officer, with a face as red as his tabs, who was arriving to be an umpire or make an inspection, or some other useless exercise.

Then, one or two of the men Jack had met at Norris Castle recognized him. He heard them shout in good-natured surprise: 'Spook! There's the Spook!' Almost immediately, the jeers and catcalls turned to cheers, perhaps not for Jack but for what his arrival represented. He would not arrive in a staff car with a driver simply to join them on another night landing along the Dorset coast. His presence *must* mean they were going to see action at last.

Jack came aboard, waving back to them, grinning at this unexpected welcome. He was hardly inside, when a crane lifted away the gangway, and the round-edged sea-door clanged behind him. The *Princess Beatrix* made ready to cast off. Blacky was waiting for him on the entrance landing.

'Hullo,' said Jack, glad to see him. Then he remembered something, and put his hand in his back pocket. He took out two pound notes and handed them to Blacky.

'Boy! Knock me down! I never thought I'd see these again,' said Blacky in amazement. '*And* this month, just as you said. You really *are* a Spook. You got inside knowledge?'

'Of course. I'm a walking oracle.'

'Then walk along with me,' said Blacky. 'You've a cabin to yourself, which is more than I have.'

The cabin was a small hutch with a bunk which pulled down from the wall and a zinc washbasin with a yellowish mirror above it. Jack opened a drawer, and put his packs inside.

'So we're really going this time?'

Blackwell nodded.

Later, at a briefing, Jack learned that the orders were exactly the same, apart from the fact that British Commandos would be used instead of paratroops, and there would be no aerial bombardment before the landing. The regiment would still go ashore at Pourville, which had the same code name: Green Beach.

The headquarters ship from which the entire landing—from Orange Beach, beyond Varengeville-sur-Mer in the west to Yellow Beach at Berneval in the east—would be controlled, was the destroyer *HMS Calpe*. Aboard this ship, General Roberts and his staff would be in direct radio contact with each of the Canadian regiments involved and also with the tanks, with British Commandos, other Naval ships, and the RAF control room at Fighter Command's No. 11 Group at Uxbridge. Carrier pigeons would also be taken aboard *Calpe*

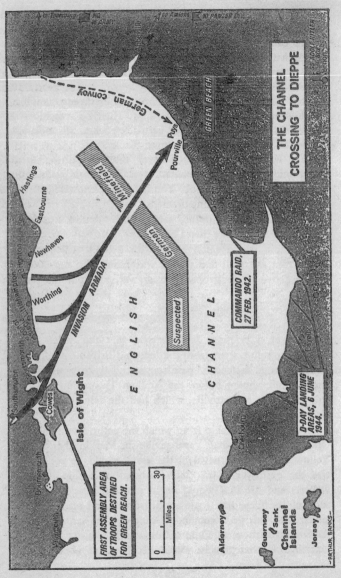

THE CHANNEL
CROSSING TO DIEPPE

ENGLISH CHANNEL

GREEN BEACH

German convoy

Pays

Pourville

Minefield

German

Suspected

INVASION ARMADA

Hastings
Eastbourne
Newhaven
Brighton
Worthing

Southampton

Isle of Wight

Cowes

Bournemouth

FIRST ASSEMBLY AREA
OF TROOPS DESTINED
FOR GREEN BEACH.

COMMANDO RAID,
27 FEB. 1942.

D-DAY LANDING
AREAS, 6 JUNE
1944.

Cherbourg

Bayeux

Alderney
Guernsey
Sark
Channel Islands
Jersey

Miles
0   30

—ARTHUR BANKS—

to despatch messages back to England should any of the radio links fail.

Once ashore, the South Saskatchewan Regiment's first objective was to establish a bridgehead through which the Queen's Own Cameron Highlanders of Canada would pass on their way to attack the airfield at St Aubin on the road to Arques-la-Bataille, which was believed to house the headquarters of a German division.

Photographs of Pourville were passed round. These concentrated on the town, not the radar station, and showed a stretch of shingle, with the River Scie emptying into the sea, a cluster of houses, and high white cliffs to the east and west. Jack now began to appreciate just how difficult his task was going to be. The earlier pictures that the wing commander had shown him in London had concentrated on the RDF station. Now he saw that these cliffs on which it stood were sheer and several hundred feet high. Snipers and machine-gun nests embedded in caves and holes could decimate anyone on the beach in daylight. Jack was also surprised to see how small Pourville was; literally a straggling cluster of houses built around a sharp bend in the road from Dieppe. A hotel stood seaward of this bend, a church on the other side of the road, that then swung up a steep hill and divided; one branch went left to Petit-Appeville, another village, and the other led up to Varengeville on top of the cliffs.

Right down on the beach at one end of a promenade, stood the casino and behind this a small building with mock-Tudor beams, that contained the electric light generators. The main street had houses and a few shops on either side of it, and a row of tall houses faced the promenade. Larger, isolated houses peered out of trees on the hillside overlooking Pourville, and others—probably farm dwellings—were scattered in the fields and rising land towards the RDF station. The River Scie seemed little bigger than Regent's Park Canal; the bridge across it was about thirty feet wide, and flat, with concrete balustrades on either side. Not that this mattered; he and his men were due to land east of the river, right under the cliff on which the station stood. He was glad of this, at least. It would be suicidal to attempt to cross that bridge, for obviously it would be covered by guns trained along fixed lines to cut down anyone unwise enough to try.

Each company in the regiment had its own special objective: 'D' Company would go east to capture a farmhouse known as the Farm of the Four Winds, set up on a hill and dominating the road to St Aubin; 'C' Company would move south-west and destroy a motor transport repair workshop and machine-gun positions, and then capture the German officers' mess and remove any prisoners and documents they could find; 'B' Company would go straight through Pourville, clearing out the Germans, and then examine a barbed wire compound beyond it, and finally turn east; 'A' Company were to go east up the road towards the RDF station on the hill that overlooked Dieppe, to deal with coastal batteries which commanded the frontal landing at Dieppe, being undertaken by other Canadian regiments.

The carrier platoon was leaving behind its Bren-gun carriers, small tracked vehicles powered by Ford V8 engines. Instead, armed with Tommy-guns, the men would be attached to 'A' Company as before, as a Special Force under their usual platoon commander, Lieutenant Leslie England. Their task was to help take out strong points on the way to the RDF station, and then give cover to Jack and his team. All companies would later head back towards the beach, where landing craft would be waiting to take them off.

Jack was unhappy at the news there would be no preliminary RAF bombing. He wondered whether the Canadians realized what this could mean, especially to the regiments making the frontal landing at Dieppe? Like him, they knew of anti-invasion defences that ringed the British coast: oil jets to set the sea alight; submerged coils of barbed wire to cut to pieces anyone wading through shallow water; sharpened dragon's teeth stakes in the beaches to rip tank tracks; the hidden mines, and the large and small guns laid on carefully calculated fixed lines so that everyone on the beach would be under constant fire. Was it unreasonable to suppose that the Germans would not give them an equally rough reception?

Jack came away from the briefing and looked down on the dock beneath. Fatigue parties of soldiers in shirtsleeves stood about, some with arms folded, some giving the 'V' sign to friends, who waved down to them from upper decks. There was something of a carnival atmosphere about the departure that recalled newsreels of transatlantic liners leaving, sirens booming, streamers flung from ship to shore.

Unseen sailors shouted orders; others levered ropes thick as their wrists from iron bollards. Propeller blades began to flay the scummy water, and the ship, which had until that moment been an inert iron mass bound by umbilical links to the shore, now came alive with a heart and power and spirit of her own. A view of cranes, saw-tooth roofs of warehouses, and parked army trucks slid past him. Soldiers on the shore were waving still, but already they were shrinking figures. They had no part in what lay ahead; they had been left behind. For the time being, they were safe, and Jack half-envied, half-pitied them.

A knock at the door: he opened it. A steward stood outside politely.

'I understand you are the RDF expert, sir?'

'That's right. What do you want?'

'Captain's compliments, sir. Would you kindly report to him on the bridge?'

Puzzled, Jack followed the man along the packed deck to the bridge companionway. As he walked, he felt the ship tremble beneath him as engines increased speed. As Jack climbed up to the bridge, the ships began to pass the old chequered forts that marked the approach to land, and gradually the shore receded, and on both sides other vessels joined the flotilla. As he entered the bridge, air-raid sirens began to wail. He thought instantly of his radar station at Hope Cove; of friends in other radar stations around the coast tracking the intruders, just as they would be tracking these ships sailing south, reporting their position, their speed, and direction.

The captain turned towards him.

'You're a radar man, I understand?'

'Yes, sir.'

'Then I wonder if you can help me? The ship's set has broken down. Not that we can use it now, in case Jerry picks up our signals, but I'd be grateful if you *could* do anything.'

Jack went into the radio room. The air was alive with static; Morse code squealed messages and music poured in from hundreds of miles away. He removed the back of the set; inside, the valves were cold. He made some quick checks, but it was impossible for him to diagnose the fault, let alone repair it without testing facilities and time. He explained this to the captain.

Jack stayed up on the bridge for half an hour, watching chalky white cliffs grow smaller behind him, and finally sink away beneath the sea. It was a perfect summer evening, and as he recognized south coast beaches where he had spent so many happy camping holidays, they revived nostalgic memories, all the sweeter because he realized he might never see them again.

He thought of his father, whom he had last seen shortly before he died, early in the war. Jack had arrived at the hospital during a night raid; he had just been promoted and his father was thrilled. And once again, he had made the point he had said so often: How great a country England was, and how worthwhile fighting for against all-comers, especially Nazis. Standing there, with the wind in his face, watching the bows dip and rise slowly against the evening tide, Jack admitted to himself the real reason why he was going on the raid. It was what his father would have wished, what his father would have done himself if he had been able. He was trying in the best way he knew to pay back his father's debt to a country that had given to his family life and hope and freedom.

Down on the mess decks, troops were already checking rifles and Sten-guns and priming grenades with which they had been issued since coming aboard. Others sharpened bayonets like butchers preparing for business. Jack saw Red squatting on a bench, his Sten-gun dismantled and the pieces opened out on a newspaper on the floor. He was muttering angrily to himself.

'What's the matter?' Jack asked him.

'Every bloody thing. We thought we were just doing another dummy run. Ford I, they called it. So many of us didn't bring our own Stens. Now we've been given these.'

'What's wrong with them?'

'They're a goddam crude gun to begin with,' explained Red. 'Mass-produced so quickly that rivets are left sticking out, and they can jam. But when you have your own Sten, you file these bits down and polish out the roughness. These goddam guns are raw, still in the grease they were packed in at the factory. Twenty rounds out of these buggers and they'll jam. That's why I'm trying to file down what I can. And a lot of other guys are doing the same goddam thing.'

Elsewhere, inevitable poker games were starting. Some soldiers bought bars of chocolate—a rarity without coupons— and cigarettes and tins of fruit from the ship's canteen. Jack bought two cans of South African peaches, a luxury he had not enjoyed since the war began. As he finished the second tin, a hand touched him lightly on the shoulder. He turned. A sergeant he had never seen was facing him.

'Yes?' Jack asked him.

'I'm Roy Hawkins,' explained the sergeant. 'Field Security. I've come to look after you.'

'I've already got ten men doing that,' replied Jack.

'Now you've eleven,' said Hawkins simply.

Both wondered what to say next, for both could read the thought in the other's mind: *This sergeant may kill me. I may have to kill this guy.*

'See you, then,' said Jack. 'They're treating me like a lord here. I've even got a cabin to myself.'

'I'm going to find the OC of "A" Company,' said Hawkins.

Jack walked along the deck, and bumped into Cecil Merritt.

'Jack!' said the colonel, holding out his hand in welcome. 'Come in and have a talk.'

Jack followed him into his cabin. The noise of engines drummed through metal ventilators.

'So we've made it at last,' said Merritt, unbuttoning his battledress blouse. 'Your first time abroad?'

'Yes.'

'Let's hope it's not your last.'

They both laughed awkwardly.

'Tell me,' Merritt went on, 'what exactly *is* all this RDF stuff? What have you got to do there?'

'I can't tell you,' said Jack. 'You might get captured.'

'Well, that's more than *you* can say,' said Merritt. 'I was thinking, if I knew more, maybe I could help you more.'

'The less anyone knows, the better.'

They chatted for a few minutes and then Jack said good-night and walked out on deck. Jim came up and leaned on the rail by his side. They stood in silence. How many aboard would live to see another sunset? A bell clanged somewhere, and the wake from the propellers churned a luminous path behind them.

'Back in the Isle of Wight the fellow I call Silver said you had a quotation for every occasion. Have you one for this trip?'

'I can't remember who Silver was,' replied Jim slowly. 'Oh, yes. He must be . . .'

'Don't give me his name,' said Jack quickly. 'No names. But what about some words of wisdom now?'

'Depends on your mood and your attitude,' replied Jim. 'You could have Henry's speech before Agincourt about gentlemen now abed holding their manhood cheap because they are not here, and so on.'

'I'd rather be abed,' said Jack simply. 'Spare us that.'

'Me, too,' said Jim. 'I can't think of anything off the cuff, Jack, except maybe something one of your English writers, Thomas Middleton, wrote in the seventeenth century, "It is vain to quarrel with destiny".'

They stood in silence for a moment thinking, and then Jim went on: 'I *can* tell you something about the River Scie, though.'

'The Scie?' asked Jack puzzled. 'What do you mean?'

'The river that runs out from Pourville. It's a pity we won't have time to investigate it.'

'Why?'

'Because back in the days of Louis XIV, in the seventeenth century, one of his court, the Duchesse de Longueville, had a row with the citizens of Dieppe, and they chased her out of town. They damned nearly got her, too, but her horse was just that bit faster. The animal stumbled as it forded the Scie, a bag split open and she lost a fortune, 10,000 silver crowns, whatever that was worth, in the mud.'

'Better than losing her life,' Jack said.

'That's destiny for you,' said Jim.

Again they stood in silence for a moment. Above them, the wind hammered a canvas dummy funnel that sailors had built to alter the silhouette of the ship. The flag of a neutral country flew from the stern—another attempt to baffle any surprise German reconnaissance plane. Jim turned to Jack shyly.

'Did I ever show you a picture of my girl?' he asked him.

'No.'

'I've brought one with me.'

Jim opened his breast pocket and took out a photograph. Jack peered at the picture in the dusk. A pleasant plump homely English face looked back at him.

'Charming,' he said. 'Beautiful girl.'

'Isn't she? Say, think she'll like it in Canada?'

'Why not?'

'There's so much goddam space there we could easily be fifty miles from the nearest house. Snowdrifts up to the roofs in winter. Bit different from Sussex, where she lives. But we have some things I think she'll like.'

'Probably you're the main one,' said Jack, and slapped him on the back.

The rails were lined now with troops, looking out at the empty darkening sea. Thank God we're going into action, Jack thought, wondering, as he often did, how his relatives who stayed behind in Poland were faring; if, indeed, they had escaped the camps and were still alive. *At last*, we're going to give something back . . .

He went down to a mess deck and sat on a form, watching Lofty prime grenades, carefully slipping in the fuses, and then hooking each grenade by its handle to his belt. Hawkins materialized by Jack's side.

'I could use a few of those,' he said.

'Help yourself,' said Lofty, not even looking up. 'Have four on me.'

'Thanks.'

Others joined them and sat down; Bud handed round a packet of cigarettes.

'Where you from?' asked Hawkins.

'Regina way.'

'And you?'

'Fort McMurray.'

'I'll give you all a tip,' said Jack suddenly.

'About all you have given us, Spook. Well?'

'It'll cost you nothing, but it might save your lives. When you're in the landing craft, either take off your helmets or keep your heads well down. Not only because of bullets, but because RDF sets pick up metal better than any other target. And the higher the metal, the easier it is. So keep your tin-hats low.'

Minutes lengthened. Men drank mugs or mess-tins of cocoa, smoked cigarettes, loosened their boots and fell asleep on tables, in hammocks, on the floor. Jack walked back to his cabin; Frenchie was sitting on his bunk, tunic unbuttoned, smoking a cigarette. Around him, spread out on a copy of the *Daily Mirror*, was a Sten-gun in pieces. He was removing the packing grease with his handkerchief.

'Where you been, Spook?' he asked.

'Having some nosh—and a look at the ship's RDF set.'

'What's wrong with it, then?'

'It's not working.'

'So what does that mean?'

'Nothing. It mustn't be used anyway. Captain'll stick to the compass, like the old navigators. No chance of us turning back, if that's what you mean.'

'No.'

'Wish there were?' asked Jack.

Frenchie shrugged, stubbing out his cigarette on the basin.

'Yes and no. I've never been so close to Jerry before, and we're getting closer every minute. It feels kinda lonely out at sea. Only wants one Jerry plane to spot us and we've had it.'

Or a Jerry radar, thought Jack; that would be even worse, for it would give the defenders much earlier warning of their approach.

'Ever been to France?' he asked Frenchie, to change the subject.

'Nope.'

'Looking forward to it?'

'Always a first time,' said Frenchie non-committally. 'What about you? What I can't understand is how you ever agreed to do the job on such goddam terms—come back alive or be shot by them or us. You get a lot of dough for taking the risk?'

'Hell, no. Probably less than you. You're in the Canadian Army, remember. Much better pay than the British.'

'You in the British Army, then?'

Jack shook his head.

'Thought not. Your battledress isn't too good a fit.'

'Don't try to pump me, Frenchie, said Jack. 'I can't tell you anything.'

'You can,' said Frenchie. 'Tell me what you're thinking.

Jack paused. He was thinking of his childhood, which was surely an odd thing to recall at that moment? He remembered the weekly ritual of lighting candles on Friday evenings, after the reading of Kiddush and the short service his mother and father conducted. He remembered the regular Sabbath evening meal of Lockshen (vermicelli) and chicken soup, with roast or boiled chicken, even more affectionately, since this was eaten in a holiday atmosphere, for all work ended before sunset every Friday.

When Jack was five, and he could already read English, his father appointed an elderly Rabbi friend, who had suffered badly during the pogroms in Poland, to teach him the elements of Judaism. The Rabbi was a tall, stately old man with a long black beard and a long black coat to match, who patiently pointed with his pencil to each Hebrew word in the

Siddur, repeating it slowly until Jack pronounced it correctly.

He had a habit which fascinated and repelled Jack: he took snuff. The little boy would watch intrigued as the pungent-smelling powder vanished through the old man's whiskers, first up one nostril and then the other. But he tolerated the Rabbi because he enjoyed his stories of Biblical heroes, such as Judas Maccabeus and David, which he persuaded him to tell. The old man always drew a moral from every story. In the case of David and Goliath, the moral was not to be afraid in life: the bigger the bully, the harder he will fall.

'I was thinking about life at home,' Jack told Frenchie simply.

'Know who you remind me of?' Frenchie asked him. 'Guy I read about once who crossed Niagara Falls on a tightrope. Some newspaper reporter asked him what would happen if he fell. He seemed amazed at that. Goddam ridiculous question, he said. You *know* what would happen. But I'm not *going* to fall. See you on the other side.'

'See you there, too,' said Jack.

'May God go with you,' said Frenchie, his voice suddenly husky. 'With both of us.' He put his hand inside his battledress blouse and pulled out a rosary. 'May the Mother of God look after us.'

'I'm a Jew,' said Jack.

'There's only one God,' said Frenchie. 'We all worship one God but sometimes under different names. Remember the words of the 91st Psalm? "A thousand shall fall at thy side, and ten thousand at thy right hand; but it shall not come nigh thee".'

'I sang that as a boy in the synagogue many times,' agreed Jack.

'Like what I said,' replied Frenchie confidently. 'The same God, and He's on our side.'

I wonder if the Germans are also praying? thought Jack uneasily, but he did not voice his thoughts. Some questions were better left unasked when danger and death drew so close.

The *Princess Beatrix* was due to stop between eleven and

twelve miles out from France and tranship the troops to the landing craft that swung like huge, square-nosed, ungainly life-boats from davits on either side. This distance had been calculated in the belief that the German radar would not be able to 'see' down to wavetop height. The landing craft, with their low superstructures, should be able to come in safely beneath their beams. At about midnight, Jack swung himself off his bed, washed his face with cold water, packed away his razor, lather brush, bar of soap, flannel and cloth in his small pack and gave it to the quartermaster-sergeant. Webb made out a label for the pack.

'I've still got this blue pack,' said Jack. 'It'll stand out a mile. Can't you change it?'

'Impossible. Not a spare one anywhere.'

'What about giving me a couple of Div. signs for my shoulders?'

These were small blue squares of cloth. Without them, he would be marked as someone who was not a member of the Second Canadian Division.

Webb shrugged.

'It's too late, Spook,' he replied. 'We simply haven't got any.'

'Well, see you.'

'Good luck.'

On the way back to his cabin, Jack met Bud.

'You may need this,' Bud told him and handed Jack a navy blue canvas inflatable Mae West life-jacket. Jack took off his battledress blouse, put on the life-jacket, and then the blouse on top of it. At that same moment, the ship's Tannoys announced that everyone should slightly inflate their Mae Wests, since they were about to cut through the German mine-fields. All were told to stand by as the danger was very real. The *Princess Beatrix* pressed on at high speed, a sailor assuring a rather sceptical group that her bow would sever the cables and then the bow wave would help to deflect any mines that might come too close. Then they went through, and were quite safe. Close behind them, other ships entered this gap in the mine-fields. The *Princess Beatrix* was leading, as the South Saskatchewan Regiment was due to land first in the half light.

Lofty approached them, waving a typewritten piece of paper.

'Training programme for the week, friends. Look what we're missing. Today we should have had cliff climbing, platoon in attack and semaphore messages. Tomorrow we're down for PT, arms drill and cliff scaling.'

'I don't reckon that's so far out still,' said Jack. 'I'll put money we'll all have our fill of running, cliff scaling and arms drill before tomorrow's through.'

About twenty miles south, in the village of Varengeville, on the cliff-top west of Pourville, two papers were pinned on the notice board outside the company office of the German No. 813 gun battery. One was General Haase's Order of the Day, the other gave details of the training programme for August 19.

0645–0700 hrs — *Frühsport* (morning P.T.)
1045–1145 hrs — *Geschütz Exerzieren* (gun drill)

Jack was glad that the reluctance of his escort to talk to him while they had been in the *Invicta* before the first raid was cancelled, had now disappeared. Maybe the thought of imminent action and the sense of danger had sharpened all their senses and thrown them closer together.

'You fit?' Lofty asked him cheerfully.

'For what?' said Jack.

'For what they can give us?'

'I won't be a drag on you,' said Jack.

'You done any kind of training then?'

'I was in a Commando camp in Scotland. Not Achnacarry, where you were. Another one.'

'But Frenchie says you're not in the Army. How come you could do that?'

Jack smiled. He could not tell him how he had deliberately given up his annual leave so that he could be posted quite unofficially to the camp.

Bud hawked in his throat and spat into the sea.

'Only goddam thing I didn't like up there,' Lofty went on, not pushing the question, 'was crossing a river swinging from a rope like Tarzan!'

'Shouldn't be any of that where we're going,' said Jack reassuringly. 'I remember when I was a kid I was mad about climbing trees and drainpipes, and so on. I'd come home from school and creep round the back of the house, climb up the drainpipe, go hand over hand along the gutter, and then in through my bedroom window, and down the stairs. I'd try and surprise my mother when I walked into the kitchen.'

'Did she ever find out how you did it?'

'She did. She came out of the house one day—and saw me hanging from the gutter. Poor old mother. She fainted!'

Lofty laughed.

'Reckon she'd faint again if she could see you now, Spook.'

He and Bud walked off with nods that were more than a farewell; they were nods of approval. Jack felt he had been accepted, and with this knowledge came a sadness. He knew so little about these men and had no chance to learn any more. After their brief, strange association, they would go their separate ways. Those who survived to recall this odd episode of a man who knew too much to be taken prisoner would only do so vaguely, because they had no proper name for him either, only Jack or Spook.

Far beneath the rail, the sea spumed with phosphorescent foam. He had seen similarly luminous spray at night along the shingle beach at Whitstable, which he knew from the aerial photographs was just like the beach on which they would land. He thought again, as he had thought sitting in Leicester Square after seeing Air Commodore Tait, of little seemingly isolated incidents in his life. His love of running, swimming, cycling, that had made him fit. The fascination of radio that had absorbed him since boyhood. What had prompted him to take a Commando course instead of going home on leave? Why had he learned bayonet training with Forbes-Smith instead of playing cards or going to the cinema?

He recalled Jim's words about destiny. Was it too far fetched to think—as he thought, breathing in the salt-laden air—that his life by chance, providence, maybe even by design, had been but a long preparation for the task that was facing him on the darkened beach twenty miles ahead?

And what about the men who were going to land with him? Was this the reason Bud had left his lumber camp, that Jim had abandoned his studies, and Red had ridden in from the prairies? Was it for this that Charlie Sawden had come in from Consul; that Graham Mavor had abandoned the bank, and Silver had given up his peacetime job? Was this the moment that would utilize the skills of Les Thrussell as a marksman? Had this been part of their future pattern of life that had also led Lofty to learn sharpshooting with the travelling fair, and Smokey to practise knife-throwing, when he would far rather have been in regular work?

A uniformed steward knocked discreetly on Colonel Merritt's cabin door.

'Come in,' the colonel called, starting up suddenly from sleep.

'Your breakfast, sir,' the steward said gravely, carrying in a tray with a pot of tea, a cup and saucer and three biscuits on a plate.

'And there's something else, sir, which I feel you may find useful during the day.'

He produced a medicine bottle and Merritt read the label with surprise: 'Sloan's Liniment: For the relief of Rheumatism, Sciatica, Lumbago, Cramp and Stiffness.'

'But I don't have rheumatism, sciatica, or any of these other complaints,' he said.

'No, sir. Neither does this bottle contain Sloan's Liniment. It's whisky, sir. Compliments of the captain. And the best of luck.'

'Please thank him for me.'

Much cheered, Colonel Merritt buttoned the bottle carefully inside the top pocket of his battledress.

Down on the mess-decks, troops were being awakened in less luxurious fashion.

'Come on now, let's have you. Hands off your cocks and pull on your socks.'

'Wakie, wakie!'

'Show a bleeding leg, you lot!'

Men were swinging out of hammocks, stretching cramped limbs and flexing muscles, queueing for mess-tins of hot, sweet tea. The air was foul with breath and sweat and the peculiar, metallic, oily smell of a ship running hard. The main lights had all been extinguished, and in their place red bulbs glowed dimly, adding to the sense of drama. Engine-room bells clanged; officers spoke into voice pipes. The hull trembled less violently, and then ceased to tremble at all, so that they seemed suddenly to be drifting on the open tide. Engines barely murmured beneath their feet, as soldiers filed along the red-lit passages, up gangways, and out into the warm darkness. They spoke in whispers and moved quietly, although they were still roughly twelve miles from shore.

Naval petty officers barked strange orders. Sailors with hammers stood by to punch out metal pins that locked hawsers holding the landing craft. Meanwhile, the landing craft crews, four men to each, with one officer for every three craft, waited ready at their stations. The landing craft, Jack thought, appeared peculiarly unseaworthy. They were roughly thirty-six feet long and ten feet wide, each able to carry one platoon, plus all its equipment. Some were built on an American pattern, entirely of wood, and offered no protection to any armament larger than a stone. In others, the officer or petty officer in charge controlled their craft from a small shelter in the stern.

Soon all were in the water, the dual exhausts of Ford V8 engines burbling like speed boats prior to a peacetime trip around some summer bay. Sailors aboard the mother ships cut the scrambling nets and the soldiers began to climb down carefully, hand over hand, cursing as they scraped knuckles on the rough, scaly sides. Jack watched Thrussell; then Mavor, his blond hair above his ears; then Red and Bud and Charlie and Jim and Silver and Frenchie and Lofty. Last man down was Smokey, chewing gum. He carried his knife at his belt.

'After you, Claude,' said Roy Hawkins, with mock politeness.

'No, after you, Cecil,' said Jack, finishing the radio catch-phrase.

'Wait a minute,' a voice of naval authority ordered Jack from the darkness. 'You're not in that craft.'

'I am,' retorted Jack.

'You bloody well aren't. One platoon's aboard already. You're in craft Number Four, behind.'

'You're wrong. I'm the RDF man.'

'Sod the RDF man. You're in craft Number Four, I tell you.'

Argument raged in muted tones on the darkened deck, while scores of Canadians milled past them over the rails, down the scramble-nets, into landing craft. Jack swung himself over the rail.

'I'll have you on a charge,' promised the voice furiously.

'Have me where you like,' said Jack. 'But later.'

'What's the trouble?' someone already in the landing craft asked him.

'Nearly missed the boat, that's what.'

'We'd have waited for you, Spook!' assured Lofty.

They all crouched down inside the hull. Sea-water slapped grey sides only half an inch away, and the smell of petrol from over-rich exhausts blew over them. To one side lay dark water they could only hear and a continent they could not see. To the other, held off by sailors with boat-hooks, towered the mother ship's vertical hull, sheer as an iron wall. Dimly, Jack could make out some faces peering down at them over the rail, pale shapes in the darkness.

'All right down there, you lot?'

The question was asked in a voice little more than a whisper.

'Aye, aye, sir.'

'Okay, Number One?'

'Okay it is, sir.'

'Cast off.'

A bell tinkled, recalling conductors on open-top buses along the Mile End Road and blue and white tricycles with men selling Wall's ice cream: 'Stop me and buy one.' But 'to buy one' now was RAF slang to be hit by a bullet, maybe to die. Jack shrugged away the thought.

The petty officer in his hut-like control box opened both throttles. For a second, the wooden craft trembled, while sea-water boiled beneath the stern. Then they were away. And all around the mother ships in the dimness of the early hours, they could sense, rather than see, other ships darting away, trailing faint arrowheads of phosphorescent foam—from No. 3 Commando on the far east to No. 4 Commando under Lord Lovat, on the far west.

In a village hall, some miles inland from the French coast, out of sight and sound of the sea, a gramophone needle dipped, a record turned, a tenor voice sang metallically through the loudspeaker:

> *Vor der Kaserne, vor dem grossen Tor,*
> *Stand eine Laterne und steht sie noch davor;*
> *So wolln wir da uns wiedersehn,*
> *Bei der Laterne wolln wir stehn,*
> *Wie einst Lili Marleen, wie einst Lili Marleen.*

Couples began to dance. Some were officers in white summer mess-dress, others were civilians, incongruously wearing white dinner jackets. Around the walls stood non-dancers, drinks in their hands, humming the tune. Dim lights whirled through blue wreaths of tobacco smoke. The girls were members of the *LN-Helferinnen* (the Women's Auxiliary Air Signals Corps). Their partners in civilian clothes were German war correspondents and photographers who had spent the previous two days interviewing these girls, on and off duty, for illustrated articles about their work to boost recruiting and reassure dubious mothers.

The men in uniform were Luftwaffe pilots from No. 3 Air Fleet. The weather report for August 19 had promised a fine morning, but a gloomy and overcast afternoon. These conditions were not considered conducive to any offensive operations by the RAF, so one pilot in three had been granted twenty-four hours' leave, and this was as pleasant a way to spend it as any. Periodically, couples would come out of the hall, through the two blackout curtains, pause to breathe the warm air scented with fresh hay in the August darkness, and then they would go off, arms linked, to the shelter of hayricks and the trees.

Behind shuttered windows sealed against any tell-tale chink of light, middle-aged French farmers and their wives lay awake in houses nearby, annoyed by the music and powerless to protest.

> *Unsre beiden Schatten sahn wie einer aus.*
> *Das wir so lieb uns hatten, das sah man gleich daraus.*
> *Und all Leute solln es sehn,*
> *Wenn wir bei der Laterne stehn,*
> *Wie einst Lili Marleen, wie einst Lili Marleen.*[1]

The wind was colder now out at sea, and sharp with salt spray. Occasional waves, higher than the rest, butted against the bows or sides of the landing craft, drenching battledress and soaking the faces of the men inside.

As Jack's eyes grew more accustomed to the near-darkness, he could make out the dim silhouette of the wheelhouse. He glanced at his watch; the hands pointed to twenty-one minutes past three, British Summer Time. They were due to go in at ten minutes to five: action lay barely eighty-nine minutes ahead.

Bud pushed a sheaf of papers at him; each was the size of a piece of toilet paper.

'What's this for?' Jack asked him.

'Got something in French written on them,' Bud explained. 'It's too dark to read now. We're to give 'em to any French

[1] Copyright 1940 and 1955 by Apollo-Verlag, Paul Lincke, Berlin. Text printed with permission of the original publishers. Words by Hans Leip; music by Norbert Schultze.

people we see—telling them this is only a raid, not the invasion. Warning them to keep away, not to get involved.'

'Maybe I should have taken that advice myself. But it's too late now.'

'Damn right, Jack boy,' agreed Lofty. 'It's too goddam late now.'

Five coastal German motor ships were heading south from Boulogne for the safety of Dieppe Harbour, escorted by three small wooden motor boats with powerful engines, known in the German Navy as submarine-chasers. They were numbered 1411, 4011 and 1404. Aboard the leader, No. 1411, First-Lieutenant Wurmbach, the convoy commander, noted that the wind was west-south-west, Force Two, freshening. Just after 0300 hours, the wind changed direction, blowing away the rumble of their own engines, and to his surprise Wurmbach heard the sound of other engines, not in the convoy.

Keeping radio silence, his ship's signal lamp flickered the recognition signal agreed between convoy and commander before they set off. This *could* be another German convoy, about which they had not been informed, or it might be from British motor torpedo boats, which frequently raced across the Channel, shot up what targets they could find, and then hared back to England, relying on their speed to get away.

No reassuring signal burned through the darkness in answer to Wurmbach's lamp, so presumably the ships were alien? But—how could he be sure? This was a difficult moment. The ships might be friendly and had not replied for a number of good reasons: their leading lookout was asleep or simply had not seen the lamp; he had replied, but his own lamp had failed; he had momentarily forgotten the correct acknowledgement to the challenge.

All these plausible, comfortable reasons passed through Wurmbach's mind. He decided to give them a little more time to reply. Ten minutes stretched to twenty, and then he added five for good measure, but still no reply came. Wurmbach waited with increasing unease until twelve minutes to four, and when he still had no response, he felt certain these ships were enemy; accordingly, he fired a star shell.

Immediately, the whole astonishing collection of landing craft heading towards the coast was exposed, and no sooner had both sides seen each other than their navy escorts opened fire. The fresh night air was suddenly bitter with cordite, loud with the hammer of guns, and screams and shouts from the wounded. Tracer bullets scored the sky like long red darts and dazzling, orange-cored circles of fire marked direct hits. Wurmbach was in no doubt of this flotilla's purpose. He shouted one hoarse, dreadful word to his radio operator: 'Invasion!'

The urgency of the danger overruled all need for radio silence. Desperately, the operator tapped on his key and then swung the switches to hear if his transmission had been received. But there was nothing in the tiny rocking radio room aboard No. 1411, trembling with near misses, with the sea boiling like a geyser all round, nothing but the shrill squeal of empty static.

'The aerial, *mein Kommandant*!' he shouted. 'It's been shot away.'

'Can't you get a message through by any other means?'

'No, sir.'

'Make a signal to 4011. Ask whether his radio can still transmit.'

Back came the answer: 'No. Aerial out of order.'

Wurmbach made a signal with the lamp, ordering his colleagues to head instantly for Le Tréport, instead of Dieppe, to disembark their wounded. Then he ordered the four remaining ships in his convoy—one had been sunk—to head in close to shore and make for Dieppe at high tide.

Guns were still thundering on both sides, and there had been casualties among the landing craft. Wurmbach had seen direct hits and heard the unforgettable roar and rush of steam from a bursting boiler. As he stood there, his feet widespread against the rocking of his tiny craft, the irony of the situation overwhelmed him. No doubt the shore forces would dismiss this action as one of the routine engagements that happened every week, but he knew differently. He alone knew the extent of the danger that threatened, for he had seen scores of boats, pointed like arrows at the Continent's coast. And yet despite all the sophisticated radio equipment with which the German Navy had lavishly provided him, he had no means to warn anyone on shore of the danger racing towards them.

British Navy ships escorting the Jubilee force also had been uninformed about this convoy, through an unknown technical breakdown. At 0127 that morning, and again at 0233 (British Double Summer Time) radar stations at Newhaven and Beachy Head both reported that enemy ships were moving along the coast towards Dieppe. This information was transmitted, but inexplicably the Headquarters Ship, *HMS Calpe*, did not receive it. Other British ships, which had picked up the radio message correctly, waited in vain for orders from *Calpe*. When these orders did not arrive, they assumed that the convoy to which the signals referred was unimportant: Jubilee sailed on.

Someone touched Jack on the shoulder. Lofty. He held a bottle in his other hand.

'Swig?'

'What is it?'

'Rum. Do you good, Spook.'

'I hate it.'

'Maybe it won't hate you, though.'

Someone handed the water-bottle to Jack. He swallowed, choking at its strength.

'That's Navy stuff, boy,' said Silver approvingly. 'Grog, you Limeys call it.'

All the landing craft carried a supply of rum, which had been issued in case of necessity. Murray Osten had found before his LCA left the mother-ship that he had one bottle of rum more than should have been drawn for his company. He tossed with the naval petty officer issuing the bottles to see who would keep it. Osten won. He handed it to his Company quartermaster-sergeant who was returning to England in the *Princess Beatrix*.

'Keep this safe for me,' he told him. 'I'll give you a drink when we get back.'

By no means all the troops drank even a tot of rum before they landed. Sergeant Major Dunkerley was personally convinced that water would be of much more value on a hot August day, and many other soldiers like him preferred to have water in their water-bottles. But in those last pre-dawn moments, Jack was grateful for the spirit which ran like a welcome fire through his cold body. Suddenly the whole sky erupted in a blaze of bright greenish light. Everyone ducked instinctively. From the east came a sudden unexpected staccato chatter of guns. A flare was falling, trailing a tail of gigantic stars that lit up the sea, the distant rim of the coast, the wideness of the horizon with the sudden eye-catching intensity of an arc lamp.

Jack took off his tin hat and peered over the side of the hull. The whole flotilla of infantry landing craft, larger craft with tanks aboard, flat-bottomed vessels known as flak ships, bristling with anti-aircraft guns, stretched in every direction. The merciless flare laid them all bare as a scalpel lays bare a bone. He could see the long wash from propellers, puffs of exhaust smoke, a beard of steam growing at a funnel. Surely it was impossible for watchers on the coast not to see this invasion fleet? Jack sank down in the craft again as the flare died. Guns went on firing, chattering, arguing with iron tongues. The flicker of muzzle flashes lit up some of the nearer craft in silhouette.

'What the hell's happened?' Jack whispered.

'Christ knows,' replied Red. 'Reckon we're spotted, though.'

'I doubt it,' said Bud hopefully. 'A man can't see very far out to sea from shore, and we're probably still five or six miles off.'

'I wish we were sixty goddam miles,' said Frenchie.

'Me, too,' said Red. 'Stuff this for a game.'

There was silence, and then one of the younger soldiers

said nervously, in a voice dried by fear, echoing the thoughts of the majority: 'We're for it now.'

A sergeant turned to him.

'That's what we came for, lad,' he said gently.

'You speak for yourself, sarge,' retorted Charlie from the stern. The others started to laugh, and the tension broke. The landing craft churned on.

High up on the cliffs the latticed Freya aerial reflector turned slowly to the left, paused and then went through another semi-circle to the right, paused and turned again. Underneath the giant reflector that locals said reminded them of a listening ear, was a small cabin that turned with it. Inside this sat the bearing operator, ready to read the aerial angle should any target come up on his screen.

Down below, in a blockhouse built of red bricks, covered with feet of solid concrete poured and made by the Todt Organization, sat more of the station's crew. One was a range-reader, another a plotter who wore a head-and-breast tele-phone set connected by special land lines to their command post in Puys, a mile beyond the town, and to the *Flug-meldezentrale*, the air operations room in Dieppe, the analysis centre, known as the No. 1 Unit, in a ground-floor room of the Golf Hotel, half a mile nearer to Dieppe.

The Freya fed four Würzburgs, that extended in a line from Les Petites Dalles to St Valéry-sur-Somme, about a hundred miles north-east of Fécamp, all the information it received about distant targets. These Würzburgs would then deal with any hostile plane or ship that came within their range and capabilities.

In the analysis centre, all information from these radars, and details of anything spotted by watchers with binoculars, was recorded on a General Situation board. This was a table on which the positions of fighter planes, ships and convoys were shown by models or plaques that were moved across a map of the French coast. The operators worked three watches and their task was delicate and vital. Plots from the Freya had to be accurately correlated with plots from the Würzburgs, otherwise one aircraft giving three tracks would in fact appear to be three separate planes. This was a problem caused by the curvature of the earth, and magnified on an enormous scale it disallowed the original non-precision Freya from working satisfactorily with the Würzburgs to locate individual bombers.

As each track was recorded, the different commands—fighter, bomber or coastal—would speedily identify their own aircraft, and any intruder by air or sea would quickly be picked up.

The commander of the whole radar section, known as the 23 *Funkmess* (Radar) *Kompanie Luftgau Nachr*. Regiment/Northern France, was a 28-year-old lieutenant, Willi Weber, who had taken command of the company seventeen months earlier, having previously been adjutant of a sister-regiment. Weber was a professional career officer. He had been born in Berlin, and passed his matriculation there in 1933, with the main subjects of physics, mathematics and chemistry. Before joining the army in 1936 as an infantryman, he had worked briefly in Berlin as an international forwarding agent. When he enlisted he had been drafted into the infantry because at that time all officers of the German Air Force had to serve their initial training with an infantry battalion.

In 1937, he was formally posted to the Air Force, and trained in military air intelligence at Berlin-Gatow and Berlin-Kladow. He had served throughout the Polish campaign, and then as adjutant to the *Luftgau Nachrichten* Regiment, Belgium/Northern France.

Weber's orders were to serve the local fighter squadrons first with information of any intruders, and then the Navy, and, as he put it, 'all comers'. The Freya 28 had an aerial range of 150 kilometres on a wavelength of 2.40 metres. It could not see down to the level of the waves out at sea beyond five or ten miles, but owing to its height on the cliff-top, it was able to pick up ships with a superstructure, according to size, up to a maximum range of thirty-eight kilometres or about twenty miles.

The Freya was the key to the early warning of any air or

sea attack from the Channel, and after the Bruneval raid, it had been reinforced with more guards. All radar operators off duty, apart from their sleep and relaxation periods, had also to help in the defence of their station. A wall of earth had been thrown up around the concrete blockhouse, partly to conceal it and partly to shield it from attack.

In the graveyard watch at 0345 on that morning the operator spotted a target about thirty-five kilometres from Dieppe. Weber was informed immediately.

'Five columns of vessels out at sea, sir.'

He gave the map grid reference.

'Are they moving?'

'No, sir. Stationary.'

Weber, in his headquarters at Puys, checked on the map. Five columns of ships presented too large a target for there to be any mistake. One ship, yes, there could be an error; one column, possibly; but not five columns. He kept in constant touch with the station. The ships remained stationary for about an hour, and then all began to move inland still in these five distinguishable lines.

To Weber, who had absolute confidence in his colleagues and their equipment, this could only mean one thing—the expected invasion, or at least a landing in considerable strength with five different groups involved.

At 0445 hours he put through a call to the 2nd Convoy Security Division of the Navy, who were responsible for determining the nationality of all doubtful vessels. The officer at the other end checked his files.

'I don't know about five *columns*,' he said sceptically, 'but there are five *ships* due from Boulogne at Dieppe at 0500. They have three sub-chasers as protection. How do you know there are five columns?'

Here Weber had to pause. Radar with the German forces, as with the British, was still ultra-secret and no inkling could be given as to how they actually found their targets. This meant that should any doubt arise as to the existence of a target, he was in no position to explain scientifically how he knew that what he said was accurate.

'I can only repeat,' he said, 'that these are not five simple ships, but five columns of vessels. With respect, this cannot be a small convoy coming from Boulogne. If they were, they would appear from the east. These are coming from the north.'

'You are mistaken,' replied the naval officer coldly. He rang off.

Weber checked again with his station. The ships were steadily drawing nearer. He felt the same frustration that Lieutenant Wurmbach had experienced out at sea when he had spotted the approaching flotilla but had been unable to warn his colleagues on shore.

Weber made another telephone call to the duty officer of 302nd Infantry Division at Envermeu, which was responsible for this particular part of the coast-line.

'Sorry to wake you at this hour,' he said almost apologetically, after explaining who he was, 'but I have to report five columns of unidentified vessels steadily approaching the coast. If they keep their present course and are enemy, I would estimate they are heading for Dieppe over a front of about twenty-five kilometres.'

'What does the Navy say?' asked the duty officer, instantly awake.

'They think they are a convoy due from Boulogne.'

'Are you sure they are not?'

'I am not sure of anything,' replied Weber simply, 'but my calculations suggest that these could not possibly be part of a convoy of ships. There may be nothing in it, of course, but I thought you should know.'

'Thanks,' said the officer, and immediately alerted his superiors. As a result, Army and Air Force units went into action. While the coastal battery at Varengeville was overwhelmed by Lord Lovat and his Commandos, who destroyed their guns and carried off several prisoners, much fiercer opposition awaited the Canadians and the other Commandos. The battery at Varengeville was controlled by the Navy; the rest came under Army orders.

The naval duty officer in Dieppe, by refusing to believe

Weber's warning, was quite unknowingly repeating the scepticism of the American officer at Pearl Harbor nine months earlier, who had wrongly assured his radar operator that planes heading towards the base must be friendly.

In both cases, the machines had given long and accurate warning, but the men who controlled them had misread their message.

—FIVE—

The sky was still dark; soon it would be grey. Men crouched in the landing craft, eyes narrowed against the wind, peering towards the land they were steadily approaching. In the deep gloom, Jack sensed rather than saw a sheer wall of cliff ahead. From the rear of the LCA, the petty officer had also seen it; a bell clanged furiously, and they cursed its noise under their breath. Surely any sentry on shore must hear it? Both engines roared full astern, and water churned like a mill-race beneath the stern.

They had come in too close, and too far east. The RDF station was almost certainly on top of that cliff, Jack thought, his heart pounding with the fear that the bell or the noise of their engines must have alerted its defenders. They reversed out a little way and then made a ninety degree turn to the west. The LCA wallowed heavily, broadside on to the incoming tide. Slowly, she began to beat west, running parallel with the beach towards Pourville. The darkness was thinning now. One soldier glanced at his watch; just after twenty to five. In less than ten minutes they would be ashore—and then what?

Sergeant Major Ed Dunkerley, looking round the men in his craft, found himself wondering what they were thinking, what they were feeling. There was no outward sign of their thoughts on their faces; earlier, one or two men had shaken hands with each other, but that was all. Dunkerley watched the cliffs grow whiter as the dawn came up, and he thought to himself, almost with surprise: Why, it's very much like England.

A light was turning on the cliffs. It appeared bright to him, like a searchlight seeking out ships behind them. But to Jack, seeing it from a different angle, and from farther along the beach, it seemed only a dim, winking light. This was the Ailly lighthouse, lit specially to guide in the German convoy from Boulogne.

Sergeant Blackwell, carrying his big pack filled with signalling gear, crouched in his landing craft with the Signals Platoon, scanning the shore warily for the first sign of movement. Near him was Private Frank Paul Forness—known in the regiment as Hank. At High School before the war, Hank Forness had been a member of the SSR Militia, and had immediately volunteered when his regiment was called for active service. He had always wanted to be a soldier, and now he was realizing his ambition.

To his right, the lighthouse winked at intervals, and he could see the dim mass of land gradually grow closer and clearer, and a faint glow from what appeared to be a window in a building half way up a hillside. Slowly, the shore took shape, with vague outlines of houses and larger buildings. Then from almost straight ahead, he saw a cluster of bright lights, like a Christmas tree in the sky. They seemed to float gently up and down as they travelled equally slowly towards him. As they approached, they appeared to pick up speed, and then, with a noise like a bundle of dry sticks breaking, they streaked overhead. For the first time in his life, Hank Forness realized he was under fire by tracer bullets.

Aboard Jack's landing craft, a soldier whispered urgently to him.

'Message from the captain,' he said. 'Pass it on. Get ready to go in.'

In each landing craft, soldiers now began to stretch cramped muscles, flexing elbows and shoulders, moving instinctively—and almost imperceptibly, for there was so little space—towards the sloping ramps. As the LCA reached shallow water, these would go down and they would all be out. And, then, as General Roberts had urged them, they wouldn't stop running until they reached their target.

'Have another swig,' invited Frenchie, and passed Jack his water-bottle. Jack put the round, sharp-edged neck to his lips, gulped down a mouthful of neat rum, and passed back the bottle in silence. No one spoke now; the time for talk was behind them. Jack could hear their combined breathing, like the breathing of some gigantic animal, with other noises: a click of brass buckles, boot studs squealing on a metal part of the floor, the slam of a rifle bolt. Their engines were barely whispering now, and waves beat impatiently against the stern as the LCA turned towards the beach.

Men checked that magazines were firmly locked in unfamiliar rifles, that safety catches were off, actions cocked, bayonets fixed securely. Tommy-gunners and Bren-gunners patted for the hundredth time the two oblong webbing pouches at their belts to reassure themselves that they contained loaded magazines. These were the automatic, almost reflex actions of trained soldiers; Jack guessed that they probably did not even know they were making them.

'Five seconds to go,' came the whisper, passed down the craft, mouth to ear, mouth to ear.

'Everybody ready now,' said a voice of command in low tones from behind the angled ramp.

'All right, Platoon Sergeant?'

'Yes, sir.'

'Well, good luck, everyone. This is it.'

A metallic clang of gears, the whirr of a tooth as a ratchet ran free, and the ramp screamed down on two metal cables. It splashed down clumsily on to the beach with a great gout of foam. Engines raced, propellers churning full astern to stop the LCA sliding on up the shore and grounding completely.

'Follow me!' shouted the officer. Everyone rose behind him, uncoiling like runners at a mass-start race. Then they charged up the beach, legs pounding like pistons, metal boot studs and heels hammering on the stones like a herd of maddened cattle. The beach was steep; running up it was as difficult as climbing a hill of walnuts in a nightmare.

The crunch of the shingle reminded Jack of running along the beach at Whitstable, as a boy, past the moss-covered breakwaters near the oyster company's sheds. Green Beach had the same salty seaweed smell, and the same summer morning dampness. He reached the shelter of the sea-wall. His bodyguards were spread out, on either side, watching him. Apart from the Canadians the whole shore seemed quiet, and darker than it had appeared from the sea.

Roy Hawkins was surprised to see some small boats drawn up on the shingle to his right. He had no time to discover what they were, but they seemed so out of place that he wondered whether they might conceal an ambush or a defensive position. Behind them, landing craft were already hastily backing off the beach. As the LCA bringing in the Signals Platoon let down its ramp, a German machine-gun opened up, raking the shingle with ricocheting bullets. Many of the platoon were wounded, Blacky severely in one foot. Hank Forness and a friend, John MacLeod, were among the few who escaped unhurt, and they rushed up the beach to the sea-wall. This was about eight feet high, with coils of wire laid along the top. Soldiers with wire-cutters immediately climbed on the shoulders of their comrades to cut a way through. Hawkins saw some of the Canadians attempt to breach it with a Bangalore torpedo—a long metal tube filled with explosive—which they flung up and across it. The tube lay trembling as though on a giant spring, and then the fuse flickered feebly and went out.

On all sides, Jack heard the patient snip, snip of wire-cutters, like busy barbers trimming metal hair, and then he saw a white notice with one ominous word painted in black: *MINEN*. Others had also seen similar notices strung at intervals along the wire coil which, like the thin, bony vertebrae of some huge serpent, extended along the whole length of the sea-wall. Hank Forness and John MacLeod moved along it, away from the crowd of troops waiting to go through the narrow gap that was being cut. Fifty yards away, a ladder leaned against the wall with a gap in the wire at the top— possibly left to allow German troops access to the beach.

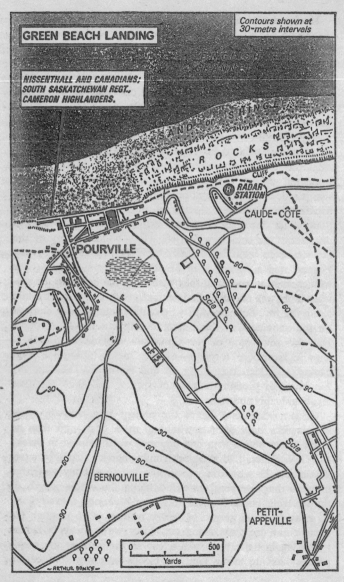

GREEN BEACH LANDING

Contours shown at 30-metre intervals

NISSENTHALL AND CANADIANS; SOUTH SASKATCHEWAN REGT., CAMERON HIGHLANDERS.

ENGLISH CHANNEL

SAND or SHINGLE

THE ROCKS

CLIFF

RADAR STATION

CAUDE-COTE

POURVILLE

Scie

BERNOUVILLE

PETIT-APPEVILLE

0   500
Yards

— ARTHUR BANKS —

132

MacLeod climbed up the ladder and so, in Forness's opinion, became the first SSR to be over the wall and into Pourville.

Despite the firing behind and above them, the little town was quiet. They could see no movement whatever, so they raced across the road into a shed and peered out of the window, feeling very much alone, and with a sense of anti-climax, wondered what to do next. MacLeod saw a cow, and suggested that they shoot it. Forness thought that the noise might attract attention, and talked him out of the idea.

Lieutenant Buchanan, the adjutant, surveying the little village from the beach, thought how peaceful the whole scene seemed. Almost immediately, this comfortable illusion was shattered, for guns began to fire from emplacements in the cliffs, and the lightening sky erupted in flickering orange flashes of flame. The Canadians could now see a line of roof-tops and gables and crooked continental chimneys in these brief bright moments, while tracer bullets painted red and green streaks across the sky. Watching these pyrotechnics, Buchanan heard one Canadian shout cheerfully, 'Gee, this is better than the Fourth of July!'

Another, remembering the rehearsals and the practice assault landings called out in mock consternation: 'These Heinies are using live bullets! Heh, where's the umpire?'

'No place for forty-eight hours' leave,' shouted someone else.

Frenchie turned to Jack.

'Don't think I'll stay that long,' he said quietly.

'Me neither,' said Jack. And as he spoke, he realized that if he were still there after forty-eight hours, it would be as a corpse.

Colonel Cecil Merritt, with the officers and men of his Battalion Headquarters, sprinted up the beach towards the garage that had been selected as the first site for their head-quarters, about one hundred yards beyond the sea-wall.

Someone had given Dunkerley a Sten-gun and insisted he took this along with him. So, holding his rifle in one hand and the Sten in the other, Dunkerley followed them out of their LCA, heading to the left, with a sergeant and a platoon of

133

men behind him. They all reached the sea-wall safely and leaned against it for a moment, while their men brought up scaling ladders, and climbed up them and over the wire.

The first RAF Spitfires were now flying in very low from the sea, guns blazing. Dunkerley had time to marvel at what appeared to be a cone of fire directed up at the planes from Dieppe, and then he was climbing the ladder himself and was over the wall. He led his party across an open space, and they took cover in the semi-basement of a house. In the shadowy half-light some figures ran past them. Who were they—friends or foes? Luckily, friends. They moved on to the left, and saw a group of Canadians talking to a French civilian who was crouched down against a paling fence.

'Who is he?' Dunkerley asked them.

'He's telling us the Germans are waiting for us,' came the grim reply.

Jack found a gap in the wire. Up he went, and through it, with his group of men close behind him. Across from the promenade stood a row of houses. It was still fairly dark and machine-guns were firing, but with the confused crackle of the shots and their echoes, it was difficult to say exactly where they were sited. They flattened themselves against the wall of the nearest house, hoping for a lull in the firing, trying to get their bearings.

Above Jack's head, an alarm clock began to ring in a bedroom, loud and unexpected as the engine bell aboard the LCA. At the same moment, the window shutters crashed open a few feet above his steel helmet. A middle-aged woman peered out, confused and bewildered by so much noise so early. Then she saw the troops.

'*Mon dieu!*' she cried in terror, and hastily slammed the shutters shut.

Outside the mussel-encrusted stone elbow that shielded Dieppe Harbour from the open sea, German tugboat No. 32 rocked like a short fat duck on the rising tide. Her commander, *Sonderführer* (Boatswain) Achtermann, had just taken aboard

Navy Pilot Hederich, and both men stood in the small wheel-house, feet braced against the roll of the tug, eyes fixed on the dim, slowly lightening horizon. They were waiting for the recognition signal from sub-chaser No. 1411, leading in the convoy from Boulogne. Then they would steam out to meet her, transfer the pilot, and the tug would be back in harbour before sun-up.

The tide was due to turn in three minutes, there was no mist, and the convoy was expected to arrive in three-quarters of an hour, at 0500 Continental time. Then to their surprise and concern, instead of the small sub-chasers and the five little ships they expected, they saw the dark shapes of unfamiliar destroyers and a host of other smaller craft approximately one and a half nautical miles away.

But whose these vessels were, neither man knew, except that they were obviously not the ships they were waiting to guide into harbour. They might be a German naval force off-course—or they might not. And if they were not—who or what were they, and why were they there? All possible answers to these questions were disturbing. Hederich accordingly gave orders to make port immediately.

While the tug was turning, sentries stationed along the coast also heard distant engines out at sea. At 0435, the Dieppe Naval Signal Station reported: 'Unknown vessels to the front of Pourville.' The station flashed that night's recognition challenge to them, but there was no reply. The Signal Station, and the routine German naval patrol boat on protection duty outside Dieppe harbour, both fired warning rockets to advise other stations along the coast that unidentified craft were in the area. And still no response whatever came from the steadily approaching ships.

The duty officer in the Signal Station decided to relieve himself of responsibility in the matter. He telephoned his immediate superior, the local port commander, who passed on the warning—'unidentified vessels approaching'—to the naval signals duty officer at Le Havre. Let him decide what to do. This officer immediately referred the problem to the Channel coast commander at Trouville, who passed it on to the supreme naval authority, the admiral in charge of Naval Operations in France, at his headquarters in Paris. But while the message was still in transit across northern France, the authorities in Le Havre belatedly decided to act on their own initiative. By then, from Puys, east of Dieppe to Varengeville in the west, the drone of many engines echoed along the coast. In concealed look-out posts along the cliffs watchers with binoculars strained their eyes to see friendly and reassuring recognition lights. They saw nothing but the dark outlines of vessels heading inshore. At 0505, orders came back along the channel of communication from Le Havre to the port commander, to the Signal Station at Dieppe: *Open barrage fire.*

Immediately, the special signal rocket was discharged. High up in the August sky, far out over the shining sea, it exploded into seven green individual stars. On that signal, all German artillery opened fire on fixed lines across the beaches.

The cliffs on either side of Pourville, a honeycomb of weapon emplacements, with machine-guns trained on different sections of the open beach, blazed with blades of flame. Bullets streamed into the sea over the heads of Jack and his companions, pocking the water, spraying the shingle, splintering stones, chipping pieces off the concrete sea-wall. Some SSRs were still beneath this, and in the growing light, they saw that it was made from big stones roughly cemented together; minerals and quartz glittered like imprisoned diamonds in the stones. To their right, white cliffs, reminding them of the Sussex coast, swept away to a headland, while the sea pounded in on rocks beneath. To their left, beyond the muddy mouth of the River Scie, stood another hill scarred by strips of grey concrete and the flat roofs of gun emplacements. On the peak of this, the Freya aerial turned slowly, like a gigantic ear listening, pausing, moving on.

Red, crouching next to Jack, suddenly pitched forward as though he had seen something immensely valuable on the ground and must at all costs pick it up. Jack shouted to him. Red did not answer. Jack shook him; Red rolled slackly on his side. He had grown a small hole like a birthmark over his right eye; it was rimmed with pink skin, although the rest of his face was suddenly sallow, the colour of wax. A little blood seeped stickily out of the hole. He was quite dead.

It was lighter now and other LCAs were still landing and more Canadians poured out on to the beach. Some dropped wounded on the shingle and others in the sea, writhing hump-backed in their pain. Battalion headquarters was already set up in the garage, alongside two dusty cars up on blocks; no petrol was available for civilians in occupied France. The signallers, headphones on, turned their sets, oblivious to the slaughter all around them. Shells landing in the roadway out-side and by the sea-wall, sent up gouts of concrete dust that drifted down slowly, covering tin hats, faces, men's shoulders, with powder, making everyone look strangely alike. Jack found it difficult to recognize all the members of his group; they found him easier to spot because of his blue RAF pack, his white hair, and the fact that he wore no divisional flashes on his sleeves.

A shell whistled through the air like an express train leaving a tunnel, and Jack threw himself flat on the promenade, mouth open to protect his ear-drums from the blast. He could hear the radio operator in the garage patiently repeating into his microphone: 'Ack, Beer, Cork, Don. Over to you. Over.' Then the shell exploded, and the air was thick with dust and rubble and cries and shouts of pain and fear. The sea wind cleared it slowly, like a heavy morning mist, and Jack saw the backs of houses straight ahead across a flat piece of rough land. They had sharply pointed roofs and spires above the windows, and their shutters were open, banging against the wall. German soldiers, some in vests and shorts, were still firing down at them from open windows.

Hawkins saw civilians wearing night-clothes clustered at front doors. A fat Frenchman wore an overcoat over pyjamas. He had a cigarette in his mouth, but had forgotten to light it in his amazement at watching the troops land.

'Get out of the way! Get under cover!' Hawkins shouted to them in English, but they could not understand him or their own danger. To the right was a road, and a steep bank with houses built into it. In a garden a cherub stood near an ornamental fish pond; a plate with the street name, Rue de la Mer, in white letters against a blue background, was fixed on a wall. Just beyond these houses, the road forked left into Pourville. To the right it climbed a steep hill. Jack could see a church spire and garages cut into the hillside; ornamental flower pots hung from beams on a terrace. Something was hideously wrong with the whole scene, and it took Jack a moment to grasp just what it was.

They had landed in the wrong place.

The LCA had been too far east before, and had nearly hit the cliff. Now they had been dropped off too far west, on the far bank of the River Scie, exactly opposite the German-occupied houses they should so carefully have avoided. He was at least a quarter of a mile farther from the RDF station than they should have been, possibly more. To reach it would mean fighting through German defences all the way.

The beach behind them was already a shambles. One landing craft had suffered a direct hit and drifted, burning. Soldiers who had survived the hail of fire on the shore and crossed the wire, were now falling on the hard red asphalt of the road. Out at sea, clouds of black oily smoke poured from a destroyer's funnels to help cover the Camerons' landing. The early morning wind blew this smoke like a dark mist across the beach towards Pourville, softening the outlines of roofs and buildings, mercifully concealing the agonies of the wounded, the grotesque attitudes of the dead—and the full strength of the German opposition.

The sound of guns and low-flying aircraft woke Paul Brunet in the flat above his flower shop in the Rue de la Barre, Dieppe. So much firing must be something serious, not just another exercise; this could be the reason for all the minor clashes out at sea and the frequent RAF reconnaissance flights. He put on a plus-four suit, because somehow this seemed more business-like to wear in an emergency than a suit with floppy trousers, rammed his Passive Defence helmet on his head and went out into the street. Someone called up to him excitedly from a semi-basement: 'The British are here!'

The British? Was this indeed the long expected landing? Brunet saw other people cautiously coming out into the street to see what was happening. He looked along the narrow Passage de Saint Remy towards the church. Three soldiers in what appeared like British uniforms—actually they were Canadians—saw him at the same time as he saw them. With his helmet camouflaged in the German style and his curious continental knickerbockers, they thought he must be a German. Anyhow, this was no time to take chances. One raised his rifle and fired. The bullet pecked a splinter of stone from the wall above Paul Brunet's head. He ducked back into the main street. After serving his country in two wars, it would be unthinkable to be shot by an Ally!

Half a mile east from Paul Brunet's shop, several men wearing naval uniform, all members of the Naval Construction Inspectorate, waited in the office of the harbour commandant with their commanding officer, Naval Construction Engineer Weiss, for the telephone to ring. Their task in the event of invasion was to blow up Dieppe harbour. Surely this must be an invasion—so why were their orders delayed?

The harbour captain, Lieutenant-Commander Meinhardt, was waiting out on the swing bridge to the outer port with a charge already laid, in case any Allied warships attempted to force an entry. Other demolition teams stood by the flood gates of the Duquesne Basin and the pumping station near the Canadian Basin. Explosive charges were always in position at both these points; new firing cartridges had been laid that morning so that they could be instantly ignited. All that was required was the order. But the telephone did not ring, and so they waited in tense and uneasy silence, smoking cigarettes, watching the black telephone on the table, ready to pounce on it at the first tinkle of the bell.

At 0600 hours, Sergeant Fritz Mezger was sitting in his pyjamas on the window-sill of his billet, a house on the hill halfway between Dieppe and Pourville. The sound of guns had brought him from his bed, and now he waited, like the men in the harbour commandant's office, for instructions.

He was the ammunition sergeant attached to Divisional Headquarters, and because he dealt predominantly with supplies of shells and cartridges and grenades and other devices of war, he sometimes referred to himself wrily as 'an accountant of death'. His was a crucial position when an invasion might need to be repulsed. Or could this be simply another exercise to test their defences? General Haase was determined they should always be on guard.

When the guns continued to fire, Mezger realized that this was no practice landing. He mounted his motor-cycle and rode into his headquarters in Dieppe to see whether his services were required. The telephone lines were cut and radio contact was proving difficult, but ammunition supplies were adequate. Because of the general emergency, he was ordered out with the infantry to help round up wounded Canadians.

All over Pourville, windows were now opening, and puzzled German soldiers were shouting: 'Was ist los?'

Was this yet another practice raid sprung on them without warning by an over-zealous corps commander? A door in a house banged open and half a dozen Germans ran out. One was pulling on his jacket, holding his Schmeisser machine-gun in his other hand. Another tugged up his trousers as he ran. Behind Jack, Smokey raised his Sten-gun and squeezed the trigger. A stream of bullets spattered the wall. The men went down like rubber toys, waving arms and legs. Smokey spat his wad of gum out of the side of his mouth and replaced the empty magazine with a full one. Jack found it almost impossible to accept that these could be real people, alive one second and dead the next. But then Red had been alive and now was dead. Jack was experiencing the peculiar sensation that comes to men the first time under hostile fire, that he was somehow not involved in all this, but watching it from a distance, an observer only mildly interested. These bullets would not hurt him. If he kept very quiet, the enemy would not even notice him, and everyone could go home.

'Come on!' shouted Murray Osten, breaking this dangerous daydream. 'Get moving! They'll have the range if we hang around!'

At his words, men in 'A' Company rose from the ground and from their individual hiding places in doorways and against the walls of buildings. Jack raced with them across the open space behind the houses. Rifle and machine-gun bullets sprayed the earth like hoses, but none hit him. He leaned against a wall on the far side, trying to get his bearings. He knew the general layout of Pourville from the photographs, but in the early morning, shaken by blasts and explosions, with the air foggy and bitter with cordite, it was difficult to reconcile a black-and-white photograph with the reality of red-tiled roofs, white fences, grey shutters powdered by years of summer, plus the total incongruity of flowers, and telephone poles with glass insulators, like strange, glittering fruit.

Forness and MacLeod fell in with a section from 'B' Company, and almost immediately came under fire. Everyone went to ground. Forness ran forward to the protection of the wall of a house. He lobbed a grenade up through a second-storey window, and the explosion blew out panes of glass in jagged splinters across the road. Then, with his rifle and bayonet at the ready, he opened the nearest door and found himself in a semi-basement. A flight of wooden stairs led up to the floor where he had thrown the grenade. He slung his rifle over his shoulder, drew his revolver and began to climb the stairs, slowly, carefully, fearful of what he might find upstairs—or who might be up there, waiting for him.

A door was half open. He waited outside it and listened to the unexpected crackle of burning wood inside; his grenade must have started a fire. Should he burst in, or should he stay where he was? He was about to move, when he suddenly thought how stupid it would be to run in on a number of armed Germans with nothing more in his hand than a six-shot pistol he had never fired before; and so he carefully tiptoed down the stairs and rejoined the section.

He asked the section commander for a loan of his Tommy-gun, but the corporal was reluctant to part with it. While they were arguing, the fire inside the building spread, and a German officer appeared through the front door carrying a briefcase in one hand, with the other arm practically blown off his body. He was escorted down the beach for medical treatment. Forness watched him go, appalled at the damage he had done to a fellow human being.

To the right of the church, and about 200 yards from the beach, the road climbed steeply out of Pourville and then divided into two. The left branch led down to Petit-Appeville and St Aubin and the airfield. The other road climbed on up the hill into the trees towards Varengeville, where Lord Lovat's Commandos were already attacking the gun battery.

Much closer to the beach, and to the right of the Hôtel de la Terrasse, a narrow track led up the cliff. Gates to houses that commanded a magnificent view of the whole beach opened on to this pathway, which was just wide enough to take a car. It levelled out at the top of the cliff near one of the most imposing houses in Pourville, La Maison Blanche. This was an immensely solid building of whitewashed stucco, with an entrance lodge to the right of double gates that opened into a wide courtyard. From the promontory on which it stood, German officers who were billeted there were proud to show guests one of the finest sea views in Northern France.

The officers had held a party on the previous evening and throughout most of the night to celebrate a promotion, and despite Field-Marshal von Rundstedt's warning about that particular date being suitable for enemy raiding operations, and Colonel-General Haase's Order of the Day urging special vigilance from August 10 to August 19, some had slept late. Against all orders, too, a number of local girls, who had been invited to the party, had been persuaded to stay the night. Now, at the unexpected rumble of guns, and the unmistakable sounds of warfare actually on the beach, these girls started up in terror. What was happening? Hadn't they better get dressed and go home?

The officers were not greatly concerned by the firing. They explained that this happened frequently, owing to hit-and-run raids by British motor torpedo boats. If that was the cause, the commotion would end as suddenly as it had begun, when the boats sailed away. At the worst, it would be just another confounded landing practice, but La Maison Blanche was so high above the beach that clearly there was nothing to worry about. Then the officers heard an insolent drumming of alien boots along the corridors. Locked doors burst open under rifle butts. Many officers and orderlies, starting up half-dressed or naked, never reached their feet. As the girls screamed and screamed again in mindless horror, Canadians fired at two yards' distance or bayoneted their escorts. They rounded up five girls, some only wearing bras and panties, others with creased dresses hastily pulled over dishevelled, uncombed hair, sobbing in terror and reaction at the sight of violent and ugly death. A grinning corporal shepherded them out of the house, across the yard, and down the curving path towards Battalion Headquarters.

Hank Forness moved off on his own, and kicked open the door of the nearest house. The little hall, barely bigger than a passage, was empty. So was the kitchen, and the living-room downstairs. Cautiously, as he had been trained, he went up the wooden stairs, and opened the first door on the landing. The room contained an old-fashioned double bed, and to his astonishment, a Frenchman and his wife sat up like two clockwork figures, eyes wide in astonishment and fear. The Frenchman raised his hands in the air and began to shout. Forness understood little French, and certainly not this torrent of supplication that poured out at him. He looked into the only other room at the top of the house, found that empty, and returned to the bedroom.

'Good,' he said, meaning to reassure the Frenchman. '*Bon.*'
The Frenchman smiled and let his arms drop.
'*Ah, bon,*' he said, relieved.
'*Bon* it is,' agreed Forness, and came out into the street.

* * *

Across the road from the church, at the end of the house behind which Jack and his party were sheltering, stood the Hôtel de la Terrasse. It was a white stucco building with a big bow window, behind a neat privet hedge and a wall, on which was written: 'Recommandé par le Guide Michelin'. The terrace from which the hotel took its name was above the bow window, where little red pots, overflowing with flowers, hung from the beams. A second terrace with a white-and-brown handrail was built outside some bedrooms that overlooked the sea.

In one of these rooms, Monsieur Emile Sadé, the owner of the hotel, lay asleep. His son, Michel, and his son's wife, had both gone to Paris on the previous evening. Michel Sadé had been serving in the French Artillery in 1940, when he was taken prisoner near La Rochelle. He had escaped, and made his way back to Pourville, where he now worked with his father in the hotel. There were no tourists, of course, but they had to look after a number of senior Italian and Belgian workers who were involved with the construction of new fortifications being built by the Todt Organization, the German forced-labour group.

Suddenly, Monsieur Sadé woke up. He had heard loud noises in the street leading up from the beach: explosions and shouts, and the rattle of gunfire. Strange lights flashed through the curtains, and dozens of men in heavy boots seemed to be running past his hotel. What could be happening? There would be serious trouble if lights were showing in the blackout; or maybe those German officers up at La Maison Blanche had brought their confounded party into the town? In that case, there might be trouble for him. He flung open his bedroom window, and shouted down at them angrily, thinking that they must be drunks.

'What the hell are you lunatics doing with those lights?' he bellowed. 'In the name of God . . .'

A Frenchman shouted back excitedly: 'Don't you know? The Tommies have landed! You'd better take shelter!'

Tommies! Monsieur Sadé dived into his clothes. Other bedroom windows and doors were also opening, and Italians and

Belgians tumbled out sleepily into the corridors. By now the hotel walls were shaking with the constant rumble of big guns; little puffs of plaster dust dropped from ceilings. There was only one place in all the hotel strong enough to survive bombardment; Monsieur Sadé herded his guests in silence down the main stairs, then on down a set of brick steps worn smooth at the edges, to the cellar. The air down there felt chill and somehow metallic; dusty wine bottles in the racks pointed necks like cannons at them. The cellar roof was curved with metal hoops, encrusted with rust. They all stood in the damp semi-darkness, avoiding the little piles of crystalline deposits that Monsieur Sadé had carefully spread on the stone floor for mice to eat, instead of nibbling his wine-bottle corks and labels. They waited, saying nothing, looking uneasily at each other, with the shouts of orders and running of feet in the street above them, aware of the growing anger of guns in a battle they could hear but could not see. If Monsieur Sadé had heard Private Forness, he would have agreed with him; *bon* it was.

At the same moment, across the cliffs at Varengeville, the Mayor, Monsieur Charles Abraham, came out of the front door of the Café du Val d'Ailly. He had heard the sound of guns and seen flares in the sky, and wondered at the reason for all this commotion so early in the morning. One of his staff saw him standing in the doorway, and ran up excitedly.

'The British are here!' he explained.

'The British? Are you crazy?'

'What's this, then?' the clerk asked him triumphantly, and held up an empty Woodbine packet.

The most direct route to the RDF station from Pourville was over the bridge, on the east side of the town. There were two ways to reach this bridge; either behind the Hôtel de la Terrasse and the row of houses, or up to the church and then left along the road in front of them. Jack waited, back flat against the wall, wondering which would be the safer. For a moment the firing dwindled—either because the gunners had to reload or the dust cloud from smashed walls and chipped stones prevented them from seeing their targets—and he decided to risk crossing the road.

'Run!' he yelled. As he moved, he heard the shriek of a shell overhead, and flung himself flat on the road; he had heard similar sounds in the blitz, and knew there was no time for anything else. The road reared up and punched all the breath out of his body as the shell landed, showering them with chips of tile and stones and brick-dust.

For a few seconds, he lay gasping for breath, and the firing started. The noise was shattering; the constant iron thunder of big guns, of shells bursting, and the chatter of machine-guns, hammered all thoughts from his head. He tried to speak, to shout, but who could hear his words? The constant crash and roar was deafening.

He gathered himself up and raced to the shelter of houses across the street. Others followed him. The nearest front door was locked. A boot against the handle, Bud's rifle butt against a panel, and they were standing inside a kitchen that smelt of garlic and Gauloises and stale cabbage water. Jack went on through into an inner room. Those tins of peaches aboard *Princess Beatrix*, with the long, cold run-in, the charge up the beach, and then the ferocious firing, had combined to produce a pressing physical need.

'Where are you going, Spook?' Lofty asked him, as he began to climb the wooden stairs. 'What are you going to do?'

'Have a Tom Tit. Always told to travel light in the Boy Scouts.'

Jack found a crude lavatory on a half landing: two stone footprints green with urine, and a malodorous hole between them. He crouched over it, trousers around his ankles. The walls, he noticed inconsequentially, were covered with grey paper stamped with embossed fleurs-de-lys. Window hinges above his head had rusted half open. The whole house shuddered, and shutters rattled like loose teeth as another shell landed.

'For Chrissake, Jack, you all right?'

'Yeah. But got no paper.'

Boots came running up the stairs.

'Have this on me.'

Bud handed Jack a sheaf of the leaflets they had been given in the landing craft. He read: '*Français! Ceci est un coup de main et non pas l'invasion*'.

True enough.

'Best bloody use those can be put to, Spook,' said Bud. 'You fit now?'

'For anything,' replied Jack, pulling up his trousers. They ran down the stairs together. Nothing moved in the road outside, except swirling black clouds from smoke canisters. Through its coils they could see wounded men scratching the ground feebly in an extremity of pain. A Canadian signaller began to run across the open space from the garage. The square shape of the No. 18 set on his back, with its long trembling antenna, marked him as a target from 1,000 yards. Halfway up the cliff, a German sniper crouched in a foxhole with rounds of smokeless cartridges laid out neatly in front of him in five-round clips on a folded newspaper to keep them out of the dust, raised his rifle. It was a Mauser Kar 98K, fitted with a Zeiss telescopic sight. The Kar stood for *Karabiner*, or carbine; the K for *Kurz*, meaning short. His rifle was basically a shortened model of one that had first been introduced in 1908—nearly eighteen years after the British Lee-Enfield that the Canadians were carrying came into use.

Like all good marksmen, the sniper was unhurried. He knew that to kill a signaller would cause a far more serious loss to the enemy than almost any other soldier, for he was an essential link between one unit and another, between a commander and the men he commanded. He held the Canadian for a second in the fine crosshairs of his sight, following him as he ran, aiming slightly ahead of him, so that the target would run into the bullet. Then he squeezed the trigger. The signaller jumped in the air like a marionette on a spring, and dropped back under the weight of his set. His arms and legs moved briefly, then were still. Only the radio antenna trembled like a fallen lance.

The morning was light now, and in between curtains

drawn back in ground floor windows, Jack could see homely things: a vase of marigolds; a crucifix next to a photograph; a polished brass clock on a wooden mantelpiece. Beyond these houses stood the bridge and some huts on the far bank, and concrete pill-boxes with horizontal firing slits. From the nearest, little spurts of flame sprayed towards them: bullets danced in the road, scoring smoking grooves in the red tarmac.

'We'll never get through while that bastard's there!' shouted Jim against the crackle of fire.

'Concrete's a foot thick at least,' said Frenchie. 'We can't shift 'em unless we can get a mortar.'

'I'll shift him,' said Charlie firmly. 'Here, hold my rifle. I'll take the bastard out.'

He threw his rifle to one side. Bud caught it expertly. Charlie took two grenades from his belt, gripped the pin-rings between his teeth, and spat them out. He waited until the firing ceased briefly, while the machine-gunner replaced his empty magazine, and then he ran towards the pill-box, crammed both grenades through the slot, and started to run back before the explosion.

Several men in the group were wounded; one badly, in the back of his neck. Blood spurted out down his tunic with every beat of his heart.

'Let's get them under cover,' suggested Hawkins. They half carried, half dragged them into the downstairs room of an empty house and ripped off their jackets, and tried to stop the bleeding. Suddenly they heard a great shouting outside, even above the crash of guns.

'For Chrissake, don't throw that!' yelled Mavor.

Jack rushed out. The Camerons had landed and some were in the street. Mavor was struggling with a soldier about to throw a grenade through the window.

'They're not bloody Jerries in there! They're our blokes!'

On the seaward side of the bridge the Germans had blocked the mouth of the river with a wall, and the water looked deep. To the right, the fields were soft and swampy because of this dam, impossible for tanks and difficult to run through in a hurry. Willows and other water-loving trees grew on both banks.

High up on the far bank, beyond the marsh, plump Normandy cattle grazed peacefully, not even bothering to raise their heads at the sound of the guns. Beyond them again on the skyline, Jack could see concrete blockhouses dug into the ground except for their roofs; big gun-barrels pointed like metal fingers at possible targets against the merging greens of fields and trees and hedges. He saw that some Canadians had climbed down, and splashed or swum their way through the muddy water and climbed up on the other side. The bridge was the quickest and easiest means of crossing, but it was still raked regularly from emplacements on both sides of the road near the RDF station as advance parties of 'A' and 'D' Companies had found to their cost. The bridge was already thick with bodies, as though a company of men had lain down to sleep between the balustrades. At the far end, Jack could see Colonel Merritt shouting to his men to cross over between bursts of fire. If they hesitated, he would take off his steel helmet and, swinging it by the strap like a schoolboy's satchel, he sauntered towards them shouting: 'Come on, boys! Come on, let's go get 'em!'

At this example, Canadians sheltering in doorways and against houses, would start out, shouting, and race across. Those who reached the other side immediately flung themselves down in ditches to engage snipers and give cover to those behind them. Others were hit and stumbled on or tripped over the dead. Bullets danced like metal hailstones around Merritt, but incredibly none hit him. He stood unscathed, still swinging his tin hat by its strap, an inspiring sight that for Jack epitomized courage and leadership and something else again; the indomitable spirit of man.

Merritt shouted: 'We *must* get ahead, lads! We need more men up front as quickly as possible. Who's coming with me?'

Jack heard a sergeant reply: 'We're *all* going with you.'

'Then let's *go*!'

He led them up the road, and Jack thought: If he can survive, so can I.

He turned to his bodyguard.

'In the next lull I'm doing a Duchesse de Longueville,' he told them. 'I'm going to cross that river.'

Frenchie was next to him. He nodded agreement.

'See that?' he asked Jack, jerking his head towards a lock-gate with a board nailed to it: '*Pêche Interdite*'.

'Pity it doesn't forbid shooting, too.'

Les Thrussell, in a doorway ten feet behind them, turned to a fat small soldier who had crept into the doorway with him for shelter.

'Listen,' Thrussell told him seriously, 'I've got to get up there with these other guys, and quick. If you're moving, too, go now. I'll keep you covered.'

'Goddam it, Thrussell,' protested the fat little man. 'I don't mind dying, but I don't want to die alone. *You* go first.'

'Right,' replied Thrussell, and he went.

They all started to run at the same time, feet pounding heavily on the tarmac, then hollowly over the bridge. Jack's mouth was dry, his back muscles braced in an instinctive, involuntary reaction to bounce off any bullets. Mavor, keeping up with him, abruptly stopped running and fell forward, his arms outstretched, like a man diving. Les Thrussell dropped down beside him and rolled him over, but he was already dead.

Thrussell opened Mavor's field-dressing pocket and took out an escape kit; they had been given it to share back in the Isle of Wight, and the compass and the Horlicks tablets might come in useful. He crammed the pack in his own pocket, then ran after the rest of the party. Leslie England, at the head of the Special Force, was also hit. His Tommy-gun spiralled out into the river, his heels flew up around his ears and he fell heavily. Murray Osten went down on one knee by his side.

'You hurt, Les?' he asked him urgently, as bullets hammered the balustrade just above their heads, flicking chips of concrete everywhere.

"Course I am, you damn' fool,' England retorted with spirit. 'What do you think I'm lying here for?'

Murray Osten started to run again, relieved his friend was able to speak, sorry he could not stop to help him, for his duty lay ahead, up the hill. As he ran, a bullet hit him in the shoulder, and its impact threw him off balance. He reeled against the parapet, slipped and fell over the side, down into the muddy water.

'Come on!' Merritt shouted at him encouragingly. 'Up out of that! Stop mucking about and get on with the war!'

The cold water revived Osten, and he climbed gamely up the other bank, streaming wet, weed hanging from his belt.

'Follow me!' he shouted, and went on running.

The road was about twenty feet wide, without any cover, and raised up on a slight bank or spine above the grass on either side. Sergeant Ralph 'Red' Neil, who took over command of Special Force when Leslie England fell, led his men along the left side of the road; Jack and his group took what meagre cover they could find to the right. They all sank down thankfully in a storm ditch, their insteps pressed flat on the ground, to lessen their target area.

Jack looked ahead up the hill. The Freya aerial was still turning, and looking much larger than it had appeared from the beach; but then they were probably 200 yards nearer to it. There was depressingly little cover ahead: some shallow hollows in the ground, a small gorsebush, a clump of nettles, and then rectangular weapon pits, neat as newly-dug graves. A German steel helmet suddenly bobbed up, like a light grey coal-scuttle; its wearer took quick aim, and then ducked down to safety. All the snipers were using smokeless bullets, so only if Canadians actually saw movement, or the sudden glitter of sun on a rifle's brightwork, could they locate their position.

They had no need to guess at the positions of mortars or the bigger guns. They gave themselves away by the flashes of flame from their muzzles, but the knowledge was useless. What good was a Lee-Enfield rifle at such range, or the puny two-inch mortars that already were running short of shells?

Jack turned carefully and looked back down the hill towards Pourville. Merritt was still by the bridge, and encouraging more people to cross it by his example—and although he remained in the vortex of bullets, amazingly he was still unharmed. To Jack's right and inland, a few houses stood with their windows open, shutters peeled back like eyelids. Some had ornate turrets and intricately decorated eaves, Tudor style beams and imitation towers; a nightmare of French provincial architecture—and a nightmare for another reason. At the open windows, German soldiers appeared briefly to fire and then bobbed down again out of sight, living figures in a deadly Punch and Judy show. Jack looked up the road again. Straight ahead and slightly to the right stood a single storey building with a flat roof. Machine-guns were already firing at them from two slits in the wall, raking the open ground ahead of them carefully, methodically. If they lay where they were, they were certain to be hit.

At dusk on the previous evening, Captain Richard Schnösenberg, commanding a defensive area around Puys, had ordered his troops to take part in an exercise against a possible Allied landing. Since he had already called practice alerts on the Sunday and Monday his men were unenthusiastic about a third. How many dummy runs did the captain need? What was up with him—after promotion?

This resentment showed in a number of ways—orders misinterpreted, near enough being good enough, snide remarks made where superiors could hear but not see the speakers. The rehearsal did not run as smoothly as Schnösenberg wished, and since he was a determined man, and an extremely efficient officer, he extended it into the night.

The sky seemed unusually clear, and he noticed with some annoyance that a large gun, which they called an 'anti-landing gun', had been left on the beach, when he had ordered it to be pulled into position on the cliffs. Accordingly, he ordered his men to hoist it up. There was some grumbling at this, and the exercise dragged on until three o'clock in the morning. The troops were about to stand down, when they heard distant firing out at sea. There was really nothing strange in this, although a brother officer thought that it seemed louder and more menacing than usual.

'Let them shoot,' said Schnösenberg briefly; he had also had enough. They all returned back to their quarters, but about four o'clock, when Schnösenberg had undressed, the other officer came to see him in his room.

'Captain,' he said uneasily. 'They are *still* shooting.'

'If you don't want me to sleep,' replied Schnösenberg tartly, 'we can call for *another* exercise.'

In fact, that is what he did, so that at dawn on the Wednesday morning, after less than three hours off duty, his men stood ready for action. His command post was on the cliff between two moles that extended from the beach. Because of the early morning mist, Schnösenberg could not see the ends of these moles, but he could make out vague shadows moving out at sea, and he reported this fact to the Naval Signal Section, 100 yards away. They thanked him for the information and explained that this would be the convoy due from Boulogne, and was nothing to worry about. Other lookouts farther along the coast had apparently made the same mistake.

Then, while they were still talking, the fog suddenly lifted and right ahead both officers saw a navy ship flying a white flag with a red cross and the Union Jack at one corner: the British Navy. Schnösenberg's discussion with the officer in the Naval Signal Station ended abruptly; his troops opened fire immediately.

Captain Schnösenberg's command post was one of the targets of the Royal Regiment of Canada, under the command of Colonel Douglas Catto. Within an hour the Canadian regiment was decimated, for the fire that opposed them was withering. But Catto stubbornly refused to admit defeat. He rounded up the few officers and men who were still unwounded, and together they began to climb the cliffs to try and wipe out the German machine guns on top.

Schnösenberg could see them coming and was so deeply impressed by this display of individual bravery against hopeless odds that he ordered his men to shoot only to stop the Canadians, not to kill them. Finally, Catto and about twenty-five men were halted as much by thick broom growing in the cliffs as by German bullets. They could neither go forwards nor back, and so were forced to surrender.

Colonel Catto, as their commander, was brought over to meet Captain Schnösenberg. Admiration crossed the bridge of war: the two officers saluted each other smartly, and then shook hands. And the colonel congratulated the captain on the efficiency of his troops.

—SIX—

The noise of heavy guns firing from the cliffs and the drone of many aircraft woke Valère Muyssen in his farmhouse on the hill between Pourville and the RDF station. For a moment he lay listening, in case this was simply another invasion exercise, but the crump of shells and shouts from the shore were not make-believe. This was something different; this was war. He shook his wife awake, and she went in to rouse their two daughters. They all dressed hurriedly in the darkness.

Muyssen, a Belgian of forty-eight who had served as an officer in the Belgian Army during the First War, believed that an allied landing must be taking place, and he had already made plans for such a welcome event. He took the spade he had kept handy in the kitchen for this moment, and began to dig several long shallow trenches in the soft earth near the back door. It was obviously dangerous to stay in the house, and they had no cellar where they could shelter, so trenches seemed the best compromise. When the trenches were about eighteen inches deep he called to his wife and daughters, and they came out and lay down in them.

Muyssen ran a small-holding with sheep and cows, and his concern was also for his stock, which provided his livelihood. He was Flemish, the son of a schoolmaster, and as a young man he had never intended to farm. In those days, Flemings in Belgium were regarded almost as second-class citizens. Most educated people spoke French, and as a boy Muyssen had to learn Greek and Latin from French instead of from his own tongue. His ambition then was to make his career in the

Belgian consular service, and with this in mind, he took a degree from the University of Louvain. Then he met and married a French girl and abandoned this ambition, because her family, in the way of many French country families at that time, did not relish the idea of their daughter living abroad, perhaps hundreds or even thousands of miles away from France. Muyssen therefore settled in Dieppe to be near his wife's parents, and after taking various jobs, he bought a farm outside Pourville. When the Germans occupied the area, he lost a number of sheep to local dogs that had been abandoned by their owners, whose homes had been requisitioned, but the Germans had not interfered with him or his family.

The four Muyssens lay uneasily in the trenches that Valère thought uncomfortably resembled new-made graves, watching the white vapour trails of planes overhead. From this strange vantage point he could also see soldiers in British-type battle-dress running across the bridge over the Scie. It was humiliating for an old soldier to lie there and watch young men die so quickly and in such numbers, and brought back his own experiences in Flanders; sights and sounds that he had deliberately buried in his mind for twenty-four years, now came vividly and terribly to life. He could see other soldiers, foreshortened by distance, dodge from house to house in Pourville. Then a party of ten or eleven soldiers approached, dropping for cover behind patches of nettle or in shallow holes, waiting for mortar shells to burst, and then leaping up and, heads well down, running on while clods of earth from the last explosion were still raining down around them. Muyssen's farmhouse was to the right of the road, and these men were coming up the hill on his side of the road.

The air cleared; they were barely thirty yards away. Some carried small machine-guns; others, rifles of the type he had seen in the First War; one, a mortar over his shoulder; another, a revolver. Instead of the khaki packs of his comrades, this man carried a blue pack on his right hip. And he had no badges of rank on his uniform, no markings of any kind. They must be English, Muyssen thought; at least, they wore English uniforms. But in his time, only officers carried revolvers, so who was this man, carrying an officer's weapon, but not wearing an officer's stars or crown?

'What's happening?' he called out in English. 'Who are you?'

'Canadians,' one of the men shouted back. 'Who are *you*?'

'A farmer.'

'Like us, then. How come you speak English?'

'I learned it at school. In Belgium. And in the Army in the last war.'

'Keep away from us then, buster. We're not stopping. This is only a raid—not an invasion.'

'Good luck!' Muyssen called to them, sinking back into his trench, wishing he were young again, in action, fighting a young man's war.

'Good luck to you, too, mate,' the man with the blue pack cheerfully replied.

Jack dropped to the ground and flattened himself against the grass to present the smallest possible target to the bullets. The others lay on either side of him, doing the same thing. Far ahead of them, up the hill, a German moved in a slit-trench, near a pillbox. Charlie raised his rifle to take aim, then suddenly fell forward, hit in the forehead. As he dropped, his trigger finger tightened, the rifle fired up and then clattered down, out of his dead hand. A Canadian sergeant behind them began to shout.

'Let's have the mortar! Get the mortar!'

There was a mortar but no more bombs for it. A Bren-gun chattered bravely, but the Germans in the pill-box were protected by a foot of concrete; the bullets danced uselessly off the wall, scarcely chipping it.

'I'll show you how we'll deal with this,' Jack heard someone say grimly, and Colonel Merritt strode forward. As he walked, he pulled the pin from a grenade. He had calculated that the gunners in the pill-box must have a blind spot to right or left, and risking this, he walked up to the concrete wall. When the firing stopped momentarily for the gunner to reload, Merritt lobbed in a grenade and dropped down again for the explosion.

Osten led 'A' Company across the grass along the edge of the road towards the crest of the hill, with the turning Freya aerial on their left. Other machine-guns swung on to them and they all dropped to avoid the fire. From the village, the hill had appeared smooth, and shaved of all grass, but climbing it, Jack discovered thankfully that it was pitted with little gulleys and hollows just deep enough to shelter a man. Directly ahead of them all, several huge oil drums filled with concrete and bound with barbed wire, had been rolled across the road. Wire strands stretched from them over the fields. They would have to run between these blocks, and the gaps were certain to be covered by guns farther up the hill, just as the bridge had been.

'Get some smoke!' shouted Ed Dunkerley.

One man lit a smoke canister and threw it into the wind. The little khaki can, the size of a tin of beans, trundled forward slowly and then erupted in billowing clouds of black smoke. As Dunkerley lay in a shallow ditch waiting for the smoke to thicken, he felt a quick tug at the sleeve of his jacket, as though someone had pulled it. Then a burning sensation spread across his chest; he had been hit.

As smoke blotted out the road block, an officer shouted, 'Follow me!' and they were up and running, until the smoke and the obstacles were behind them. They had gained several yards—and had lost almost as many men. As they dropped down on the grass again, a bullet tore the heel from one of Dunkerley's boots. His leg jerked as though pulled by a wire, and his ankle went numb. Gradually feeling returned and with it a sharp fiery pain; the bullet had scored the base of his foot.

Overhead, Spitfires and Luftwaffe planes were turning and wheeling and diving, with a chatter of cannon and machine-guns. At times a parachute would billow white against the blue sky. Dunkerley watched as cross-fire chipped to pieces the few stunted bushes remaining on the hill. Then he saw bullets spurt into the dust all around him, coming so quickly that before he could roll out of their way, he felt another sharp gouge of pain in his right hip. His leg lost all feeling, and faintness overcame him. Two mortar bombs dropping behind him and one in front, possibly fifty feet away, jerked him back to reality. The Germans were bracketing them, seeking the range; the next shot could be fatal. Some soldiers, bemused by the noise, constant and deafening, by the earth trembling as bombs landed, and the choking haze of smoke and dust, began to falter.

'Come on!' ordered Dunkerley urgently, forgetting his own wounds. 'Let's *go*!'

He led them up the hill, and the next bomb fell harmlessly behind them. In several small hollows injured men had crawled away to die; others were helping the wounded. Somehow, a handful of them reached the wall outside an abandoned pillbox. A Canadian dropped down beside Dunkerley. His mouth, one side of his face and one hand were so thickly covered with blood that it was impossible for the sergeant-major to estimate the severity of his injuries. They lay in the early morning sun, grateful for temporary shelter, faint with pain and loss of blood.

'You know something?' the soldier asked him slowly, speaking with difficulty because of his wounds.

'What?' asked Dunkerley.

'Just this, sar'-major. Never again will I curse at you and your bloody discipline. Now I *know* what discipline means.'

They lay, weakened by wounds, watching the battle as though it was all a dream that would presently melt away like the pain and the drifting bitter-smelling smoke. Above the roar of guns, Dunkerley heard the faint trembling cry of a goat tethered somewhere beyond a ruined building. As a farmer himself, he wondered what had happened to its owner; who would milk that goat, and when? And, forgetting his own situation, he felt compassion for one wretched, harmless, terrified animal caught in the cross-fire of two opposing armies.

In Battalion Headquarters of the German 571st Infantry Regiment, in the fifteenth-century castle high above the cliffs between Dieppe and Pourville, the Commanding Officer,

Lieutenant-Colonel Hermann Bartelt, made a decision: he would call in his outlying company, at present on detachment at Ouville-la-Rivière, seven miles west of Dieppe.

While it was impossible to say how the battle on the beaches would end, early reports agreed that the invaders were suffering heavy casualties. Even so, they were fighting tenaciously and still might gain a foothold. Despatch riders confirmed that a number of military telephone wires had been cut, either deliberately or by shelling. If the colonel waited too long he might not be able to call up his reinforcements. He therefore ordered that the telephone line to Ouville be tested. It was still intact, so he spoke to the major in command, and explained that the British were landing at Dieppe and Pourville, and accordingly he was to send a strong detachment to the area immediately. They were to come by road to Hautot, about four miles from Dieppe, and then over the cross-roads at Petit-Appeville, two miles from Pourville.

Colonel Bartelt assumed that the British were landing because the Canadian Army wore British-style battledress, and no Canadian prisoners had yet been taken and interrogated. He selected this particular point, where the road to Pourville from Paris crossed the major arterial road from Dieppe to Le Havre, because the invaders would pass this junction if they intended to go inland.

The major commanding the detachment at Ouville welcomed these orders. Now not only would his men have an unexpected chance of distinguishing themselves in action, but they could also test under active service conditions his claim that they could travel speedily, silently, and without need of petrol points or complicated mechanical maintenance. For his columns were equipped with bicycles.

Immediately, he ordered all men to parade with their cycles in the road outside the headquarters. They formed up smartly in full battle order, with water-bottles, small packs, rifles, gas-capes, steel helmets, automatic weapons, plus spares and bandoliers of extra ammunition.

Orders were read out, and the officer in charge of the detachment gave the command to mount. Each soldier, per-

Flight Sergeant Jack Maurice Nissenthall taken in 1943.

Captain Murray Osten, Commander of 'A' Company, South Saskatchewan Regiment, from which ten men were chosen to 'protect' Nissenthall. (Photo. M. Osten)

Lieutenant-Colonel Charles Cecil Ingersoll Merritt, VC, QC, the Commanding Officer of the South Saskatchewan Regiment, who was awarded the VC for his leadership at Pourville. (Photo. Imperial War Museum)

Air Vice-Marshall Sir Victor Tait, KBE, CB, who briefed Nissenthall on his mission.
(Photo. Personal Collection)

Professor R. V. Jones, CB, CBE, FRS, a major contributor to Britain's successful radar war effort.

The war-winning cavity magnetron valve devised in 1940 by Professor J. T. Randall and Dr. H. A. H. Boot. 'Its unique ability to transmit microwaves at very high power enabled radar equipment to be built that was infinitely more powerful and accurate than anything previously designed'.
(Photo. J. M. Nissenthall)

The radar station, now fallen on to Green Beach from the cliff top site
where it stood for over thirty years.
(Photo. William Heinemann Ltd.)

Green Beach, Pourville, seen from the cliff-top site of the radar station.
(Photo. William Heinemann Ltd.)

The bridge over the River Scie. In August 1942 there were no houses to provide cover, and the bridge was soon completely blocked by the bodies of dead and wounded Canadians.
(Photo. William Heinemann Ltd.)

The road into Pourville from Petit-Appeville. Jack and the remainder of his bodyguard were pursued along this road by the 571st Infantry Regiment, mounted on bicycles.
(Photo. William Heinemann Ltd.)

The German <u>Kommandantur</u> at Envermeu, twelve miles from Dieppe, headquarters of the 302nd Infantry Division under Major-General Konrad Haase.
(Photo. William Heinemann Ltd.)

August 19, 1942, after the landing, a destroyed Churchill IV. These tanks were fitted with extensions to their exhausts to facilitate deep water landing.

German soldiers with a wounded Canadian prisoner. *(From contemporary German pictures)*

Field Marshall Gerd von Rundstedt, German Commander-in-Chief West (centre) discusses the enemy landings with officers of Army Group West. *(From a contemporary German photograph)*

Jack Nissenthall, (left) Les Thrussell and James Leasor outside Les Thrussell's house in Moose Jaw, Saskatchewan, 1973. *(Photo. William Heinemann Ltd.)*

fect in drill motions he had practised to complete precision, stood, right foot on the pedal, and then, as one man, they swung their left legs over the saddle.

But what had not been practised was cycling with such heavy equipment, with the dead weight of extra ammunition and mortars. The military bicycles were designed to carry an accoutred rider, but were not all strong enough to bear all this in addition. On one cycle after another, spokes tore out of wheels, and the wheels collapsed, throwing their riders on to the road.

The reinforcements from Ouville took two hours to reach Hautot, barely five miles away.

Jack lay in a storm ditch on the inland side of the road, about 100 yards from Ed Dunkerley, with his bodyguard spread like a human fan around him. He savoured pleasantly incongruous scents of summer: fresh hay from the fields, warm grass, white flowers with a strong sharp scent which he had last smelled as a boy on Kent cliffs. He wondered inconsequentially what they were called. How were their seeds carried across the Channel—and did they originally belong to France or to England?

The sky above was filled with fighter planes; empty cartridge cases rained down all round them. The noise was as loud as ever, but either he had grown more used to it, or his ears had become dulled, for he accepted it now as an unavoidable background; like working in a steel-works, wearing ear-muffs.

Cautiously, he raised his head and scanned the hill behind him to see how other SSRs were faring. Near the concrete blocks, the road was dotted with bodies, some wearing khaki and some in field grey. None was moving. Around them lay the detritus of dead soldiers; a litter of rifles, steel helmets, smoke canisters; an abandoned two-inch mortar, a smashed radio set. Smoke still rolled majestically over the water, where blazing landing craft drifted aimlessly, pivoting on submerged rocks until some unseen eddy tugged them away. He could hear distant shouts of orders and counter-orders, the rattle of machine-guns, the crack of rifles, the hollow thump of mortars. But whether they were Canadian or German, it was impossible to know, and lying there in the hot morning sun, the rum on his empty stomach began to spread a strange drowsiness through his body, so that the matter seemed curiously unimportant and irrelevant.

He looked up towards the RDF station, which he could now see more clearly. It was a solid concrete building, surrounded by a high blast wall piled with earth and sandbags. Beneath the aerial was a small cabin which moved with it, and contained the operator. Jack noted that, unlike comparable British radar aerials, the Freya aerial did not once make a complete revolution, to sweep inland, but only turned within 180 degrees. This was possibly because it was unable to do so owing to the thick cable connecting the cabin on its turntable with the concrete blockhouse underneath. This meant that the Germans were still using a direct co-axial cable connection to the transmitter whereas British sets had long since gone over to a rotating electro-magnetic coupling which allowed the aerials of Chain Home Low and Ground Control Interception sets to make complete circles through 360 degrees unfettered by cables.

Machine-gun posts and trenches for riflemen were dug into the ground between the station and a barbed-wire fence surrounded it. Although Jack knew what he had to do, he felt half hypnotized by heat, by reaction from the sights and sounds around him. He forced himself to his feet, and his bodyguard rose with him. The road turned to the right, wider here, with a strip of stones on one side. In peacetime, this had been intended for motorists who wanted to pull off the highway and sit in their cars, washing down their pâté and *baguettes* with a bottle of Bordeaux, admiring the view. Now the open patch of gravel simply meant another hazard to cross.

They still kept to the right of the road, so that it could give them some cover from machine-guns around the RDF station. Other Germans were also firing at them from across the fields half a mile away, towards the Farm of the Four Winds, but they kept moving fast, and no one was hit. They reached the first bend in the road where it curved right, then left on its way around the cliff-top to Dieppe. Down the far side of the bank on which the road was built, Murray Osten had set up his company headquarters and an artillery observation post in a hedgerow. They were screened by the bank from the defenders of the RDF station and only open to firing from across the fields from behind them.

Jack saw that Murray Osten's face was pale and drawn. He must have lost more blood than he realized from his wound; the wet red patch on his battledress was twice the size it had been down the hill. But however ill or weak he felt, Murray Osten outwardly appeared as ebullient as ever. He waved one arm in the direction of the RDF station.

'There's your goddam target, Jack!' he announced dramatically. 'There's your station! Take it—if you want it!'

His remark was so unexpected that Jack laughed.

'I'll do my best,' he replied.

'We haven't enough men for a frontal attack,' Osten went on. 'That station's encased in concrete couple of feet thick. We'll get some artillery down on it. I've asked the FOO[1] here to radio to the Navy, giving our map reference, but we've had no results so far. Part of my aerial's been shot away.'

Jack crawled carefully up the bank to reconnoitre. Sharp-edged flints nicked his knees beneath his thick battledress trousers. At the edge of the road, he paused, for now he could see the station from a different angle. Twelve-foot high coils of barbed-wire lay round it, rusting in the sea air. Behind them, an inner screen of single wires stretched across wooden posts. At the centre was the octagonal concrete compound, with only one narrow way in; this faced them, heavily screened by an extension of the blast wall. Above the square concrete building, the metal aerial, a mass of fine girders, grotesquely large now he was so close, turned to and fro like the spread wings of some huge prehistoric bird, searching for prey.

[1] Forward Observation Officer.

He could imagine the crew inside their dark room, secure in the comforting safety of concrete above them, beneath them, around them, working under naked electric bulbs. The tube would show the familiar blips of light, pale green against the dark green background; then the quiet, unhurried voices of the bearing operator, reading off the ranges, and the plotter, speaking into the head-and-breast telephone set connected by direct line to the central air operations room in Dieppe. Mugs of coffee and thick china cups stood on metal desks, with the corporal's report book, and, in a corner, an oscilloscope used for set maintenance. But they would not have time to notice any of these things, for the continual dog-fights overhead were keeping them as busy as one-armed paperhangers.

There was his RDF station, all right, the layout strangely reminiscent of Rosehearty, and only about 100 yards away. How many radar experts in Britain—Jones or Preist among dozens—would willingly have changed places with him, to be so near such a treasure-house of enemy secrets! Jack was inwardly astonished that he was the man who was actually there. On duty at Hope Cove, he had often wondered about his opposite numbers along the French coast; about their equipment and their techniques, and knowing the Freya's wavelength and having been told by Preist at Malvern the approximate height of the aerial, he had used Watson-Watt's method to calculate a theoretical performance chart. Now, theory had become practice; he was on the verge of discovering whatever secrets that blockhouse contained. His overwhelming interest in what he might discover drove all concern about his own dangerous position from his mind. He slithered back down the bank.

'I've got to move up closer to it,' he told Osten, shouting into his ear against the roar that surrounded them. 'Give me all the cover you can.'

Osten nodded to two Bren-gunners. Other Canadians who carried spare Bren magazines, unbuttoned their pouches so that they could hand over their full magazines when the gunners ripped the empty ones off their reeking barrels, and threw them back to be refilled.

Jack turned to Thrussell and Hawkins.

'Ready?'

'Yes,' said Thrussell quietly.

'When you are,' said Hawkins.

'Then it's now,' Jack told them. He picked up a rifle from a dead soldier, checked the magazine—eight rounds inside, and one up the spout, safety-catch off. He cocked the action and began to crawl forward, cursing the blue RAF pack that slid around from his back to his side, getting in the way of each tree stump or sawn-off shrub.

He had covered about fifteen yards before they were spotted. Bullets raked the ground around them.

'Back!' Jack shouted urgently.

They slithered backwards as fast as they could.

'Near thing,' said Jack briefly.

'As Wellington said about Waterloo. More or less,' said Jim.

More bullets spattered around them.

Hawkins said: 'There's no sense in trying to go up there with a handful of men. A whole company of Jerries are around the station, and dug in so's you'd need a tank to shift them!'

Hawkins was right. They would only be dead heroes if they attempted to reach the station on their own from that position. They moved back for about thirty feet from the road, where a few bushes provided some thin cover from snipers across the inland fields. Behind them, a narrow lane, hardly wider than a path, led down to Pourville between high grassy banks. The hedges had not been cut that summer, and in places they met across the top of the track, making a dark tunnel dappled with patches of sunlight. Jack glanced at the Canadians around him. Many were wounded, and even if they were all fit they simply did not possess enough fire-power, with First War Lee-Enfields, and untried Stens and Brens, to come within yards of the concrete emplacement surrounded by a wall of barbed wire. In a charge, they would simply rush to certain death with no hope whatever of securing their objective. Jack decided to go back to Battalion Headquarters near the beach to see whether he could radio a destroyer to bring down fire on the area, or find any mortars that could do the same thing.

Jack pulled off his blue pack.

'Keep that safe,' he told Lofty.

'I'll come with you,' said Thrussell.

'So will I,' said Frenchie. Jack looked at them, glad of their company, yet wondering why they wanted to escort him. Was it to save his life—or to make sure that if he were wounded, he lost it?

The lane was surfaced with loose, whitish chips of crushed stone and gravel, that felt curiously slippery underfoot, like running on wet moss. Several times, they slithered and almost fell. Jagged pieces of falling shrapnel cut green twigs above their heads, and leaves fluttered to the ground like confetti as bullets sliced through hedge tops.

The path ended near the bridge. Jack had hoped that it led into Pourville by some back road, but they would have to cross that bridge, now blocked with bodies. It seemed unlikely that anyone could still be alive in the mass of blood-stained khaki-clad soldiers, yet even in the urgency of the moment Jack could not bring himself to run across them. The swamp seemed impassable, so he jumped up on the nearest balustrade. Bullets flicked pieces of concrete from the supports under their feet, but none hit them. They jumped down on the other side and raced through Pourville, towards the garage, where Battalion Headquarters had originally been set up. The cars inside were now covered with dust and rubble, roofs and mudguards dented by fallen masonry. All the windows at the back of the building had been blown in; splinters of glass covered the floor. Canadian wounded lay on stretchers or gas-capes or sat propped against the far wall, faces greyish-green from shock and loss of blood.

'Where's HQ now?' Jack asked the nearest Canadian. The man pointed feebly towards the casino near the beach; he was too weak to speak. Part of the top storey of the white casino building had already been shot away, but the floor beneath it had held. Jack went through the frail door into an entrance hall. Posters in frames advertised the attractions of Dieppe, Le Touquet, Cinzano, Dubonnet. Ornamental electric light brackets hung down from the walls by their wires. The glass was smashed in the windows, but their frames still held, edged with jagged glass slivers. A Canadian radio operator crouched on the floor, tuning his set.

'Got to get a message through to *Calpe*,' Jack told him breathlessly. 'Artillery wanted now on Study.' This was the code name for the RDF Station.

'You joking?' asked the signals man, not even looking up at him. There had been no radio contact with the headquarters ship for some time. He was about to say more when they all heard the whistle of a mortar shell and flung themselves flat. The shell exploded on the promenade, maybe twenty feet away. The building rocked crazily; lumps of concrete and plaster rained down. The signaller blew dust from the dials on his set and calmly began to repeat his call-signal into the hand-microphone. Outside, on the waste land over the tarmac road, Jack saw another radio operator dead, his set still strapped to his back.

'They're aiming for them deliberately,' said the operator. 'They're even using our own goddam transmissions to pinpoint where we are! Reckon that's how that mortar nearly had us just then. We're giving ourselves away every goddam time we speak. Some Jerries are using our wavelengths, telling us to retire, or giving us a lot of junk about what's happening.'

'Haven't we any recognition code words?' Jack asked.

'Sure, but so much is going on, they're not always used. And in any case, while we're trying to figure out whether a message is genuine, they work out our position and mortar us.'

He looked up from his set and pulled off his earphones.

'No reply,' he said bitterly. 'Either their set's dead, or ours is. It's been like that all morning.'

'Christ!'

Jack looked about him in desperation. He must find more men or heavy supporting fire if he were to smash his way into the RDF station, but how and where?

Through the shattered window in the back of the room he

could see the cliffs. Snipers were methodically firing down at any movement they could see. He ran outside into a small courtyard at the rear of the building, sheltered by a wall from the snipers' fire. Some wounded had been carried here, and they lay uncomplaining on gas-capes or the dirty concrete, half in the sun, half in the shade.

Ten or twelve French girls were also in the yard, incongruously wearing sleeveless cotton summer dresses. Some carried baskets of tomatoes and long French loaves. Others had calmly set up a table with plates of tomatoes and sandwiches, and china jugs of water and wine. They had filled the Canadians' mess tins and were holding them up to the wounded to help them drink. The sight of their young pretty faces and frocks more in keeping for a picnic, emphasized the ruin and destruction all round them. One girl turned to Jack and spoke rapidly, but he could not understand what she said.

He turned to Frenchie who was nearby.

'Don't they know we're not staying—that we're going back today? That it's dangerous for them to be here—not just from the risk of being shot?'

'Of course. But they want to come back to England with us. They're begging us to take them back.'

'But that's impossible. Haven't they read these leaflets?'

'They're still hoping.'

'For God's sake, get them out of here,' said Jack. 'It's a death trap between these concrete walls. Can't you make them clear out before it's too late?'

'They won't go. They're determined to come away with us to England. They have risked their lives to help us.'

Jack shrugged his shoulders. Mercifully, this wasn't his problem, but it was clear from the number of landing craft already sunk offshore or shelled and drifting aimlessly, that the Canadians would be lucky if they managed to escape themselves, without taking back any French civilians. Even if they could all reach landing craft—which would be difficult enough on an ebb-tide, running under fire through shallow water for a quarter of a mile—there would simply not be sufficient vessels to transport them all to England. He sat down against a wall in the shade and took off his steel helmet, which he had rammed down over his scalp to keep it on when he ran. It had given him a headache, and he smoothed back his sweat-soaked hair. Reaction from climbing the hill and discovering the virtual impregnability of the RDF station made him unspeakably weary and lethargic. He swallowed one of his two pep pills; maybe that would help. A French girl handed him a ripe tomato, and he bit into it gratefully and nodded his thanks.

The wish of these girls to escape to England made Jack acutely aware of the fearful danger of his own situation. He had agreed to come on this party—what an incredibly inane description!—readily accepting the peculiar conditions involved, without really imagining that there was much risk of them being implemented. Now he remembered the old Polish Rabbi telling him how David slew Goliath. But what would have happened if David's sling had snapped? Now that would be a Biblical story with a totally different ending. David had taken a calculated risk—and he had survived. Jack had also agreed to a calculated risk, but maybe his calculations had been at fault?

The extraordinary thing was that when he used to buy a suit or even a tie or a shirt before the war, he would look at all kinds of patterns and judge one against another before he decided. But when it had been casually proposed that he should come to France dressed as a soldier, on the understanding that if he could not return alive, then he agreed to stay there dead, he had immediately acquiesced—as though he accepted this sort of ludicrous proposal as completely reasonable.

Surely, when the moment came to escape, even if no landing craft were left, these Canadians would not cold-bloodedly kill him? But then, why shouldn't they? They had accepted their orders, just as he had accepted his. It was too late now to vary the terms. He recalled Frenchie's quotation: 'It is vain to quarrel with destiny'. Was his destiny to die on this foreign shore? The only way to make sure it wasn't, was to beat them

—Jerries and Canadians alike—and damn well do what he had come to do. And then escape—somehow.

'Come on,' he said gruffly. 'Let's get out of here.'

'Where to?' Thrussell asked him.

'Back up to Murray Osten. We can't get any help down here.'

'So what can we do up there?' asked Frenchie.

As they started to run across the open space outside the casino, a mortar bomb landed near the sea-wall and blew all three off their feet. Jack could not see Thrussell or Frenchie, for dense dust blotted out the sunshine, coating his throat, thick as a bat's fur. He gasped for breath, and then crawled to his feet and began to run, staggering and coughing, through the main street, over the bridge, up the long track between the hedges and dropped down thankfully on the bank next to Murray Osten. Frenchie joined them.

'Where's Thrussell?' Jack asked him hoarsely.

Frenchie shrugged. He was too exhausted to speak. Jack remembered the mortar bomb: the blast, the heat and dust, the shattering punch of the explosion. That must have hit Les, he thought. Poor devil. Nearly half of his group were dead already, and what had he achieved? A couple of runs up the hill under fire, and beyond that—nothing, nothing at all.

'Get your message off?' Osten asked him.

Jack shook his head.

'The signaller tried, but his set's US.[1] Give me some more covering fire, and I'll try to crawl round the back of the station again on my own.'

'You haven't got a hope.'

'I'd have more if we had smoke. Got any?'

'Nope. Only more wounded. Either these goddam snipers are coming closer, or their aim's improving.'

Jack stood up.

'Where are you off to?'

'To try and find some smoke canisters.'

'I'll come with you,' said Smokey.

[1] Unserviceable.

He was not the companion Jack would have chosen. Smokey had unstrapped his water-bottle and held it up to his mouth.

'What are you drinking?'

'Rum.'

'You must be mad in this heat.'

'I'd drink rum any time.'

Jack set off once more down the path. Now he could hear Germans shouting orders from the fields; they were much nearer than they had been even a few minutes earlier. Unless he could reach the RDF station very soon, the entire hill would be overrun. He and Smokey sprinted through the main street. Tiles and lumps of masonry, even front doors blown off hinges, had been scattered about as though after an earthquake. Then they saw Colonel Merritt. His face was pale and strained; he had deep dark circles round his eyes. Jack was shocked at the change in him.

'We need more men up there,' Jack told him, pointing to the hill. 'And mortars and smoke. Otherwise we can't attack the station.'

'I'll give you all I can,' Merritt replied at once. 'But look what they've done to my boys. They have torn them to pieces.'

He gave a gesture that embraced the dead and the dying. The casualties had been high—and what had been achieved?

He shouted to a corporal leading a section a few yards away; one man carried a two-inch mortar.

'Come on! Follow him to the RDF station!'

Jack led them back over the bridge and across the fields, but now the Germans were barely three hundred yards away, and their fire was growing far more accurate. Only a few of the reinforcements reached 'A' Company.

Jack sank down wearily on the hot dry ground. It was senseless to attempt to attack the station with the small force they had. He would have to crawl round the back on his own. There might perhaps be a blind spot in their defence just large enough to allow one man to approach any exposed telephone wires. One man could succeed where even two would be seen. And he had now decided on the only way of extracting the secrets from the Freya.

During the previous autumn, British listening stations along the south coast, monitoring every German radio transmission, had picked up regular messages from Freya operators. They would speak in code on their radio-telephones or operate their Morse keys, giving details to their control centres of the plots of approaching aircraft. It had been a relatively simple matter for cryptographers in Britain to break these codes, and from then on British radar scientists were able to analyse the capabilities and strength of Freya stations. These radio transmissions had stopped abruptly, when the Germans followed the British custom of connecting radar stations to control-rooms by land-lines. If these lines were cut, Jack knew that the operators in the Freya station facing him, tracking the heaviest air battle of the war, would be forced to go over to radio-telephone or wireless telegraphy transmission immediately—otherwise they would be unable to pass on any information to their control-room, and so would create a serious gap in the whole German radar screen at the height of a ferocious air onslaught.

Yet the moment they spoke by radio-telephone, mobile monitoring outfits along the Sussex and Hampshire coast would tune to their transmissions. These would be recorded and analysed, and from the mass of figures and code letters, the experts would soon discover whether this particular Freya had been modified and improved and was the precision instrument some suspected it now must be—or whether it was still the relatively unsophisticated set whose secrets they already knew.

If the operators did not go on the air, this would be because they knew they could safely opt out and hand over their task to some third quite unknown station or stations working on another wavelength. So either way, much would be learned. The Freya would either yield up its own secrets—or it would reveal the existence of a third radar chain.

'Give me what cover you can with your Brens and Stens,' he told Osten. 'I'm going up on my own.'

'You're crazy, Jack. You'll never get there. The moment you move up that hill, they'll have you.'

'I've got to risk it. If they don't get me, your blokes will. It's not much of a choice either way, is it? I'm going.'

As the pep pill poured adrenalin into his blood, Jack felt taut, keen, almost light-headed. He also felt a dull ache deep in his stomach. He had never liked rum, and now, with the heat and the exertion of repeatedly running up and down the hill, he liked it even less. What a moment to have indigestion!

'We're coming with you,' declared Hawkins, slamming a round into the breech of a Lee-Enfield he had taken from a dead soldier.

'You betcha,' said Lofty.

'Don't be bloody fools,' Jack told them. 'Keep me covered instead.'

At 0625 hours, the telephone rang in a sparsely furnished office in the sitting-room of a house outside Amiens, about eighty miles inland, and the headquarters of General Wolfgang Fischer, commanding the German 10th Panzer Division. The duty officer scooped up the receiver, expecting no more than a routine call. To his astonishment, a colonel from 15th Army headquarters spoke excitedly in his ear.

'The British have landed at Dieppe on a twenty kilometre front, extending from Varengeville to Berneval,' he announced. 'Tenth Panzer Division will hold itself in readiness for all eventualities. The situation is still somewhat obscure, but the order for full alert can arrive at any minute. You will immediately operate *Alarm-Stufe* II (No. 2 Alarm). Now put me through to the GSO I.'

This was the General Staff Officer, Grade One, a colonel, who dealt with such matters on behalf of the general. The duty officer, who also controlled the internal telephone exchange, pushed in the plug for the colonel's extension, and turned the buzzer handle. When the GSO picked up his telephone, a little metal eyelid would drop over his extension number on the switchboard. But there was no reply; the number continued to stare back accusingly at the duty officer. Surely the colonel could not still be asleep with the telephone ringing by his bed?

He buzzed him a second time, in case he might be in the bathroom, but again there was no answer. This meant that the colonel was not in his quarters; he had presumably slept out, against all orders, during the danger period of 18/19 August. Perhaps he was spending the night with a girl-friend? This was the duty officer's first thought. His second was to discover the colonel's whereabouts in the few seconds at his disposal. Feeling a twinge of sympathy for his superior if he were to be caught out on this one night of the whole war, the duty officer spoke again to the colonel from 15th Army.

'He is not answering his telephone, sir.'

'Is he sick?'

'I do not know, sir.'

'Very well. Then put me through to the general's adjutant.'

'Very good, sir.'

This time the receiver was picked up immediately. The duty officer thoughtfully replaced his own telephone. Within seconds, the general's adjutant was calling him.

'Sound Stand-to,' came the order. 'See that all commanders are issued with maps for the Dieppe area. And clear the line to 81st Army Corps.'

The officer dialled the military exchange and asked for a line to corps at Canteleu. There was a few moments' delay, and then a puzzled operator replied that the line was dead; either it had a fault or the wire had been cut. There was no telephone connection to corps. The duty officer reported this information to the general's office.

'Then contact them at once by radio.'

But no arrangements had been made in advance for radio contact between the two formations, so this was also impossible. And there was worse to come. A search of the map store of the 10th Panzer Division Headquarters showed that it possessed no maps whatever of Dieppe. Other coastal areas, yes; but not Dieppe. The general was furious. What kind of nonsense was this? No contact by telephone or radio with

174

corps, and no maps of the coast they might have to defend that day against a full-scale Allied invasion?

'*Get* maps,' he demanded ominously, as though they could be made to materialize miraculously. No one envied the officer who had the task of explaining to General Fischer that the nearest available maps were at the divisional depot in Lille, seventy miles away, but it had to be done. A driver was roused from his bed, given a small truck and another soldier as escort, and told to drive to Lille as quickly as possible, and return with as many maps of Dieppe as he could find in the depot. The driver asked whether he should report back to divisional headquarters. No one was quite sure, for if these landings were serious, the division could by then have moved north. Finally, the driver was instructed to return to headquarters first, and if the division had gone, to overtake them on the road to Dieppe.

Meanwhile, buglers were sounding Stand-to and orderly corporals ran from room to room, hut to hut, waking up the heavier sleepers. All trucks, all armoured vehicles were to be made ready for an early departure.

At the same time, farther inland at Vernon, the SS Adolf Hitler Brigade was receiving similar orders. Sepp Dietrich's headquarters possessed large-scale maps of all surrounding areas; and his men were ready to move within minutes, all rations issued, all spare petrol cans filled, tyre pressures and engine oil levels checked. Then they stood by their vehicles, patiently awaiting further orders, as the morning sun climbed slowly and strongly up the sky.

A Bren-gun chattered, then a Sten. Murray Osten's riflemen began to fire single shots. Jack knew that they were short of ammunition, and unhooked two grenades from the belt of a dead Canadian and hung them by their handles at his own belt. They could come in useful—if only to stop himself being taken prisoner.

Lofty handed him his pack of tools and radio-testing equipment, and Jack swung it to one side to keep it out of his way. Then he picked up his rifle and raced across the road.

On the other side, he flung himself flat in the ditch. Above his head, strands of wire, a relic of peacetime days, trembled in the wind. This fence must have marked a boundary of private land, for a painted notice was nailed to a tree. Jack read it with ironic amusement: *'Chasse gardée. Entrée interdite sous peine de poursuite.'* Well, he was going to take the risk.

His blue pack had slid forward under its weight of tools, so he pushed it back again, and crawled on his belly beneath the bottom strand. A buckle on the pack caught on the wire and he struggled desperately to free himself. Sweat poured off him, for if a German spotted him, he was dead. Jack gave one huge thrust forward, the wire twanged like a gigantic violin string as the buckle ripped, and he was through.

He lay for a moment, trying to control his breathing and the racing of his heart, for he still had to crawl at least another fifty yards. As lungs and heart calmed, he began to move slowly and carefully, pulling himself forward crocodile-fashion on his elbows. The ground was rough and hard and steep. Jagged flints and the sharp sawn-off stumps of shrubs and bushes cut his hands. His Mae West felt like a strait-jacket around his chest, but it was impossible to stop and loosen the tapes beneath his blouse.

Every few yards, he lay prone, face flat against the earth to minimize himself as a target, while he regained his breath. Once he glanced behind him. Across the road, he could see half a dozen steel helmets, and as many rifle-muzzles. They all seemed to point at him unwaveringly, like a row of accusing fingers. His body-guards were keeping him in their sights, even if the enemy had not yet got him in theirs.

Jack was now only a few feet beneath the first rim of the hill. He raised his head carefully to see exactly how far he still had to go. The edge of the cliff was about 100 yards away. Beyond the grass lay the sea, still partially obscured by smoke, with crippled landing craft drifting aimlessly on every current. To his left, the road curved away. So far as he could see, the RDF station had no defences at the back. The slit trenches either faced Pourville or towards the road. Presumably the German planners who had sited the gun-posts had considered, reasonably enough, that attack would come only from either of those two directions. Jack crawled forward for another few feet and lay still. Overhead, German and British planes wheeled and dived, guns chattering. Jagged edges of shrapnel dropped all around him, thudding into the soft soil. He crawled on, all sense of time and distance forgotten; nothing mattered except that he should not be seen. Everything depended on it: success or failure, his life and death.

Then he saw the wires he had to cut; eight of them, in two sets of four, stretching from a square opening in the wall to a strong metal triatic mast. The station was built on a slope, and to carry these wires out of the compound a short mast was needed. Because of the angle of the road, one of its legs was shorter than the others. The wires led from the mast into armoured cable that went underground. Jack slid his pack round, took out his biggest set of wire-cutters and pushed a second pair into his back trouser-pocket in case he dropped the first. There would be no time to select another set. Cautiously, he undid the buckle on his pack and slipped the strap off his shoulder, still lying on the ground. Raising himself up slightly on his elbows, he examined the wall.

It was completely blind, and he could still see no machine-gun posts or even a slit trench on this side of the station. He took a deep breath, jumped to his feet and began to climb up the short leg of the mast. This was easy enough, but it would bring him into instant view of anyone patrolling the rear of the compound. He got to the top, reached out with the clippers and snipped the first wire. It dropped to the ground. Then he cut the second, the third, the fourth. As he cut them, firing broke out overhead. Bullets whined like metal mosquitoes about his ears. He did not know whether they were aimed at him, or behind him at 'A' Company, but this did not affect the situation. He could be killed quite as easily, either way, for they passed frighteningly close.

He cut the next two wires, but the last two were out of his reach, fixed to a wooden strut. He leaned over, and gripped the seventh wire. It was thin and strong, the German equivalent of British Army Don-8, and it supported his weight,

even swinging him up and down gently as it stretched. He
snipped the remaining wire and then, as the firing increased,
he cut the last wire from which he was suspended. He fell
about fifteen feet, rolled over to break his fall, and leaving
his pack, went on rolling down the hill until he reached the
road.

A stream of bullets lifted the topsoil all round him, but he
was safe. I'm fireproof, he thought, exhilarated by what he
had done. Like the colonel. Fireproof. They *can't* hit me.
And in this dangerously euphoric state, induced by a confused amalgam of heat, danger, reaction, relief, rum and
Benzedrine, Jack raced over the road and dropped down with
Osten and his men.

The WAAF sergeant who had escaped to England with her
Jewish parents from Stuttgart in 1938 sat on a canvas-backed
chair next to the RAF flight sergeant who had lost his whole
family in the first air raid on Warsaw.

They were both in a khaki-painted caravan, parked up on
the Downs near Birling Gap on the Sussex coast. In front of
them, on a wooden table that ran the whole length of the
caravan, stood two radio receivers and two gramophone
turntables, with thick wax discs. They wore earphones and
their hands constantly adjusted the controls of their sets.
The walls of the caravan were papered with maps of the
French coast; certain towns and hills had been ringed in red
or blue crayon on a cellophane cover that was fixed over the
top of these maps. The caravan had no windows; only three
circular ventilators in the roof that spun in the breeze from
the sea. A lorry with a generator for their batteries was
parked nearby, and a set of complicated receiving aerials. An
RAF orderly was brewing up tea in the shade of the lorry.

The WAAF sergeant moved a switch. The wax disc in front
of her began to turn; the arm hovered above it tremulously
for a second and then dropped. The needle began to cut a
new groove. The Polish flight sergeant noticed this and
removed his headphones.

'Something?' he asked her in German. It was the tongue that came most naturally to both of them.

The girl nodded, still busy with the controls.

'Plots,' she said briefly. 'New station's just gone on the air. Very loud and clear. They say they've had trouble with their land-lines. Damaged and temporarily out of order.'

'Where is it, exactly?'

She moved more controls, trying to fix the origin of the transmissions, now being recorded on the disc. With her other hand she scribbled some numbers on a pad and tore off the sheet of paper. The flight sergeant took it and stood in front of the wall map, checking the grid references.

'West of Dieppe,' he said. 'Must be that Freya 28. They haven't used radio-telephone for months. That should be useful. Better contact HQ immediately.'

Up on the hillside, across from the RDF station, the strong morning sun felt fearfully, sickeningly hot. The wounded lay, eyes dulled by pain, faces grey from loss of blood.

Jack said, 'I'm going back to Pourville and then inland to the crossroads at Petit-Appeville. If the tanks have landed at Dieppe, they're due to come round there. If we can persuade even one tank up here, he can blow that blast-wall to pieces and we can get inside the station.'

He had still not entirely abandoned his aim. A tank was the only way in which it could be accomplished without mortars or a naval barrage. They set off down the path. Lofty, his left sleeve cut off, so that he could bind a field-dressing around a wound in his arm; Smokey, tippling from his water-bottle, swirling the rum around his mouth like a gargle; Jim, white-faced and silent; Bud, Frenchie and Silver, watchful, missing nothing, saying nothing; and, on the perimeter, Roy Hawkins.

'I kept you in my sights the whole time, Spook,' Smokey told Jack thickly. 'And if I missed with a bullet, reckon I'd have got you with my knife.'

'Save that for Jerry,' said Jack. 'I'm going home on the boat this morning.'

179

'You'll be lucky,' said Bud. 'Look at that shambles down there on the beach.'

They had come within sight of the sea. The tide was going out fast, leaving the shallow water dotted with bodies, that turned with every eddying current. Sun glistened on wet tin hats, on the bright parts of Brens and Sten-guns abandoned on the damp shingle. The breakwaters were like huge old, green, rotting teeth, dug into the stones, and long dark patches of seaweed striped the sea, already iridescent with oil from burning landing craft. The tide was too low for any more craft to approach close to the beach, and whenever the blunt bows of enterprising LCAs would probe tentatively out of the smoke towards the shore, fountains of water would immediately gush up around them like geysers as the German artillery swung in on this new target.

To escape would mean running out through this ebbing, shallow sea for 300 yards or more before the water would be deep enough to swim, and all the time, under an increasing hail of cross-fire pouring down from the cliffs. Bud was right. Getting away wouldn't be easy. But then Bud could afford the luxury of being captured. Jack *had* to escape—or die.

—SEVEN—

Although Jack was not a soldier, he had instinctively assumed command of his group.

'Cut every wire you see,' he ordered. 'The Jerries must have observers telephoning everyone's whereabouts to their mortars and artillery.'

As he spoke, he snipped two pairs of telephone wires nailed to a tree above him. The others ripped more wires from posts, then ran down the narrow path and over the bridge, so accustomed by now to death that they barely gave a thought to running over the backs of corpses who only minutes before had been their friends.

Colonel Merritt, crossing the bridge seconds later, was surprised to see a pair of unusually light brown boots sticking out from among the fallen soldiers. Only one person in the regiment had worn boots that colour on the raid: Les England, commanding Special Force. Was he also among the dead? Merritt crossed over and pulled away some other bodies. England was not dead, but he was badly wounded. Some stretcher-bearers came hurrying past, and the colonel ordered them to carry the lieutenant down to the beach. Fortunately, they reached it as a landing craft managed to come in close under the smoke screen, and England was taken off almost at once. But his ordeal was not yet over. A torpedo hit the ship to which he was transferred, and the vessel quickly sank. Below decks, apparently trapped, and having seemingly escaped death by bullet only to meet it by drowning, Les England saw the gaping hole blown in the sinking hull by the torpedo, and the sea a lighter green on the other side.

Desperately, despite his agonizing injuries, he swam towards this hole and out through it as the hull sank beneath him. He held his breath and floated to the surface. Within a short time, another ship picked him up, and he reached England and hospital that evening—owing his life to the distinctive colour of his boots.

Jack's party reached the main street safely. The pavement was littered now with tiles shaken off roofs by blast or shells. They paused by the little church built of huge stones, no doubt gathered up from the beach and set in alternate rows, three or four deep. The brown paint on the wooden porch had faded and blistered. Jack read the date on a plate set in the wall: 1648. The sun shone bright blue and red and orange through stained-glass windows; inside, a candle burned on the homely wooden altar. They flattened themselves along the church wall, and waited, feeling the stone warm beneath their hands, and thankful that the building shielded them from firing farther up the hill. A notice about Mass, written in French and German, was pinned on the oak door.

Roy Hawkins removed his steel helmet and wiped sweat from his forehead. It seemed incredible to be sheltering in a church doorway from men of his own age whom he could not even see, and would probably never see, let alone meet, but who nonetheless would kill him if they possibly could; always provided that he did not kill them first.

None of them, on either side, knew whether their lives could be counted in minutes or in years, yet they accepted this unquestioningly. And all around them, other people's homes, containing perhaps all the possessions they had collected in a lifetime of frugality, had been damaged and destroyed—for what? To keep a stretch of beach or to take it? Hawkins thought wearily: This is senseless. And he wondered whether anyone else thought the same, not only on his side, but among the Germans? Jack's quiet English voice brought him back to reality.

'Just beyond this church, up on the left, you'll see where the road divides. Left-hand fork goes down to St Aubin and

Petit-Appeville, which is only a village astride the main Dieppe to Le Havre road. The tanks must come to Pourville along that road from Dieppe, because they'll never risk the road up by the RDF station. So we'll head out and meet them at that crossroads. Okay?'

'We'll never make it there,' said Lofty. His wound had grown painful, and he had lost more blood than he realized. His face was pale, eyes sunk into their sockets and red as live coals.

'We've not much option,' retorted Jack.

'We're with you, Spook,' said Smokey. His voice sounded slurred, thick and soft as syrup.

'Good. But lay off that rum, or you won't stay with me.'

'I'll stay.'

Smokey's face damp with sweat, dark as old brandy, was thrust up close to his own, eyes narrowed against the bright sun. Heat and alcohol had fuddled Smokey's mind; only his great physical endurance and his fitness kept him on his feet. Jack regarded him with a mixture of distaste and admiration.

'We'll wait until they stop to reload, then we'll go. Right?'

The others nodded. Only Smokey paid no attention; he was shaking his water-bottle to discover how much rum remained. For a moment, the firing ceased, and they all sprinted across the road, and were several yards up the hill before it restarted.

The gradient was far steeper than it had appeared from the safety of the church porch, and the metal studs in the soles of their boots slipped on the smooth hot tarmac. Houses lined both sides of the road; those on the right were built into the hill, with white-painted balustrades to their verandahs and shutters closed across upstairs windows. In peacetime, families would fill these houses every August and the empty verandahs would be littered with towels and swimming costumes hung out to dry, and buckets and spades. Now, they seemed deserted; the gardens looked overgrown and untended.

Neither Jack nor anyone with him was aware of a pair of friendly eyes watching their progress with concern. Valère Muyssen, from his trench outside his house, could see right across the water meadows and for half a mile along the road. By turning his head he could also see the Germans firing at them. This was a unique view of human hunters and humans hunted. It brought back even more strongly the sounds and smells and fears he had known in the First War. The fresh earthy odour of the trench became the stench of rotting earth in Flanders; and the young men he heard shouting in English were men he had known and served with when he was young. Muyssen had received a serious head wound in that war, and was nursed in a British field hospital. As he watched these figures in British khaki uniforms running like toy soldiers along the road beyond the fields, this wound began to beat like a sullen drum. His lips moved in silent prayer: 'Look down in mercy on them, Oh Lord. Be unto them a shield and a buckler . . .'

Some Camerons attached themselves to Jack's group and they all marched in single file on the far side of the road, up against a wall which would give them cover from snipers from across the valley. In the narrow triangle of land between the two roads stood an hotel, with faded white paint and a red pagoda-style arch over the entrance. A hanging sign advertised '*Son Bar Américain*'; plants flowered brightly in stone pots. They leaned briefly against the wall, watching this building in case it contained any Germans, feeling the wall warm against their backs like oven bricks. Then they went on. Bees hovered drowsily over thick red and yellow flowers on the bank.

Jack found it almost impossible to believe that he really was in an occupied country, in danger of death, marching along an unknown road in the desperate hope he would meet a tank whose driver was not even expecting them. Surely a whistle would blow somewhere and then everyone would fall out for tea and corned beef, and march back singing to barracks? Could this really be war and not just another make-believe manoeuvre? He pulled his thoughts together.

'Come on,' he said. 'Over the road—*now!*'

They raced to the shelter of the hotel wall on the Petit-Appeville road. To their left, meadows stretched lush and green and damp, watered by the Scie. They marched on doggedly. It was very hot. Sweat soaked their shirts, dripping down their foreheads, stinging their eyes. They reached an orchard on the left of the road, where apple trees leaned over a wire fence. Jagged pieces of falling shrapnel had split the apples; the air was sharp with ripe fruit.

Suddenly, Jack wondered what would happen if they reached the crossroads and no tanks arrived? He asked Roy Hawkins what he intended doing in these circumstances.

'I'm not going to be captured,' Hawkins replied immediately. 'If necessary, I suggest we go down through France to the Pyrenees, and then get back to England through Spain.'

'We wouldn't have much chance in these uniforms, and not speaking French.'

'At least it would be *a* chance,' replied Hawkins shortly. They walked on in silence to the crossroads. To the left was an open space with goalposts where the village boys could play football, and a *pâtisserie*; to the right, a petrol station with two pumps, but no petrol. Above them, the sky was deep blue, and the guns sounded far away, their firing only a distant warning, like summer thunder. Jack could smell tar melting on the road; the crossing shimmered in a haze of heat.

They heard voices from a house on their right, and looked at each other in concern. Jack noticed a gleam of sunshine on the black paint of a car. A Citroën saloon was parked near the side of the building. This was the first civilian car they had seen, and they all had the same idea at the same time; seize it, drive to Dieppe and meet the tanks halfway.

Frenchie, Jim and Roy Hawkins ran with Jack to the car. The driver's door was unlocked, but the ignition key was missing. They would ask at the house for it. They walked up to the front door cautiously, carrying their rifles across their bodies, ready to swing them up to a firing position if need be. Jack banged on the door with his fist—there was no knocker —and then they stood looking at each other, half expectantly, half uneasily. Odd how the upbringing of a lifetime asserted itself, he thought. Even under the stress of war, you did not kick down a stranger's front door; you knocked politely and then waited for someone to open it. He felt like a travelling salesman with nothing to sell.

The door opened. A Frenchman with a small dark moustache wearing a blue shirt and baggy trousers stood in the hall. His face was very pale.

'Speak to him,' Jack told Frenchie.

'We need to go to Dieppe in a hurry,' explained Frenchie in French. 'We want to use your car.'

'Who are you?'

'Canadians.'

'How do you mean, Canadians? I do not understand.' The man looked from one to the other quickly, eyes sharp as lizards' tongues.

'Give us the keys to the car,' said Frenchie firmly. 'We have just landed at Pourville.'

'Don't frig about,' said Jim suddenly in English, and dug the muzzle of his tommy-gun into the Frenchman's stomach, who began to speak very quickly and loudly, holding up both hands, as though he was already a prisoner.

'Round the back—quick!' shouted Jim. He guessed that the man was trying to warn someone else. Hawkins and Frenchie ran round the side of the house; an unarmed German soldier was coming quietly out of the back door. They seized him and led him round to the front. The Frenchman now began to speak very rapidly indeed, shrugging his shoulders, holding his hands up to heaven.

'What does he say?' asked Jack.

'He's bewildered,' said Frenchie.

'Better than being buggered. Give us the keys.'

'He hasn't got them. Says it's not even his car.'

They were arguing senselessly, as people talk in dreams. Over the hill, guns boomed faintly and machine-guns chattered like insane metal parakeets. And all the while, vital minutes were slipping away.

'If we can't have the keys, then you won't have the car,' said Frenchie bluntly. He lifted the bonnet, seized the plug leads in his fist and tore them away. Then he smashed the distributor with the butt of his rifle.

The Frenchman began to shout, sweat glistening on his face like varnish. He was terrified.

'We'll take this bloke,' said Jack, for they could not risk leaving the young German. He was barely out of his teens, and he held up his hands obediently in surrender. Someone found a piece of string in their pocket and tied his wrists.

The sun felt hotter now, and both roads were empty. The locals were either staying inside their houses with doors locked and shutters closed, or they had all prudently fled at the first sound of guns. The Canadians lay down in a circle on the ground near the *pâtisserie*, where they could cover all four roads. They waited, rifles and Stens pointed outwards, fingers alongside trigger-guards. Telephone-wires hummed high above their heads. Jack climbed up the nearest pole and cut them.

Surely the tanks must be here soon? They began to look at each other uneasily, wondering what could have gone wrong, each man fighting his own rising tide of alarm. The strain and tension of waiting at a crossroads in occupied France, with hundreds, possibly even thousands of German soldiers presumably all round them and no doubt closing in, grew almost too much to bear.

At that moment, several German naval officers were emerging cautiously from air-raid shelters in Dieppe, near the harbour, and keeping close to the walls, they ran through the streets to the main promenade, the Boulevard Maréchal Foch, which lies parallel with the sea.

So many telephone lines had been cut or damaged, whether by shelling, falling buildings or sabotage no one yet knew, that accurate news was impossible to discover; they felt it essential to see for themselves what was happening. The beach before them was littered with tanks, equipment, bodies. Some of the tanks had stuck halfway up the steep shingle, their guns still firing, turrets turning slowly like the deadly heads of mythical metal sea-monsters, seeking new targets. Others were stationary, drowned in feet of water, guns out of action. One tank had jammed on the open ramp of the huge landing craft that had carried it across the Channel, and it stood at an angle of forty-five degrees, its front submerged under water. Another had managed to crawl up the shifting shingle to reach the promenade but there it had also stopped. Buildings along the sea front were ablaze, as were some landing craft that drifted uselessly near the breaking waves, crewed by the dead. The tanks poured out flames and shells from their guns, but to the watching naval officers, this resembled last fevered death throes. When their ammunition was exhausted, they were harmless, eunuchs of war. The steep incline from the sea had shown up a weak part of the Churchill tank design: the tracks. Their labouring engines, racing through huge clutches to force giant sprocket wheels to revolve and drag thirty tons of reluctant metal up the beach, had snapped a link somewhere on these tracks. So the tanks had stuck, with yards of useless track lying on the beach beside them, like a shining metal necklace. The Germans had not beaten them; the angle of the shingle beach could claim the victory. Of no use now were their long twin exhaust pipes like chimneys designed to allow tanks to operate in six feet of water. With every second their killing power diminished, and soon the crews of the Calgary Tank Regiment, sweating behind heavy steel armour that bore such brave names as Cougar, Cheetah and Cat, could be captured at leisure.

The German naval officers understandably found this a cheering prospect, but they were more interested in the predicament of the tanks for a more parochial reason—interservice rivalry. The German Army had recently organized several landing exercises in collaboration with naval units, which involved defence against tanks. The port commandant in Dieppe had demanded that these tanks should attempt to cross an elevation of beach gravel, and all had stuck so firmly that they could not move.

The port commandant had pronounced himself satisfied with this practical demonstration.

'Now we *know* the British cannot land here with tanks,' he said with conviction. The German Army had some reservations about this; maybe with modifications tanks could cross the shingle and come ashore? Now, not for the first time, the Navy felt that they had been proved right and the Army wrong, and the officers retired smugly to their underground fastnesses to congratulate themselves on this agreeable state of affairs.

Three miles south-west, knowing nothing of all this, Jack and his bodyguard waited impatiently at the crossroads for tanks that had never left the beach. The German prisoner stood disconsolately, his head down, wrists bound with string. He was not alone in his depression; his captors also felt a growing sense of anti-climax.

'What's the time?' asked Jack, to break this deepening spell of gloom.

'Twenty to ten,' replied Hawkins, consulting his Army watch. They had been far longer ashore than they had realized; hours had passed like minutes. Silver, Smokey and Jim sat down, backs against the rough, concrete wall of the *pâtisserie*, removed steel helmets and wiped sweating foreheads. Silver swigged some water from his bottle.

'It's hotter than the hubs of hell,' he grumbled. Maybe the locals agreed; there was still no sign or sound of life. Petit-Appeville was a painted village without movement, a crossroads without traffic. This feeling of make-believe worried them all, as they waited in the baking August heat. Each wanted to read the next man's thoughts from his eyes, but deliberately avoided his gaze in case he could read theirs. For what message of hope could they possibly find?

At 0947 hours, the telephone rang in the headquarters of the 15th Army at Tourcoing.

'Hold the line for the Commander-in-Chief,' came the brief imperious order. General von Rundstedt in his headquarters, surrounded by wall maps marked with coloured-headed pins and little flags showing the position of the German defenders and the Allied invaders, picked up the telephone on his desk as its buzzer sounded.

'Fifteenth Army on the line, sir,' his adjutant informed him.

'Very good.'

Von Rundstedt was by no means clear about the situation around Dieppe. The first report to come in from 15th Army Headquarters had reached him at 0630 hours—'According to a message from HQ 81st Corps of 0605 hours, bombs dropping on Dieppe, and enemy landing attempts at Berneval, Dieppe, Pourville and Quiberville.'

This was the first time during the whole war that there had been simultaneous daylight landing attempts along a front of about twenty-five kilometres on the French coast. It was thus just possible that these landings could be the preliminary to a major invasion. Von Rundstedt had waited, hoping that further more detailed reports would arrive to paint a clearer picture of events, from which Allied intentions might be deduced. When they did not, he had ordered 15th Army to put the 10th Panzer Division and the SS Adolf Hitler Division on an advanced state of readiness, Alarm Scale 2. He also informed the 7th Air Force Division of enemy landing attempts so that they could make the necessary dispositions to intercept any bombers that might be on the way.

Then scattered reports, some contradictory and confusing, began to come in. The chief of staff, HQ 81st Corps, announced at 0732 that the landing attempt at Pourville had been repelled, but bombing continued on Dieppe. The situation at Quiberville was 'still unclear'. Eight minutes later, at 0740, the Commanding Admiral, France, reported that telephone lines to the port commandant at Dieppe were broken. The Naval Signal Station at Dieppe sent a message by radio: 'English continue to land at Dieppe. Destroyers laying smoke on coast. Up to now twelve tanks have landed. One is on fire.' Von Rundstedt spoke to General Kuntzen of 81st Corps at his headquarters in Canteleu. What was his opinion of the enemy's intentions? Kuntzen considered the attack to be purely a local operation. It did not seem to carry enough weight to be the spearhead of total invasion. There had been no preliminary aerial bombardment, and only light naval ships appeared to be supporting the landings. Von Rundstedt wanted to be convinced, but to be wrong could be fatal. He possessed the most meagre details on which to base any firm conclusion, but if he made the wrong decision, he would take the blame. Accordingly, he passed on the items of information he had received to the German commanders in the Netherlands, Belgium and Northern France, and all forces were put on an immediate state of Highest Alertness as more contradictory messages about British fighters, destroyers, landing craft and general Allied intentions poured in.

Because the troops wore British-Army type battledress, the Germans still assumed that they must all be British. At 0940 hours, news arrived that 302nd Infantry Division had started to counter-attack. 'Little can as yet be said about the situation in Dieppe proper,' the message admitted cautiously. 'Further to the west, near Pourville, landings still seem to continue. Situation at Quiberville unclear . . . Enemy landing attempts at St Aubin still possible.'

This was more serious than von Rundstedt had expected. The farther inland the invaders reached, and the more speedily, the more difficult it would be to contain them. And in addition to the damage they might do to all kinds of targets, they might also leave agents who had come with them for this purpose, or arms for Resistance groups which were already flexing their muscles against the occupying power. Von Rundstedt decided to issue further orders immediately to 15th Army. General Curt Haase, its commander, listened in silence at the end of the line.

'Tenth Panzer Division will be placed under the command of General Kuntzen, headquarters 81st Corps, to clear up the situation immediately. Tenth Panzer Division can move vanguard at 1000 hours and main force at 1100 hours.'

The orderly officer, 10th Panzer Division, received these orders at 0951 hours; immediately, General Fischer ordered the advance guard of his division to move north to Dieppe. There was an awkward moment when the column commander asked for map references. Dieppe was a large port. Was he to proceed to the centre or to the outskirts? The driver had not yet returned from Lille with the necessary maps, but the commander was assured that as soon as the maps reached Amiens, they would be sent by motor-cycle despatch rider.

Now von Rundstedt sat in his splendid office, considering the situation; not only the military situation, but his own. He knew that the mechanical condition of the Panzer division's vehicles was dubious. They had motored for months on the Russian front; many needed overhaul and others should be replaced. Also, the general shortage of petrol had meant that new drivers lacked practice. If they were delayed by mechanical breakdown, the Panzers could be reduced to infantrymen packed into broken-down trucks, so they needed all the support he could provide. Accordingly, he made two further telephone calls. One was to General of Artillery Jodl, the Chief of Armed Forces Operations Staff, to inform him of his actions, in case he had any additional comments or suggestions to make. He had none.

The second call was to request air cover for the vanguard and command group of 10th Panzer Division, over the areas of Torcy-le-Grand and Torcy-le-Petit, at 1200 hours, and for the main force over Neufchâtel two and a half hours later. This should at least ensure that the skies above the vehicles were kept clear. Von Rundstedt felt that he had allowed for all eventualities and therefore if the tide of battle turned against his troops, he could confidently defend his decisions.

So the long column of trucks and tracked vehicles set out from Amiens, rumbling north. They had barely reached the outskirts of the city when their first mechanical casualties occurred. Half-tracks and lorries pulled out of the convoy to the right of the road and stopped. Drivers reported that engines were overheating, worn tyres were bursting in the heat. In some cases, minor maladjustments such as dirty plugs or pitted ignition points had caused breakdowns. Troops jumped down thankfully to stretch their legs. When the column commanders ordered the drivers to clean the plugs or points, or change the punctured tyres, and so get their vehicles moving again, they replied that some had no tool kits, and others who carried tool kits lacked the knowledge to use them. Worse, tracked vehicles that did manage to keep going were soon ordered to slow down, for the rubber-tyred bogey wheels over which the tracks ran were so worn that they slipped badly, and grew so hot that the rubber began to smoke. Unless the whole column kept down to a slow and steady pace they would never reach Dieppe, let alone be able to return to Amiens.

Unknown to the Germans—and to many Canadians without radio sets in working order—the code word to retire and the hour at which to begin, 'Vanquish at 1030', had been transmitted just after 0900 by the few remaining signallers, and then was passed verbally from one section to another. Gradually, the SSRs and the Camerons began to fall back towards Pourville beach to await the landing craft that should arrive to take them off. But such was the severity of the German barrage that none of the remaining landing craft could now approach the shore in safety. Black smoke rolled like a thunder cloud over the August sea. Orange flashes lit it up from behind as one Navy craft after another fired a salvo against the German guns up in the cliffs. The beach was littered with bodies; with sodden packs and pouches; with rifles, Stens, and burning landing craft, ramps down, stuck fast on the shingle, left behind by the retreating tide. No one in Pourville knew that the RAF could not be overhead by 1030, and that 1100 was the earliest they could provide cover, because of the time necessary to fly from airfields in England, and that the evacuation time was therefore postponed for a further thirty minutes.

This meant that some men from the prairies arrived on Green Beach half an hour too soon, and then had to wait, either crammed into the casino, or in the shelter of houses, or under the sea-wall with rows of wounded already lying there on stretchers.

Roger Strumm, the SSR Regimental Sergeant Major, had been severely wounded in one leg. Three men carried him away from the line of fire and laid him down under a tree. He bore his pain stoically, furious that he was no longer able to be up with the fighting, where he felt he was needed. The tree's overhanging branches, and long grass, concealed the

RSM from the sight of Germans and his own soldiers alike. Some young SSRs, turning away from the fearful carnage ahead, were thus astounded to hear the RSM's famous voice bellow at them, like a disembodied foghorn.

'I may be wounded, but I am still RSM of this goddam battalion!' he shouted. '*You turn about and get up front!*'

The men turned about immediately. Later, others carried Strumm down to the beach, and there Colonel Merritt saw him lying with rows of wounded. The colonel bent down to say he was sorry to see Strumm in such pain. Strumm shrugged; this was a hazard of war; no soldier should complain. The wound did not appear to bother him; what really mattered, what was important, was that he had served with his regiment in action.

'They said I was too old,' he replied simply and proudly. 'But—I fooled 'em!'

Jack was the first to hear the distant metallic rumble, like a grinding of raw steel on the asphalt road. Then the others heard it, too, as it grew louder and nearer, and they all stood up, faces brightening.

'The tanks! They're here!'

They ran excitedly up the slope to the crossroads, expecting to see the blunt welcome noses of the Churchill tanks coming towards them; but the main Paris to Le Havre road was empty for as far as they could see in each direction. The noise was not coming from that road at all, but from straight ahead.

'Maybe they've cut across country?' someone suggested.

'Maybe they haven't,' said Silver hoarsely. 'Look—*they're Jerries!*'

'My God!'

They stood, staring in horror as round the nearest bend in the road ahead two lines of soldiers appeared in field-grey uniforms. They carried unfamiliar rifles slung across their backs, and were festooned with mortar bombs and pouches of spare ammunition. And they were riding bicycles.

Now Jack realized the reason for the noise: flints and sharp stones had ripped their rubber tyres to pieces and they were riding furiously on bare metal rims. The riders were part of the mobile column of the 571st Infantry Regiment from Ouville. The men whose cycles had collapsed under them were still double-marching along the road some way behind.

Jack's party stood horrorstruck. The Germans viewed them with equal surprise, but acted more quickly. They leapt off their machines, flung them away and dropped to the ground on both sides of the road, to take aim. One man fired a single round at Jack's group. The bullet went wide, but it broke the spell.

'Back to the beach!' Jack shouted hoarsely, and they started to run along the road. It was difficult for the prisoner to keep up with them since his hands were tied in front of him, but he managed.

'Say,' asked Smokey rhetorically, as they jog-trotted along, 'why am I carrying this goddam anti-tank rifle while this bastard is carrying nothing?'

He reached out and pulled the German's sleeve. They all stopped running for a moment. The German soldier looked at Smokey in a puzzled way, not understanding what was going to happen.

'Cut his hands,' said Bud.

Smokey slid his right hand round to his knife. The blade was very long and sharp, and the young German looked at it in horror. Were they going to kill him? He began to shout, waving his bound wrists in a desperate attempt to communicate.

'Nein! Kamerad!'

'He thinks you're going to kill him,' said Bud.

'Not yet, we won't,' said Smokey. 'But stop him hollering.'

Bud held a huge hand over the young man's mouth. His teeth champed against it furiously as he struggled. Then Smokey's knife flickered like a sunbeam. The string fell to the ground, Bud removed his hand, and the soldier stood there, massaging his wrists sheepishly.

'Now take this and shut up,' Smokey told him as though he understood, and thrust the anti-tank rifle at him. The German shouldered it, relieved at still being alive. As they set off again, a machine-gun from behind them raked the road, snapping branches inches above their heads.

'Off the road!' Jack shouted, and they plunged away into the orchard on their right. Long grass reached to their knees, and rows of trees hung heavy with red apples. A mortar began to cough from the crossroads behind them and branches broke, showering them with fruit. Frenchie stretched out one hand to pick a ripe apple from a high branch above his head —somehow it seemed more appetizing than the apples at their feet—and then he screamed. Where his hand had been was a mass of pink splintered bone and raw flesh; blood was pumping down his battledress sleeve. He sank on his knees and fainted. Bud ripped his field-dressing from his pocket and bound the white gauze bandage around Frenchie's arm as a tourniquet.

'We'll have to carry him,' he said.

'You'll be all right, Frenchie,' Jack told him with an assurance he did not feel. 'It's nothing serious.'

'Yes,' whispered Frenchie, regaining consciousness briefly. 'I'll be all right.'

His face was the colour of a tallow candle, shining with sweat. Already, his cheeks looked hollow. Bullets began to clip the leaves above their heads, and a mortar shell landed about thirty yards away as they stumbled with him deeper into the orchard. Shrapnel dropped like jagged rain. Then a spent bullet grazed Frenchie in the temple, hardly leaving a scar. Jack opened his blouse. He could not feel a heart beat, but could not believe he was dead. Perhaps he was only in a state of deep shock?

'You after his dog tags?' asked Smokey gruffly.

'No, his rosary.' Jack held the little cross for a moment, feeling its tiny indentations damp with Frenchie's sweat, and then he let it fall on its string outside his blouse. He remembered that brief talk aboard the *Princess Beatrix* only hours before. 'It is vain to quarrel with destiny . . .' Was this Frenchie's destiny to die in an unknown apple orchard? Was it the destiny of them all to die here near Dieppe? He fought down a rising panic that threatened to choke him. He did not know a Catholic prayer, so in case Frenchie were dead, he repeated what words he could remember of the Jewish service that had been said over his father two years earlier.

'Yisgudul Yisgardush. If a man lives a year or a thousand years, what profiteth him? He shall be as though he had not been. Blessed be the true Judge, who killeth and maketh alive . . .'

Then, in the Jewish custom, Jack pulled a handful of grass and said: 'And they of the city shall flourish like the grass of the earth.'

He stood up. They would have to leave him and hope the Germans would be able to treat him. The optimism and euphoria they had all felt at the crossroads was now fast ebbing away. They were tired and dazed by the constant cacophony of artillery shells and bombs, the rattle of unseen machine-guns, the increasing nearness of death.

Inertia thickened and slowed all impetus. Their legs felt strangely heavy and their muscles were like rubber, for while the urgent message to escape beat in their brains, how could they possibly get away?

Jack opened his field-dressing pocket, took out his escape pack and handed round the Horlicks tablets. They chewed them gratefully. Then the sugar moved in their blood, and they felt more cheerful and stood up and ran on almost mechanically, parallel to the road and still in the orchard, half doubled up, as men run under fire, and barely 200 yards ahead of the pursuing Germans. They found a gate and went through it back on to the road. From one of the houses on their left, a machine-gun began to fire. To escape it, Roy Hawkins leapt the hedge at the roadside. This had concealed a ravine about twenty feet deep, and as he fell down head-over-heels, his braces snapped. Hawkins held the grenades against his belt in case they should roll away and explode, and lay dazed for a moment. Then he picked himself up and started to run to catch up with the others, holding his steel helmet on with one hand and his trousers up with the other.

They were close to the steep bank now, while the fields stretched like a patchwork quilt of different greens towards the river on their right. Mortar bombs were landing on the road ahead of them, and they sought shelter behind a small farmhouse. A flock of geese ran out of a shed, hissing angrily, heads stretched forward level with the ground, wings spread out behind.

'Even the bloody birds are on Jerry's side!' said Bud bitterly as the geese attacked them, pecking at their trousers and their knees, jumping off the ground in a furious flurry of white wings. Jack and the others kicked them off or aimed blows at them with rifle butts, but the necks of the geese bent like rubber pipes. They thronged around the men, oblivious alike to their blows and their curses. So they ran on again, level now with the road, geese hissing in fury at their heels, then crossed a fence, and left the geese screeching and running alongside them on the other side. Above their heads, more and more Spitfires were coming in, shooting up targets, turning and wheeling in the summer sky.

'Couldn't you signal to them with a mirror that we're here?' asked Bud hopefully.

'Impossible,' said Jack. 'By the time the pilot's seen the flash of a mirror, he's gone two miles.'

'Couldn't you radio them—ask them to shoot up those Jerries behind us?'

'We haven't a set.'

'There's one lying in the road.'

He pointed to a No. 18 set still strapped by its webbing harness to the back of a dead signaller.

'Keep me covered and I'll get it,' said Jack promptly. The others lay down, only their heads above the rim of the road, rifles and Stens ready, watching for the first German to come over the hill behind them. Jack ran out into the road and kneeled down beside the dead Canadian signaller. The metal buckles of the set's harness were hot to his touch. He unhooked it from the dead man's shoulders and carried it back to the side of the road. The aerial was still intact, and he pressed the switches, turned the dials, and listened to the headphones, but the set was as dead as its operator. He removed the back. A bullet had gone right through the battery and torn away the main leads.

'It's kaput,' he reported, but he slung it over his shoulder; he might find a battery from another set.

'Could you make it work?' Lofty asked him.

'Maybe. If I can find a new battery,' said Jack. 'But I don't know the wavelength of the planes or the *Calpe*. I can't work miracles.'

'We'll damn well have to, Spook, if we're to get out of this lot. Look behind you, buster.'

Across the fields, and down both sides of the road, German soldiers were now closing in behind them, taking advantage of all the cover they could find. Roy Hawkins had seized Frenchie's rifle, and he and Silver and Lofty fired at them. The leading Germans immediately flung themselves down into the long grass and fired back; the rest kept on running. Jack watched them, almost mesmerized. They had a compelling air of invincibility.

'It's running-shoes on again,' he said resignedly.

Slightly behind him, Silver gave a choking gasp, as though his breath had been strangled in his throat. He fell forward heavily, the brass buckles from his pouches scraping the asphalt. Then he slowly rolled over into the ditch.

Jack dropped down with him.

'What's happened?' he asked.

Silver could not speak. His lips tried to form words, and then his face turned pale beneath his steel helmet. He coughed, and thick blood ran down his chin, ropy with saliva. He had been hit in the stomach. He was dying. There was nothing anyone could do for him.

'Where's he got it?' asked Lofty, kneeling down beside them.

'In the guts.'

'He's out now,' said Smokey.

'Poor devil,' said Jack. He stood up; they could do nothing for him, and yet he was reluctant to abandon him. Mavor, Thrussell, Red, Charlie, Frenchie, and now Silver; six of his group who had travelled thousands of miles from their homeland, to die in ditches and fields and at the roadside near an unfashionable seaside town midway between London and Paris.

He had had little opportunity to discover much about any of them; indeed, he only knew a few by their real names. Now he would never learn much more. He wondered about their families, whether their relations in Canada would ever know how their fathers or brothers or husbands had died. But how could they? He did not even know whether they had any relations. How ironic that so many men who knew just as little about him as he knew about them should be bound to him by orders to keep him alive—unless they had to kill him!

'Come on,' he said, dismissing these thoughts. They started to run again, and kept on running until they were briefly out of sight and range of their pursuers, and then they slowed thankfully to a walk. They had nearly reached the wall of the hotel, at the junction of the roads. Beyond it, on the other side of the second road leading to Varengeville, they had a fine view of the big houses. Wrought iron gates and wide balustrades and shaded verandahs seemed a ludicrously incongruous background to being chased down the hill. How many families in peacetime August would have enjoyed the morning sun on these verandahs, sitting in deckchairs with iced drinks at their elbows?

Jim shouted hoarsely behind them: 'There's another radio set!'

'Where?'

'On the back of that poor bastard!'

He pointed back towards a dead signaller lying in the ditch on the right. Jack had missed seeing the man or the set, because his thoughts had been far away; the pep pill was still pouring adrenalin through his body, although at a slightly slower rate, and he felt light-headed. Perhaps this set might work? It was worth a try: anything was worth trying in their position, for if he could contact the *Calpe* and bring down some fire power or some air support, the pursuers might become the pursued. It was all a very faint hope, of course, but it was still a hope, and there was nothing else.

'Come with me. I'll try and get it.'

The firing had ceased temporarily until the Germans came round the turn in the road behind them. The only sound, apart from the constant grumble of distant guns, was the squeal of their own boot studs on the hard, hot road. They crouched in the ditch while Lofty crawled across the hump of the road to the dead signaller. Jack watched a ladybird crawling slowly up a blade of grass inches from his face. Then he heard a crack behind him like a dry stick breaking, and Jim gave a gasp of pain and surprise.

'You hit?' Jack asked him.

'Only a nick in the shoulder. Nothing serious.'

In that same second, Jack felt a stunning blow on the back of his own steel helmet, as though it had been hit by a sledge-hammer. A brilliant flash of light momentarily blinded him. He fell forwards, and the radio set jumped on his back as though it had been kicked. Its metal case had saved him from another bullet, but this might not save him from the next. He rolled over on his side in a reflex action, lifted his rifle and fired blindly in the direction of the shots. Then Lofty dragged the other set across the road and they slithered and ran, now in the ditch, now on the road.

A couple of hundred yards more and they would be past the crossroads and the church and into battalion headquarters. The beach was probably less than a minute away. Sounds like a landlady's advertisement for Whitstable or Southend, Jack thought. One minute sea, h & c all rooms, cruet, separate tables. A machine-gun chattered into his thoughts. A second patrol of Germans appeared round the corner from the direction of the church, and they began to move steadily up the hill towards them. They were caught between enemies behind and enemies in front.

'How many rounds have we?' Jack asked the others as they all sank instinctively to the ground. His head was beating like a giant pulse. He felt dizzy, almost disembodied, as though all this was happening to someone else entirely.

'Thirty,' said Hawkins, breaking his revolver and reloading.

'Couple of mags,' said Jim.

'Nine, and one up the spout,' Smokey replied.

'Same here,' said Lofty.

'Wait until they get nearer and we can take the lot.'

'Not too much goddam nearer,' said Lofty grimly, and squeezed his trigger. One German ahead of the rest threw up both arms and tossed his rifle away in a muscular paroxysm as he fell sideways across the road. The others dropped down behind trees, and opened fire with their machine-guns. Chips of brick and concrete showered down on Jack and his group.

If we can't get out of here, we've had it, Jack thought bitterly. What a bloody awful way to go. He could no longer see clearly out of his left eye, but with his right he suddenly spied three French civilians standing a little way down the hill. They were all men in their sixties, red-faced, stockily built, almost like an English cartoonist's idea of Frenchmen. Two wore berets, and the third, a black flat cloth cap. Something glittered in this man's left lapel. Jack blinked at it, trying to focus his one good eye. Then he realized: the old man was wearing his first War medals. They shone silver and gold under their brightly coloured ribbons. What the hell was going on? Who were these fellows? They stood in a group, looking towards the Germans coming from Petit-Appeville, just out of their line of fire.

Lofty and Jim raised their rifles and each fired a couple of shots, hoping to make the Germans keep their distance. The Frenchmen looked across at Jack and his companions as though only just realizing they were there. Then they turned slowly and again looked at the advancing Germans coming stealthily up the hill. As one group or the other fired, the old men turned their heads to the left, then right, left and right, like spectators at a tennis tournament. And all the time their faces remained grave and completely impassive.

Jack guessed that as old soldiers they must have understood that the Germans would soon overwhelm the handful of men in the ditch. It was simply a matter of time, probably only minutes at most—unless they were given a chance to run. Jack's whole body was now one huge booming throbbing pain. It was agony to move, however slowly, but somehow he must move or die where he lay. Then the firing stopped as quickly and unexpectedly as it had begun. He lifted his aching head carefully, muscles tensed warily for any new danger.

The Frenchman wearing the medals was walking up the hill towards them on his own. He walked in an unhurried way, puffing at a cigarette, apparently unconcerned at all the shooting; he might be taking a Sunday morning stroll. Near the brow of the hill behind Jack's group, a German under-officer was shouting orders to his men, who had already stopped firing in case they hit this civilian. They could deal with the invaders at any time, for they could not possibly escape, but to shoot a French civilian would inevitably mean an enquiry and awkward questions and possibly disciplinary action.

That old boy must be as deaf as a post, or blind or drunk, or maybe all three, thought Jack inconsequentially. Both groups of Germans lowered their guns slightly as he came within range. He kept on walking, looking neither to the right nor to the left, until he was across the road from the Canadians. Then he glanced at Jack, and in that instant Jack realized the extent of his courage. Their eyes met. The old man's message was clear: *I am holding their fire; get out while you can.*

He did not pause or falter, but kept on walking steadily, puffing blue smoke from his Gauloise. He stared firmly ahead again—and so he did not see Jack and the others leap from the wall and rush madly along the road, past the hotel, the church, down along the Rue de la Mer towards the sea.

'Round the back!' gasped Jack. 'Into the yard!'

They raced in single file along the alleyway. Some of the French girls were still there, bandaging the wounded, but now their jugs and plates were empty, and the yard was much more crowded than it had been on Jack's last visit; there was barely room for them to stand, so he leaned wearily against the back wall. He still could not see properly out of his left eye, and the pain was slowly spreading across to his right eye, clouding his vision. Shapes of people moved like dim images. Was he going blind? Had he been hit in the head? Vaguely, he saw a pail half full of water on the ground, and he pulled off his helmet, scooped up a handful of the water and dashed it in his face.

Immediately, the pain began to melt away; complete vision returned almost at once to both eyes. He turned the helmet slowly over in his hands. At the back was a deep dent where a bullet fired down at him from the bank had bounced off at an angle. This bullet had punched the metal against his skull and rammed the whole helmet down on his head, restricting the flow of blood and somehow depressing a nerve to the left eye.

'I'm all right,' he said slowly and thankfully. 'I'm damn well all right.'

'Course you are, Spook,' agreed Bud. 'Never had doubts myself. But what the hell's going to happen now?'

'Let's get out of this yard and have a look at that set,' replied Jack. 'There's no room to breathe here.'

They walked back along the alley and crouched down against a wall. Jack unhooked the set from his back and placed it on the ground in front of him. Lofty laid beside it the set he had found. Jack switched on this radio, pulled the earphones over his head, and began to turn the dials, but it was dead as the other one. He reached down instinctively to open his RAF pack, and remembered that he had lost that long ago.

'Give me a bayonet, someone,' he said.

Bud pulled his bayonet from its scabbard and handed it to him. Jack used the point as a screwdriver and removed the back-plate. The batteries inside seemed sound. If I had only half an hour with these two sets on my bench in the EMI workshop in Tottenham Court Road, he thought, I could cannibalize them and easily make one work out of all these parts. Tottenham Court Road. Would he ever see it again? Or Cottage Road, Bow, or Ealing Broadway, or any other part of London? He began to prise the valves out gently from their sprung sockets with the end of a bayonet.

'Look out!' shouted Jim, and Jack ducked instinctively. A mortar bomb landed beyond the wall of the courtyard, showering them all with dust. He heard cries from the wounded and from terrified French girls, and then he was up on his knees, shaking out bits of plaster and brick from the condensers and coils and valves. But in vain; the explosion had smashed two of the silvered valves.

'It's no good,' he told the Canadians, who squatted around him. 'Both sets are US. They've had it.'

'So've we if we don't get out of here soon,' said Jim. 'Jerry's everywhere.'

A sergeant ran past them.

'Jerry reinforcements coming down the hill in numbers!' he shouted urgently. 'Give 'em all you've got.'

'What with?'

'There are Brens in there!' He waved a hand towards the yard. Jack ran in, seized a Bren-gun that someone had left against the wall, and ran out with it.

'Those girls in the yard!' he yelled, 'Bring out more mags!'

The girls, and all wounded soldiers who were able to help, crammed new clips of rounds from canvas bandoliers into Bren-gun magazine pans. Lofty appeared carrying the anti-tank rifle that Smokey had made the German carry for him.

'What about the prisoner?' Bud asked him.

'He's inside. So are some others. They're not going to make a run for it.'

'I don't think it matters now if they do. What worries me is, will *we* get away?'

That worries me even more, thought Jack drily, but the best way to help himself—and all the other Canadians lying wounded on the beach or crowded into the casino or taking what shelter they could find under the walls of houses—was to hold off the Germans long enough to allow more landing craft to edge closer to the beach.

They could not come right in as they were under intense and accurate artillery fire, and also the sea was now too shallow; but each yard nearer meant one yard less for weary and wounded men to run through the water under ferocious fire. One or two Canadians had come out with Lee-Enfields to engage the Germans, who were moving in relentlessly from a wide circle. If they could only halt them, this would help the men awaiting evacuation on the beach and the men in the boats. From concealed weapon-pits dug high up in the chalk face of the cliffs to the west, enemy machine-guns chattered like angry monkeys. Jack exhausted the Bren magazine and seized another one in an attempt to distract the German gunners from the targets on the beach. When that was empty, he grabbed the more accurate anti-tank rifle and rammed its huge cartridge in the breech.

The rifle was far too heavy to fire from the shoulder, so he lay down on the ground and took steady aim at one of the dark mouths in the cliffs, from which machine-gun flames flickered like orange tongues. Forbes-Smith's rules of aiming at Rosehearty . . . The tip of the foresight in line with the shoulders of the backsight . . . first pressure on the trigger . . .

The clumsy weapon kicked on its stand as he fired. He lowered it, wiping sweat from his eyes, peering up at the cliff. The machine-gun had stopped. It did not start again. But instead other light machine-gunners were firing down at them.

Jack and his comrades crouched behind the bodies of dead Canadians, using them as a wall of flesh, firing steadily, so that even the dead helped the desperate defenders.

In the courtyard, the girls and the wounded Canadians had used up nearly all their ammunition. Some landing craft with troops on board had already escaped while others had been hit by shells and were burning. They were surrounded by dazed men who had jumped or been flung into the sea and who swam about desperately among the dead and the dying.

Then a Navy ship sailed through the drifting smoke and at point blank range lifted off the front of the cliff in one broadside. Chalk, bodies, guns, equipment fell like a child's box of toys, and crashed to the beach far below. Overhead, droves of Spitfires and Mustangs came in almost at wave-top level, attacking the JU 88s and the other multi-engined German planes that were attacking the ships. The noise was so great, it was impossible to talk in anything less than shouts, and men were pointing or giving thumbs up or thumbs down signs rather than waste their breath on words no one could hear.

Jack could see figures in field grey and coal-scuttle helmets running in from across the fields, down the hill below the RDF station, and from the Farm of the Four Winds. What about Murray Osten and 'A' Company? Were they all dead?

Inside the casino, wounded Canadians were propped up against the walls. Friends had lit cigarettes and stuck them in their mouths, but others had such serious abdominal injuries they could not smoke or even speak; they appeared all but dead already. As Jack and Roy Hawkins stood near the door, unable to go further into the room because of the milling crowd already there, a Bren-gunner picked up his gun and bravely ran with it through the doorway for a better arc of fire. A patrol of advancing Germans flung themselves flat in the dust, firing as they dropped. One bullet whined over Roy Hawkins' shoulder, ripping away the shoulder-strap from his battledress. A second hit the Bren barrel at an angle and ricocheted along the gunner's wrist. He dropped the Bren awkwardly, screaming in agony. Jack and Roy Hawkins tried to drag him inside, but he was delirious with pain and struggled against them, shouting that he must stay where he was. Outside, the Germans were up on their feet again, and racing towards them.

The room was so crowded now that there was barely space to stand, and all the while, machine-gunners from the top of the cliff who had survived the Navy broadside, poured down streams of bullets which ricocheted through the broken windows. Shots drilled rows of parallel holes high up in the far wall, and dust from the disintegrating plaster ceiling hung like fog in the hot, foul air. Some men were shouting, others groaning in agony, others searching frantically for magazines and ammunition, because surely it could only be moments before the whole building was totally overrun, and anything seemed better than surrender.

Jack unhooked the two grenades from the back of his belt and hung them at the front instead. If he were wounded, he would pull out both pins and kill himself instantly, and any German near him. Then he took out his escape set. He had only two pills left, the second pep pill and the cyanide capsule, the means maybe of life and death. He swallowed the pep pill, put the cyanide pill in his pocket, and threw away the box. Then he turned to Hawkins. He had noticed a faint movement out at sea through the smoke, about half a mile east of the casino.

'There's a landing craft out there,' he said. 'Looks like it daren't come in. If we could swim that far out, we might reach it.'

'It's quite a way,' replied Hawkins. 'Several hundred yards.'

'Better than trekking several hundred miles in Army uniform through occupied France to the Spanish border,' Jack retorted.

Firing outside intensified. More men forced their way desperately into the room; Jack was momentarily separated from Roy Hawkins.

The room felt hot as a bakery oven. Plaster dust from the ceiling hung like a fog, and the walls trembled with each explosion. Men were so crowded they were treading on the wounded, who shouted and screamed in their pain. Some wandered in holding Bren-guns, half crazed with heat, the constant thunder of the explosions, the bewilderment about what was happening. Others fought to get out to the door to set up a defensive position.

What hope had any of them of survival? Jack thought, as the second pep pill poured adrenalin through his body. He would try to reach the landing craft; that was his only hope. It was futile to accept surrender, or to die here like a beast in a pen; but surrounded on three sides by advancing Germans and with the sea behind them, what other chance had they got?

One man ripped off his battledress blouse, tore off his white vest and started to wave it.

'We'd be better off surrendering to the Jerries,' he shouted hoarsely. 'We've no ammo. Why bloody die in vain?'

Some yelled agreement. Others bellowed against.

'Stop the shooting!' shouted a man with a blood-stained bandage round his head. 'If we stop, the Jerries will stop, too. It's senseless, this. We haven't a chance.'

Jack saw a face thrust into his, a face dark as though carved in teak, polished with sweat. Smokey. He had lost his helmet, and his damp hair was matted with plaster dust.

'I'll never bloody surrender to any fucking Jerry!' he shouted. He drew his knife, elbowing the other men out of his way.

'I'll slit the bastard's throat with this—and anyone else's who wants to give in.'

'You're bloody drunk!' someone shouted, and Jack realized he was. Smokey held a water-bottle in his left hand and raised it to his lips. The smell of rum was overpowering as it slopped down his chin. He met Jack's eyes.

'He's right, Spook. I took it off a dead Cameron.'

Someone pushed past with a white vest tied around a rifle barrel.

'Get back!' said Smokey sharply. 'I'll carve anyone who surrenders. But before I do, I'll get this little bugger here.' He turned on Jack, threw away the bottle and seized him by the front of his battledress.

Jack struck his hand away.

'Who bloody well got us into this pisshole anyhow?' shouted Smokey, his voice slurred and thick. 'This sodding RDF expert. Well, find a way out of this, Spook.'

'I will,' Jack answered him.

'How?'

'Across that beach to the sea.'

'It's a goddam graveyard already. Bodies are eight deep. Can't you see? You haven't a hope. You'll get shot.'

Jack turned, hoping to see Hawkins or Jim or Lofty, but he was hemmed in by strangers; men with tired, dazed eyes, cut cheeks, bandaged heads and arms; wounded, weary men, who had seen a dozen lifetimes of violence and fearful death compressed into a few hours, whose minds were numbed, almost anaesthetized, by the constant iron bellow of bombardment.

Now, barely able to think clearly any longer, with the enemy massing on one side, and the sea stretching behind them for nearly seventy miles, they faced two terrible alternatives. They could surrender now and hope for fair treatment, or they could keep firing in this cramped stinking room, until their ammunition had all gone, and hope somehow for the miracle of rescue. Jack could not appeal to them; they had their own problems; he must cope with his. Then he saw Lofty only a few feet away; he had forced his way to the front door to see for himself how close the Germans were. Jack grabbed his sleeve.

'Help me form a group and we'll make a run for it,' he told him. 'There's an LCA under that smoke. We can take the prisoner, too.'

'I'm with you,' said Hawkins. He also realized that this was their only chance.

'Right. We'll get all the smoke canisters we can—and then go!'

Jack murmured the words of the Shema, the Jewish prayer used in moments of extreme danger and stress: '*Hear, O Israel, the Lord Thy God, the Lord is One.*'

He saw Jim make the sign of the cross and Lofty's lips, pale with loss of blood, move in some prayer of his own. This was also their moment of truth. *It is vain to quarrel with destiny.* Within minutes they could all be dead.

Other men crowded eagerly around them with advice.

'You'll be bloody well killed. Instantly. Better be taken prisoner.'

'I can't be,' replied Jack simply. 'I'm going to run for it.'

'We're with you!' shouted Smokey, waving his knife. He lunged at Jack and seized his arm.

Jack tore himself free and tried to punch him, but too many people were milling, pressing, throttling them with their bodies for him to do more than raise his fists. If he was going, he had to go now, and the only possible way out was through the window overlooking the sea. The glass had been smashed, but the metal bars were still in place.

'Break the window!' Jack yelled.

Across the heads of dozens of men, Jack saw Jim and Roy Hawkins pick up rifles and smash the metal frames with the butts.

'Who's going to run for it with me?'

A confused uproar of men shouted replies, some for, some against. Others thrust themselves forwards, wanting to know his plan.

'Only those who can run and swim!' Jack shouted back at them. 'Wounded haven't a chance. But you can all help us if you want to.'

'How?' asked a Canadian with his arm in a blood-stained sling.

'Smoke. Get all the smoke canisters you can. Chuck them on the promenade as we head for the sea.'

Jim unbuttoned the breast pocket of his battledress and pulled out the photograph of the girl he had shown Jack aboard *Princess Beatrix*. He held this carefully in his right hand, like a talisman.

'Any smoke canisters?' Jack yelled.

Someone called: 'Smoke here, buster.'

'Well, *throw* 'em!' shouted Roy Hawkins.

One went out of the front door, then a second; a third and fourth through the window. Two were damaged and lay uselessly where they landed. The other two fizzled and then erupted in clouds of smoke, but it was far too thin to provide any real protection. As Jack and the others stared in dismay at these black wisps blowing in the wind, a shell trundled over their heads from behind the smoke screen out at sea, and landed harmlessly in the side of the cliff. It was not high explosive but a smoke shell; a huge black cloud erupted from the crater like a volcano.

'Go when that smoke blows over the sea-wall!' Jack yelled. A number of men headed at once for the door, and then jumped back inside as a burst of bullets blew splinters off the lintel.

'The window!' shouted Hawkins hoarsely. Smoke was drifting over them steadily, thickening into a strange unnatural dusk.

'Now!'

Jack jumped up to the window and swung his legs over.

'You're not going without me, you Limey Spook bastard!' roared Smokey, and seized the back of his battledress. Jack fell sideways. Smokey dropped back and then vaulted over the sill after him, knife still in his hand. And after Smokey came Roy Hawkins, then Jim, and Lofty and other shadowy figures: faces tense, muscles bunched, some hatless and empty-handed, others still in full battle order, holding rifles. The German prisoner was somehow dragged out with them.

'Run!' Jack bellowed, legs pounding like pistons. At that moment, a mortar bomb or shell landed behind the casino. The shock wave of its explosion almost blew them off their feet, but although they staggered and reeled, they did not fall. Jack glanced behind him. Smoke and dust darkened the air where the casino had been. High up above this he saw rifles and beams and rubble and bodies and parts of bodies falling, almost in slow motion. It looked like a direct hit. But he was still alive, still on his two feet, running hard. A machine-gun crackled incessantly from up on the hill, and the prisoner dropped down on his hands and knees like a man at prayer, and then fell behind them, either hit or pretending to be hit. Jack could not pause to find out. And what did it matter now? The only thing that mattered was to reach the sea, and then that comforting black cloud and then the landing craft. Other automatic weapons and rifles opened up. Bullets screamed past them, as they raced in a daze of danger, veering to the left, away from the firing, towards the edge of the sea-wall. The huge coils of barbed wire were still largely intact, presenting a prickly hurdle to be taken in a stride. On the shingle, about ten feet below where beach mats had been spread in rows each August before the war, and up as close to the wire as possible to have the benefit of shelter from the wall, were neat rows of wounded Canadians. Some lay strapped on stretchers, ready to be carried out to landing craft. They lay patiently, pathetically hoping for rescue that could now never arrive. Contrary to Jack's hopes, the lines of bodies in the shadow of the sea-wall would prevent them receiving any cover in their run.

They raced on, hearts bursting. Under the thinning smoke from the shell, the gap in the wire was still about twenty yards away. A splattering of bullets chipped the concrete around their feet. More firing. A fusillade from a machine-gun. Someone screamed and fell behind him, and he sensed rather than saw a man's body roll upside down over the wire, and heard his shriek as the countless barbs ripped his flesh like fish hooks.

'Jump!' yelled Jack, as more bullets sprayed the sea-wall. As he shouted, he leapt sideways, just clearing the top of the coiled wire, and landed on the shingle in a narrow space between two stretchers. The man on his left was unconscious and uncomprehending. The man on his right was a red-haired SSR in his early twenties, his body and legs covered by a blood-stained grey blanket.

'Have another go,' he said with a smile. 'Next time maybe you'll land right on me.'

'Sorry, mate,' said Jack gruffly, and instinctively put out his hand. The other man shook his head. He could not move his own hands because of the tight blanket. Jack ruffled his red hair in an apology, and then looked up through the wire along the promenade. It was empty, but ten feet behind a body hung on the wire, head down, face turned away, blood dripping steadily from both hands. As Jack watched, something fell away from the man's right hand and fluttered down among the stretchers. Jack grabbed at it. He was holding the photograph of Jim's girl-friend. Jack crumbled it up and threw it away. As he started to run on, he heard footsteps running with him, and he glanced to his left. Roy Hawkins was keeping pace, revolver in his hand, as well as one or two others. Had everyone else been killed in that first mad dash from the casino? They bounded along the beach like two runners in a nightmare marathon, boots sinking to the ankles in the thick shingle. One hundred and fifty yards ahead, Jack could see a breakwater much stronger than the rest. Instead of just a mass of rotting moss-covered stakes planted in the shingle, this seemed virtually a wall of solid planks, thick as railway sleepers. There were some spaces and gaps in the planks, but it still offered a reasonable shield against fire from the cliffs. If they crouched down behind the planks as they ran, they might have some cover.

Suddenly Jack grabbed at his belt and dropped forward on his knees. Hawkins immediately went down beside him.

'What's the matter?' he asked breathlessly. 'You hit?'

'No. My grenades. I've dropped one.'

'For Chrissake!'

Scrabbling among the stones, Jack suddenly saw the pineapple-shaped grenade and hooked it back on his belt. They ran on together.

There were few wounded so far up the beach, but to Jack's horror he heard Germans on the promenade shouting at them. Some were standing up, taking aim from the shoulder; others were firing from a kneeling position with rifles, snub-nosed Schmeissers. Bullets streamed over Jack and Roy, behind them, in front as they raced, hearts bursting, sobbing for air. Fifty yards more to the breakwater.

Would they make it? *Could* they? 'Hear, O Israel . . . the Lord Thy God, the Lord is One . . .'

Thirty yards. They swerved to the left across the beach because the waves had pushed shingle ahead of them into a steep ridge, level with the top of the breakwater. To run up and over it would be suicidal under the hail of bullets. Then they reached the breakwater, and rusting bolt-heads, the size of fists, and green beards of moss hung with clusters of blue-black mussels, loomed level with their eyes. Down the beach now, close up against the breakwater all the way. Keep on running.

As Jack ran he flung off his steel helmet, unbuttoned his blouse, and tossed it away from him. He needed nothing that would hold him back in the sea. The summer breeze felt cool and fresh through his sweaty shirt, giving him new vigour. Then he heard Hawkins shouting behind him: 'Jack! That RAF shirt! It's blue!'

Of course. He should have insisted on a khaki shirt for the Germans would guess no soldier would wear air force gear. But how could he rip it off when his Mae West was still strapped tightly round his chest like a plump boa constrictor? Then Jack heard a German screaming orders from the promenade. Out of all the shouted words, he only recognized one: *blau*. That meant blue, so it must refer to him. Christ! He *must* get away. Get away. *Get away*. The words formed their own rhythm in time with his hammering boots.

Nearer the sea now, the pebbles were smaller and rounder and shinier and more slippery, polished by more waves and glittering amber-like beneath inches of clear water. Then the sea came over their ankles, and they were splashing through it, throwing up fountains of spray on either side, like children on the first day of a seaside holiday. The breakwater was rotten here with great gaps in the beams, and they ran doubled up to cross these open spaces as bullets peppered the wood. Some penetrated the planks, pushing out splinters of soft, sea-sodden wood like white fingers at them. Others churned the sea like a storm of hail.

Roy Hawkins threw away his steel helmet to prepare to swim. He was streaming with sweat, for beneath his battle-dress blouse he still wore his fiancée's thick woollen sweater. Now he ripped off his blouse and the sweater after it and ran, holding it in one hand, still reluctant to throw away a present that had meant such a sacrifice. But he knew the wool would absorb so much sea-water that it must only drag him down when he began to swim, and could make the difference between floating and sinking, so he let it go.

Gradually, the deepening water and their own increasing weariness slowed them almost to a standstill. Jack flung himself forwards into the sea. It was barely three feet deep and his hands scraped the sandy bottom, ribbed with the endless outlines of tiny waves. Hawkins followed him and they both half swam, half crawled like this for a few yards, then came up for air and went down again until the sea was deep enough for them to swim.

'Swim under water,' gasped Jack. 'But not in a straight line.'

The salt water stung his face, raw from chips of stone that had spattered from exploding shells. Its coolness refreshed them both, but there was no time to delay, to savour this sensation, for bullets still whipped furiously into the water all round them.

Hawkins was momentarily surprised to taste the sea or salt on his tongue. He was used to swimming in the Athabasca River, the Union Gap or the Clearwater Lake; this was the first time he had swum in sea-water. Jack and he steadily swam under water in a zig-zag course, bobbing up briefly and regularly for air. Once, Jack opened his eyes under water, and saw silvery white streaks from passing bullets and puffs of sand as they landed. Would they never escape? They were still about fifty yards from the smoke screen but through it they could now make out the blunt bows of a landing craft, half concealed by the black, oily clouds.

The LCA turned slowly, and Jack saw that the ramp was jammed half open. Water poured inboard through the gap on either side. Perhaps it was crippled? Perhaps everyone aboard was dead? Perhaps anything—but at least it floated and would give them shelter and minutes to regain their breath, to work out what they could do. They swam on steadily, resisting an intense and panic desire to thresh through the water, for this would only tire them more quickly, and neither knew how long they might have to stay afloat. They kept more to the surface now, partly because they were almost exhausted, and to submerge and come up again called for more effort, and partly because bullets seemed to be falling short behind them.

Then a shell landed ahead, right inside the smoke, aimed at the landing craft. The shock-wave of its explosion punched their bruised bodies through the solid wall of water with the force of a fall on a brick floor. It drove all breath from their lungs, so they were forced to float on their backs for a moment, gasping like landed fish, while the sea boiled all round them. As they swam wearily on into the smoke screen, Jack again saw something darker loom just ahead of him, but for a moment his tired brain refused to register what it could be. Then he realized it must be the side of the landing craft.

He tried to shout for help, but all he could manage was a croak. No one could possibly hear him, and the craft was turning slowly. Within seconds, it would be moving and they would be left to drown. He heard the drum of an engine, the thrash of a propeller, and then saw the ramp above his head. Jack gave a last kick, stretched up and gripped the metal edge of the ramp as it swung round. Hawkins was already hanging on to the other side.

He heard running feet slosh through water inside the LCA, and then a sailor was crouching down in the angle of the half-open ramp.

'It's okay, mate,' he said in broad Cockney, gripping his wrists. Slowly, he pulled Jack inboard. He lay for a moment, half on, half off, wedged in the opening, too exhausted to move further. The sailor gave another heave and he was inside, half conscious, lying in the bilge, sucking in great gouts of air. He raised himself up and gasped, 'My friend! Pick up my friend.'

Roy Hawkins was still in the water; the sailor had not seen him. Roy heard someone shout urgently: 'Get this thing turned round!'

The LCA was facing the shore, with little frontal protection. Hawkins thought in an extremity of despair, I've got this far, and they're going to leave me! He beat feebly with one fist on the side of the craft, holding on with the other and gasping desperately: 'Let me in! I'm still here! *Let me in!*'

The sailor heard Hawkins and turned and pulled him aboard. Six inches of sea-water slopped to and fro inside the craft from the jammed ramp. Wounded soldiers were lying on duck boards, oblivious of water up to their chests, with only their heads above it, too ill to move.

'You all right now, matey?' the sailor asked Jack in a Cockney voice. Jack looked up slowly and nodded. He had no strength for words. Also, he had just grown aware of a fearful pain in his side; even to breathe was an agony. Dimly, through a cloud of pain, he wondered what this could mean. Had he ruptured himself? Was he having a heart attack? Was he badly wounded, and somehow had not felt the pain because of the cold sea? He moved his hand down and his fingers closed around one of his grenades. He had been lying on it. The pain he felt was the segmented side cutting into his flesh.

—EIGHT—

'You won't need that here, mate,' said the sailor, nodding towards the grenade.

'You never know,' replied Jack, finding his voice. He was wondering now whether the sea-water had spoiled his cyanide pill, and glanced at Hawkins, sitting back thankfully against the side of the LCA, eyes closed.

The landing craft was turning with painful slowness like a clumsy, wounded sea-beast, barely capable of movement. Only one engine was running while an engineer worked frantically to start the other. Jack knew that the craft steered as much by her two engines as by her two rudders; they could not keep a steady course unless both were working.

'Bet your revolver's ruined, Roy,' he told him, almost cheerfully. If it was, at least Hawkins could not shoot him. But they both had kept their grenades; they were not home yet. Jack might still have to honour his bond.

'Any more survivors?' he asked the sailor.

'Only those you can see. We've got to keep cruising up and down until the other engine's going, so we may pick up some more. Then we're off.'

Jack looked up at the sky, blue through drifting patches of black smoke that still almost totally obscured the shore. The same sky he had seen on the beach; the same sky those left behind would also see—with this vital difference. He was watching it in freedom. His prayer had been answered. 'Blessed be His name, whose glorious kingdom is for ever and ever . . .'

As the craft turned, Jack could see white cliffs, and the

bright muzzle-flash from guns still firing. A grey cloud of dust hung like a giant mushroom over the beach at Pourville, pierced here and there by flames. From the distance, they resembled waving orange scarves. To the left, beyond the RDF station and the ridge of high cliffs, an even higher dark cloud shrouded Dieppe, and black columns of smoke towered up through it. A battle was still going on, and many Canadians would not escape. So who had won and who had lost? Then he remembered the hanging wires behind the RDF station, and he wondered; he would not be sure until he reached England.

Early that morning, the German war correspondents and photographers who had been dancing with the service girls on the previous evening, discovered that they were unusually well-placed for an unexpected first-hand view of war. They had been awakened and rushed in cars to the outskirts of Dieppe, where an officer met them to explain what was happening. The Allies—apparently mainly Canadians with British Commandos, judging from prisoners already taken—had rashly attempted a frontal assault on Dieppe and Pourville, on Varengeville and Puys. As the correspondents would now be able to see clearly for themselves, most of the enemy's tanks had been disabled on the Dieppe beach. Its steep slope and loose shingle had broken links in their tracks, which no doubt were fashioned from inferior metal; it was well known that British steel was by no means as tough as the products of the Ruhr. The high wall to the promenade had been another obstacle which only two or three tanks had been able to surmount successfully. Crews who had not already been killed would be forced to surrender as soon as their ammunition was exhausted.

British Commandos had meanwhile attacked the heavy artillery battery at Varengeville, and after overcoming heroic resistance, had apparently silenced it. Full details were still awaited, but these invaders seemed to have escaped back across the Channel. No doubt the Luftwaffe would make sure they did not reach England. At Pourville, Canadians had landed, and strong patrols had gone inland to the crossroads at Petit-Appeville. Only the courage of the mobile cyclist column from Ouville had prevented what could have been a most serious consolidation at that point.

The 10th Panzer Division had been fully alerted and was racing north to the coast. Its distinguished commander, General Fischer, had driven ahead of his troops and would be available to answer questions relating to the action after he had discussed with General Haase the most effective way that his Panzers could be brought into action—if indeed they were needed. For so well had the defenders fought that the raid had speedily been repulsed. Most of the Allied landing craft had been destroyed, as the journalists would also be able to see for themselves, and Canadians and British who had not already been killed in their craft before they landed, or on the beaches just afterwards, would shortly be compelled to surrender. Altogether, it had been a remarkable display of courage and resource by German troops and the Luftwaffe and Navy; even more remarkable because many of the German soldiers were young recruits.

The correspondents would have much of interest to write about, and the photographers a great deal to photograph. But they had all made an early and unexpected start after a late night. Refreshments would be in order first. If they would just follow him, gentlemen . . .

The journalists and photographers, several incongruously dressed in civilian clothes, and most of them unshaven and bleary-eyed, walked in the grounds of the old castle with staff officers, some of whom wore white summer mess-tunics, and held glasses and cigars in their hands, and were not at all averse to having their names and even their photographs appear in connection with what was undoubtedly a victory.

At the base of the cliffs, far beneath these agreeable discussions, the beach was littered with dead and dying; with silent tanks, guns pointing down despondently, all ammunition spent; with burning landing craft and weapons thrown away. This was the aftermath of war, the unmentionable underside of martial glory, never portrayed in recruiting posters. Many of the correspondents had not seen such fearful sights before, so much mutilation and death, all the more terrible against a summer background of sun and sea. They were imaginative men and stood fascinated and horrified, and above all thankful that they were on top of the cliff, not down on the beach.

On these littered, bloodied beaches, the men of the 14th Canadian Army Tank Regiment (the Calgary Regiment) and three Canadian infantry battalions waited under withering fire for landing craft to take them off. They waited without much hope, in silence, sheltering from bullets as best they could beneath rocks, behind tanks and in what shallow trenches they could gouge out of the shingle with their hands. They did not move more than they had to, for fear of attracting more fire. To a civilian peering fearfully down from the cliff-top, they might even appear to be only other corpses. But their spirit was not dead.

Lieutenant-Colonel Robert Ridley Labatt of Hamilton, commanding the Royal Hamilton Light Infantry, suddenly heard his sergeant major shout:

'By God, sir! Take a look at *that*!'

Colonel Labatt raised his binoculars and saw the German officers in white summer uniforms, the chattering civilians, the wink of sun on glasses, a cigar held in a delicate hand. The sight was too much for any man to bear. Instantly, he ordered two Bren-gunners to fire at this unexpected target. They hosed the grass with bullets. The onlookers scattered. For some who moved too late, this first brief glimpse of war's other side was also their last.

At 1300 hours, *HMS Calpe*, the headquarters ship, sailed through the murk and pall off Dieppe for a last close look at the beaches. Black smoke still rose above burning LCAs and town buildings like funeral pyres. Visibility was very bad from the sea, so it was impossible for the watchers, peering through this drifting fog, to realize that hundreds of men were in fact still crouching on the beach behind tanks and landing craft, either wounded or pinned down by fire from the cliffs and the rocks. From the ship, they could see no sign of life. Nothing moved except the smoke.

Up on the headland, in Colonel Bartelt's headquarters, an officer was already speaking on the telephone to divisional headquarters at Envermeu.

'I have to report that the British Navy has gone,' he said. 'A few remnants of the landing force are still holding out on all beaches. I request permission from General Haase to clear up the battlefields.'

There was a moment's pause for discussion at the other end of the wire. Then back came the brusque reply: 'Permission granted. Proceed. Report progress.'

At once, a General Order went out to all scattered sections of the German 571st Infantry Regiment; they were to make an immediate advance down to the beaches. The battle was all but over. The victory was all but theirs.

After the raid, Lieutenant Willi Weber carefully examined the radar station at Berneval to the east of Dieppe. It was intact and there appeared to be no casualties, and no attempt had been made to capture it or interfere with its operation in any way. He was relieved that nothing on the lines of the Bruneval raid had been carried out. He drove over the cliff towards Pourville, pulled off the road and walked up the hill, with its grass cut close as on a golf course, to the Freya station. A non-commissioned officer saluted him.

'What are your casualties?' Weber asked him.

'I'm sorry to say, sir, we have lost two dead and nine wounded.' He gave their names.

Weber nodded. Many of his NCOs had battle experience in France or Poland or the Eastern Front, and every off-duty soldier—even VD patients in the camp hospitals—had been called into action to defend the coast. The radar technicians had fought on the road from Pourville to Dieppe; they had died within sight of the station.

* * *

As the landing craft turned round slowly, water swirled inside it. The two pep pills Jack had swallowed were now making him feel dizzy and light-headed in the heat, and his thoughts drifted aimlessly as pieces of wood in the bilge. The engineer once again pressed the starter solenoid, and the second engine began to fire, uneasily at first, then more steadily. The LCA picked up speed, leaving the protective embrace of the smoke, and headed out to sea. Two JU 88s cruised in the sky, ready to shoot at any movement.

'Where are you going?' Jack shouted to the petty officer in the wheelhouse.

'To that flak ship. We're taking in too much water to make England on our own.'

Looming ahead on the far side of the smoke screen, a flat-decked barge, bristling with anti-aircraft guns wallowed in the tide: the flak ship. As the JU 88 pilots, now joined by two single-engined fighters, saw the landing craft and realized where it was heading, they opened fire. The petty officer grabbed a Lewis gun, and shouting and cursing, with his feet spread against the lurch and rock of the LCA, he squeezed the trigger. Empty cartridge cases showered over the deck as he fired. The CPO shouted orders to steer to port, then over to starboard, and then back to port, to baffle the bomb-aimers. Cannon shells hammered the armour-plated ramp; others bored holes in the hull beneath the waterline, and the sea came hosing in.

Then the flak ship's mass of anti-aircraft guns opened up on the German planes, and they turned and headed back to shore, leaving the landing craft sinking steadily behind them. With the constantly increasing dead-weight of water aboard, both engines labouring on full throttles could barely force it through the sea. Slowly, painfully, they reached the flak ship and bumped alongside, the water in the LCA already above their knees. One by one, the wounded were handed up, then Jack and Roy Hawkins climbed aboard, and then the petty officer and the crew. As the water rose finally above distributors and plug leads, both engines coughed and spluttered and died, and the stern slid down because of their weight. Then the blunt bows dipped and the LCA sank, leaving a stream of bubbles, streaks of oil and pieces of wood, and steel helmets floating upside down, like begging bowls.

The armour-plated deck of the flak ship burned beneath the noon sun. Lying on it, without a hat or the benefit of any shade felt like lying on a grill; the soaking uniforms of the survivors steamed in the fierce heat.

The crew turned out to be Royal Marines, largely Cockneys.

'You all right, then?' one asked Jack cheerfully.

Jack nodded.

'Thank God we're safe.'

'We're not bloody safe *yet*, mate, but we will be if we can get rid of these buggers.'

He jerked his head in the direction of Heinkels and JU 88s that now wheeled above them slightly out of range, like wasps circling a honey-pot. Then one of the JU 88 pilots noted the blind spot to the rear of the flak ship, caused by the bridge which stretched right across the stern. Almost in slow motion, he positioned himself for a bombing run.

'Wait for it,' one of the gunners yelled, as the Marine fire control officers ducked when the crews prepared to open up.

As soon as the slow-flying bomber cleared the bridge, the first puff of ack-ack exploded in front of the fuselage, the second in the aircraft. But a stick of bombs was already falling. The first bomb erupted some distance from the flak ship, the second immediately behind her, jolting the craft and blotting out the sun. The third landed just in front of them, drenching the decks in spray. Then the bomber flew on, and the Marines kept up a constant barrage from their ack-ack guns, so that the whole ship shuddered and reeled with the recoil. They all cheered wildly as the plane crept away low over the horizon, pulling a long trail of oily smoke behind it.

Then a Spitfire lost height overhead, and the pilot parachuted down. The flak ship steered towards the white parachute ballooning into the sea, but a small naval craft beat them to it, to the accompaniment of cheerful boos and shouts and 'V' signs from the Cockney crew. This familiar East End approach cheered Jack. It was good to be alive—far better for him than any of the crew could possibly imagine. The realization that he had survived, the conviction that he was now as good as home, gave him an appetite. He remembered he had not eaten anything except a few Horlicks tablets for about twelve hours.

'Got any grub?' he asked.

'Only corn' beef, mate.'

A Marine threw him a wedge-shaped tin. Jack ripped off the key and opened it, and Roy Hawkins and he clawed out the meat with their fingers. Jagged strips of shrapnel skated across the smooth deck, and empty cartridge cases kept rattling down on every side as they ate. The risk of being injured because they had no steel helmets suddenly seemed very real. It would be diabolical to be hit now by accident when they had dodged so many bullets deliberately aimed at them. They threw the empty tin over the side, and went below.

As they began to climb down the narrow metal companionway with its diamond-shaped stair treads, both men became aware of a smell so terrible that they paused. It was intensified by the grilling sun on the metal deck; a smell of raw flesh wounds overlaid with the sickly sweetness of death, the stench of faeces and vomit, as semi-conscious men with unspeakable injuries lay beyond control of their bodily functions. Jack and Roy Hawkins paused on the lower steps, looking into what had originally been a mess room. Wooden tables had been hastily pushed together, and their legs tied with ropes and strips of webbing. Doctors and medical orderlies wearing white overalls soaked with blood were carrying out emergency operations on the tables, while beneath their feet the metal floor rocked and rippled and heaved as the ship's guns blazed and bombs dropped all round. More wounded lay packed and uncomplaining on stretchers, side by side on the floor. Many were unconscious or in drugged sleep; others had faces contorted by pain, hands pressed against their stomachs or chests in desperate attempts to contain their agony.

Above them all, the ceiling of the mess room vibrated like a giant drumskin, amplifying the cacophony from anti-aircraft guns. Jack and Roy Hawkins backed up the ladder immediately. It seemed better to risk being wounded in the fresh air than to stay down below in this fearful floating charnel-house.

As the Germans advanced steadily and relentlessly towards Pourville beach, closing in on the defenders from a wide semi-circle, Cecil Merritt organized his final defensive position along the sea-wall. Behind the remnants of his regiment lay the wounded; and behind them was the sea. Gradually, Canadian fire dwindled. Ammunition was running out, and Merritt knew that surrender was now inevitable. Reluctantly, he asked whether anyone had a white flag. One of his officers, Major E. W. (Lefty) White, replied that it was very much against his grain to show a white flag. Instead, he suggested that Corporal Joe Waner, who spoke German well, should order one of their German prisoners to return to his comrades, and tell them to stop firing and accept the Canadian surrender. This was done, and firing on both sides gradually ceased.

The Canadians laid down their arms, and were formed up in three ranks behind the Hôtel de la Terrasse. Major White, seeing one of his corporals standing near him dejectedly, put his arm around his shoulders and remarked philosophically, 'Well, Alf, we will have to see if these Jerries can play ball, eh?'

The SSRs waited with resignation and dignity for whatever their future held. Some appeared relatively smart in battle-dress and battle order. Others stood on the beach in under-pants, wearing dead men's boots without socks, or with strips of Mae West life-jackets tied around bare feet as makeshift shoes. These were men who had swum out to the smoke screen, desperately hoping to find an LCA able to take them aboard, but had instead discovered that the smoke concealed nothing but miles of empty sea. As they swam out, they had torn off their boots and gaiters, their jackets and trousers, and thrown away equipment because of its weight. Then, exhausted, and with no chance of rescue, they had been forced to swim back in their underpants to surrender on the shore. But despite the shock of defeat and reaction from nearly nine hours of fierce battle in the burning heat of mid-August, their discipline was high.

Merritt, wounded at last after hours of apparently charmed life, watched with pride as Lieutenant R. L. McIlveen, one of his young platoon commanders, led his platoon down to the beach. The men marched smartly in three sections. The SSRs might have lost an action, but they had not lost their self-respect. The sight of these young soldiers, all volunteers, marching back in step, heads high, was to remain one of Cecil Merritt's sharpest and proudest memories of that day.

When Murray Osten arrived at the beach with the survivors of 'A' Company, Merritt remembered the Sloan's Liniment bottle that the steward aboard *Princess Beatrix* had given him that morning. He opened it, and they shared the whisky together thankfully. Then they set out to march with their men over the hill, past the RDF station and into Dieppe and unknown years of captivity ahead.

An ironic incident occurred when an RAF plane fired on this column of marching men, under the impression that they must be German reinforcements. They dropped in ditches and behind walls for cover, and when it flew away, formed up again on the hot empty road.

As they marched, they passed German Army linesmen already out repairing telephone wires that Jack and the Canadians had cut. And soon these lines hummed with mutually congratulatory messages from one German commander to another. At 1650 hours, when the Canadians had been taken to a hospital in Dieppe for the wounded to be treated by captured Canadian doctors and German Army doctors, before being moved to a brick factory farther inland to be interrogated and documented, General Kuntzen, commanding 81st Corps, was sending a congratulatory telegram to the 302nd

Infantry Division; *'Gut gemacht 302. I.D., insonderheit Besatzung in Dieppe!'* (Well played, the 302nd, and particularly the Dieppe garrison!)

General Curt Haase ended his congratulatory telegram with a characteristic exhortation to even greater vigilance: *'Augen und Ohren auf!'* (Keep your eyes and ears open.)

Field-Marshal von Rundstedt informed the High Command Armed Forces Operational Staff of the end of events at Dieppe with the dignified pronouncement: 'No armed Englishman remains on the Continent.' Then he sent a less formal teletype message to the units responsible for this agreeable state of affairs, 'to express to all commanders and troops who took part my appreciation and thanks. I was able to report today that the troops have fought very well!'

Over the wires to the Field-Marshal in St Germain came congratulations from his Führer in Berlin: 'I beg you, *Herr Feldmarschall*, to express my thanks and my appreciation to all participating units of the three armed services. I know that in the future, too, I can rely on the commanders and the soldiers of the armed forces in the west.'

The troops were duly gratified by all these laudatory communications, but where fighting men are concerned, words are no lasting substitute for deeds. More to their liking was the issue of one half bottle of Sekt, ten cigarettes and two cartons of biscuits to each man in the area. In addition, one day's front-line ration, on Scale 'A'—one hundred grams of bread and fifty grams of meat—was to be issued to all fighting troops, with a second liquor ration. Satisfaction over this announcement was tempered by the knowledge that Luftwaffe personnel would receive larger additional rations, and for a longer period than the infantry; but then infantry in every army always feels hard done by.

As German troops started to clear up the debris on the beaches and the streets, a batch of German reporters arrived in an ammunition and tool wagon seeking interviews for German radio programmes.

'You're too late,' Captain Schnösenberg told them without ceremony. 'It's all over. Finished. There's no more fighting.

'That doesn't matter,' replied the reporters, undismayed, 'we have any amount of recorded battle noises in the car.'

Schnösenberg was annoyed at this glib approach, and asked them not to use fake anything in an interview about such a serious affair. In the event, they ignored the captain's request. His mother actually heard their broadcast, and remarked to her son on the fierceness of the battle sounds.

Jacques Dubost, a schoolboy of twelve, home for the holidays and helping his mother with the family Café des Tribunaux, that stood in the centre of Dieppe, where the Rue St Jacques joined the Grande Rue, had also been awakened by the firing that morning.

Fascinated by the prospect of actually seeing a battle in progress, he spent hours scouting around, oblivious to danger or to shouted orders to keep off the streets. By early afternoon, when Canadian prisoners were being formed up under German guards near all their landing points, he decided he must help them in the only way he could. He ran home, collected all the spare clothes he could find, and some bars of chocolate and sandwiches intended for customers in the café. Then he took these gifts along to the prisoners and distributed them to the weary, dejected captives as they stood under guard. The German soldiers pretended not to see what he was doing.

The flak ship plunged on doggedly, hour after hour, through afternoon and early evening. Several German and British planes circled her, but they faced no more attacks. At about nine o'clock, roughly twenty-four hours from the time that Jack had left Southampton, he saw a faint rim of coast appear, very like the one he had just left; green grass covered similar white cliffs. As they drew closer, he could see the vertical CHL radar masts with which he was so familiar; they were all but home.

The wind was chilly now, and the metal deck-plates studded with round rivets that had been almost too hot to touch during the afternoon, felt cold and damp. Jack's shirt and trousers had dried stiffly in the heat, and one of the Marines had given him a battledress blouse. He was thankful for this as heat drained from the day, and evening mist shrouded the sea. The blouse had a whistle lanyard in one pocket, and the red and blue Royal Marines flash on each shoulder. Jack buttoned it up against the breeze and crouched with Hawkins out of the wind, near the base of an anti-aircraft gun-mounting. They were both experiencing reaction from their experiences, and were in no mood to talk. In any case, what was there to say? In the words of one of Jack's masters at Malmesbury Road School, who liked Latin quotations, *Iacta alea est*, the die is cast. He could not change anything now; he could only wait with burning impatience to discover whether the Freya operators had gone over to the radio-telephone when he cut their wires; and was there any mysterious third radar screen, or was that only a myth?

They dozed fitfully, now and then dreaming they were still being chased, and starting out of their sleep with thundering hearts and cries of alarm. It was nearly midnight when they awoke to find the flak ship approaching Newhaven harbour. To their astonishment and despite the blackout, floodlights were blazing inside the harbour, and other ships were queueing to enter. Signal lights flickered to and from the shore.

'What's going on?' Jack asked one of the Marines.

'Harbour master says we've got to wait out here. They can't take any more until they've unloaded all the ships already alongside. MO's choked. Says several blokes will die if we can't get them in soon.'

The flak ship wallowed for two hours on the night swell, while the sea ran past like black oil. Stomachs empty, mouths dry, bodies shivering with cold and weariness, Jack and Roy Hawkins waited with the others, in silence and gratitude that they had survived. The effect of Jack's two pep pills had now totally worn off and he felt indescribably tired. His head ached and his throat was raw, and when finally the flak ship did berth beneath the floodlights, and relays of stretcher bearers ran aboard to carry off the wounded, he and Roy Hawkins jumped down on to the shore almost with a sense of anti-climax.

The floodlights burned with a fierce bright incandescence totally strange after nearly three years of blackout, but then everything seemed strange here. A mobile canteen was dishing out mugs of strong sweet tea and free packets of cigarettes. They drank the tea gratefully, and no one questioned them.

'What now?' Hawkins asked him.

'Get some kip,' said Jack. 'It's no good milling around here.'

It was equally useless trying to persuade someone to issue him with a rail warrant to London at this hour; he would find a place to sleep and then make his arrangements to visit Air Commodore Tait in the early morning.

Exhausted, they walked slowly and stiffly along the quay. It was packed with service and civilian ambulances. They crossed sunken railway lines, passed giant silver-painted bollards, and finally entered a warehouse with a round curved roof and walls of white-painted planks that made it resemble a vast inverted lifeboat or wooden ark.

It was very cold inside; wooden crates and sacks of flour were stacked on the concrete floor. They could barely see their way in the dim light that filtered through the open doorway, but then they had not far to go, only to a corner where they both sank to the ground on sacks, loosened their boots, and slept.

The German Army had already counted the valuable equipment their uninvited visitors had left behind them. This included 1,242 rifles, 165 Brens and Sten-guns, 60 anti-tank rifles, 58 light mortars and 50 machine-guns. There were also 28 tanks, 22 heavy mortars, 6 self-propelled guns, 3 tank-landing craft, one Jeep, and several beached but serviceable landing craft. They anchored these vessels for the night, to be refloated on the morning tide. The Churchill tanks were carefully examined for booby traps, then towed up from the beaches, put into working order and subjected to the most severe tests. Months later, on the conclusion of these exhaustive experiments, a British agent was able to remove copies of the full test reports and recommendations, and forwarded them to the appropriate authorities in London. The German mechanical thoroughness was greatly appreciated; modifications their experts suggested were incorporated in future tanks.

Another discovery on the beach at Dieppe produced a more disagreeable result, as unsatisfactory in the end to Germany as to the Allies. A German officer who had watched the surrender from a concealed vantage point noticed that a Canadian brigadier standing near some other officers bent down suddenly and tried to bury something hastily beneath the shingle. The German officer immediately removed the stones and laid bare a waterproof package that contained Copy No. 37 of the complete plans for Jubilee. This beautifully printed and bound 'Military Detailed Plan', which the brigadier had most unwisely carried ashore, dealt with every aspect of the raid, and was studied closely (and in places critically) by German Intelligence officers, senior commanders and eventually Field-Marshal von Rundstedt.

General Haase, making his report on the plan, found it 'inconceivable why (the Canadians) did not support the battalion which landed near Pourville with tanks. An attack with tanks from Pourville against the hill west of Dieppe and against the Farm of the Four Winds might have been successful. . . .' Ironically, Lord Mountbatten had proposed in his original plan that tanks should land to the west of Pourville at Quiberville, and if the bridge remained intact, they would have attacked the high ground just to the south-west of Dieppe itself.

Others studying the book found a more immediately rewarding item, tucked away in Appendix L, Paragraph 4, No. B/2, which stated that, 'Whenever possible, prisoners' hands will be tied to prevent destruction of their documents'.

This was not a Canadian order, and indeed had been included against Canadian wishes simply to make sure that no risks were taken over gathering information which could be valuable. The Germans turned this discovery to considerable propaganda effect. Berlin Radio broadcast a statement announcing that, as a result of the order, 'all British officers and men captured at Dieppe shall be put in chains from 3rd September, at two o'clock'. This date was the third anniversary of the outbreak of war.

The British War Office issued an immediate denial that the hands of any German prisoner had been tied, and then added, rather feebly, 'any such order, if it was issued, will be cancelled'. As a result, the Germans agreed to call off their reprisals—only to reimpose them with effect from October 8. This was done because a small British raiding party, that had in the meantime landed on Sark in the Channel Islands, seized some German prisoners, and tied their wrists, so that they could not escape. Despite this, one did and explained the circumstances. In retaliation, as from October 10, German prisoners in Britain and Canada were also shackled. The Canadians and British captured at Dieppe were put in handcuffs from eight o'clock each morning and stayed in them until nine every night. Later in the war, when the number of German prisoners in Allied hands exceeded the number of Allied POWs in German camps, these conditions were gradually relaxed. On November 22, 1943, more than thirteen months later, the shackles were finally removed. They were not seen again.

Something was thudding regularly into Jack's ribs. He moved to avoid this, but it followed him. Reluctantly, he opened his eyes, but could not recognize where he was with the high curved roof, the crates, the sacks. Two Military Police lance corporals stood regarding him, hands on their hips, prodding him methodically in the ribs with the bright, boned toecaps of their left boots.

'Who are you, then?' the first asked him. Jack struggled sleepily to his feet, still trying to remember who he was, where he was and why he was there. He gave them his name. He was home now, so that was safe enough.

'I'm a flight sergeant in the RAF,' he added. 'I must get to a telephone and ring the Air Ministry.'

'At five o'clock in the bleeding morning?' said one of the MPs disbelievingly. 'Are you being funny?'

His companion added suspiciously: 'If you're an RAF flight sergeant, why are you wearing a Marine's jacket without any stripes?'

He turned to Roy Hawkins and appealed to him.

'Who is this bloke?' But Hawkins could not help them with Jack's background; he did not know himself.

'He's a radar expert,' he explained. 'We've been on the Dieppe raid. I'm a sergeant with Canadian Field Security.'

'What are you doing in this shed, then?'

'Getting some kip,' said Jack. 'And don't speak to me in that way.'

'Let's see your AB64.'[1]

'I haven't got one.'

'And yours, Sergeant?'

'I haven't mine here, either. I've told you, we've just come back from Dieppe.'

'How can you prove that?'

'Let me get to a telephone, and I'll be vouched for immediately.'

'Bloody odd, mate, if you ask me,' said the first corporal ponderously to his colleague. 'We'll take them over to the sarge and see what he says.'

'Let me telephone John Green,' said Roy Hawkins. 'He'll explain the whole thing immediately to your sergeant or officer.'

'Who's John Green?'

'My major. Canadian Field Security, East Grinstead.'

'You're together, then, are you?'

Suddenly, Hawkins started to laugh.

'What's so funny, Sergeant?' asked the more talkative MP.

'Nothing,' Hawkins replied, still grinning. How could he possibly explain to these two dumb cops that on the Dieppe raid he and Jack had indeed enjoyed a unique association— together? Why should they, or indeed anyone else not per-

---

[1] Army Book No. 64; issued as paybook to every soldier.

sonally involved, believe that his orders had been to protect this Cockney now wearing a cast-off Royal Marine blouse—to the extent that he must kill him rather than allow him to be captured?

They all began to walk across the sunken railway lines. The air was salty with the smell of sea. Ships were still unloading, but fewer ambulances waited, and it was light enough now to see buildings and cranes and a train in the siding. Five o'clock in the morning. Twenty-four hours earlier they had been on the far shore of this same sea, in Pourville, going over the wire above the sea-wall.

An Army car bumped towards them, and they stood to one side to let it pass. The corporals smartly saluted the Canadian major at the wheel, who wound down his door-window to speak to them. His face lit up with surprise and relief as he saw Hawkins.

'Thank God you're back, Roy,' he said warmly. 'I drove right down here to see if there was any news of you—and you're the first guy I meet!'

'I was just going to ring you, sir,' Hawkins replied.

'Hop in the back,' said Major Green, opening a rear door. Then he looked at Jack.

'Who's this?'

'The RDF expert I had to look after, sir.'

'Really?'

John Green now regarded Jack with more interest.

'I'd be grateful if you could help me, sir,' Jack told him. 'These MPs are suspicious because I am wearing Royal Marine flashes, have no paybook, and claim to have been to Dieppe with the Canadians!'

As he spoke, he realized how thin and unlikely his explanation to them must have sounded.

'That's all right, Corporal. I'll take responsibility for him.'

'Very good, sir.'

The MPs saluted, relieved to be shed of this departure from routine, and marched off in step. Jack climbed thankfully into the back of the major's car and they drove to Canadian Field Security headquarters.

When Roy Hawkins and Jack parted company at East Grinstead about an hour later, neither imagined they would not see each other for more than thirty years, when Jack flew to Canada to visit Roy Hawkins at his home in Fort McMurray, Alberta. Neither, in fact, gave the slightest thought to when they might meet again, for at half past six on that August morning, far more pressing matters claimed their immediate attention. First, Roy Hawkins had to collect his motor-cycle from King George V Docks, before someone else removed it. He put his paybook in his pocket in case he was stopped at the dock gates, wrote himself out a rail warrant, and caught the first train to Southampton. He was relieved to see that his BSA was exactly where he had left it. He swung his leg over the saddle, kick-started the engine, and set off back to East Grinstead.

Twenty miles out of Southampton, weariness gradually overcame him. Roy Hawkins nodded briefly—and skidded under an Army truck. He was thrown off, but not hurt, and the only damage was to the motor-cycle's handlebars, which were slightly bent. The truck-driver, more shaken than Roy, helped to pull out his machine from beneath the back axle, and then straightened the handlebars. Hawkins rode on slowly, now fully awake, to East Grinstead. After a bath and a brief sleep, he took the revolver out of his holster to see how much damage the sea-water had done. To his dismay, the blue metal was already raw with rust. The sergeant major saw him examining it.

'Boy! Look at that! Have you got a job cleaning that!' he said sympathetically.

'No,' replied Hawkins, 'not me.'

'Not you?'

'Nope. It isn't my pistol.'

'Then whose goddam pistol is it?'

'Yours.'

The sergeant major swore that this could not possibly be the case; his pistol was hanging up behind his office door, where he had left it. Only after he checked the serial number did he admit that Hawkins was right. Diplomatically, Roy explained why he had borrowed the weapon; even more diplomatically, he cleaned it before returning it. Then he went out to call on his fiancée Rowena to give another diplomatic explanation: why he had thrown away the precious sweater she had knitted for him.

Jack reported to Canadian Army headquarters in a country house outside Reigate. Two Intelligence officers, a captain and a lieutenant, were already busy debriefing survivors from the raid. Jack explained to a sergeant clerk that he had been at Pourville with the South Saskatchewan Regiment on a special mission.

'What about it?' asked the clerk, unimpressed by this hatless, unshaven, scruffy Cockney in a Royal Marine battledress blouse, with filthy, torn trousers and salt-whitened boots.

Would it be possible for Jack to telephone the Air Ministry in London?

The clerk replied that there was a public telephone up the road.

'This is an official call,' Jack told him.

'Yeah? Who to?'

'Air Commodore Tait, the RAF Director of Radar.'

'You a nutter or something?'

'No,' said Jack. 'Why?'

'Then what makes you think this guy will be in his office— if there is such a person and if he has an office—at this hour?'

'What time is it, then?'

'Six fifty-five.'

'It's very important.'

Something in Jack's tone swayed the clerk. He went into the debriefing room, and brought out the lieutenant to see Jack.

'What's all this about?' the officer asked brusquely. 'You in the Marines?'

'No, sir,' said Jack.

'Then why are you wearing a Royal Marines jacket?'

'Someone gave it to me aboard a flak ship on the way back to Newhaven from Dieppe.'

'Where's your AB64?'

'I haven't got one. I'm a flight sergeant in the RAF.'

The officer looked at him suspiciously, hardening his eyes. The Canadians had brought back several German prisoners for interrogation. It was not at all impossible that some other English-speaking Germans had dressed themselves in uniforms from dead soldiers and returned voluntarily as spies. He would treat this cautiously.

'Why are you dressed in Royal Marines battledress with no badge of rank if you are a flight sergeant in the RAF?'

'I had to land at Pourville—Green Beach—with the SSRs as one of them.'

'Why—if you are in the RAF?'

'I can't say, sir. It was a secret job.'

'Can you prove that?'

'Only by phoning the Air Ministry and speaking to Air Commodore Tait.'

'You have his number?'

'I have.'

'He won't be there at this hour, surely?'

'I know this must seem very odd to you, but I give you my word it is genuine,' Jack assured him earnestly. 'Please let me use a telephone, so that I can take a train to London. It is absolutely imperative I report to him.'

The lieutenant regarded him in silence, considering the situation.

'Tell you what I'll do,' he said at last. 'I'll give you a warrant *and* an escort. Now let's have your number, rank and name. I want to make a few checks, meantime.'

Jack and his escort were taken in a fifteen-hundredweight truck to the station, and they caught the next train up to Waterloo. For the first time, sitting in a compartment of civilians, Jack realized from the looks he was getting that he must seem like a scarecrow. He studied himself in the mirror above the seat. The Royal Marine for whom his blouse had originally been intended had been a much bigger, broader man, for it hung around him like a sack. The collar was so loose that Jack could see his blue RAF shirt underneath it.

His hair was matted like a bird's nest; he had no cap, and his cheeks and forehead, his nose and his chin were raw with minute grazes and cuts as though he had been sandblasted. Brick dust and chips thrown up from exploding bombs and shells had scored his face like shot. No wonder the sea-water had stung when he had submerged at Pourville. How long ago was that, anyway? Could it really only be hours? Here in this English train, travelling through Sussex, it might have taken place in another century—if it had ever happened at all.

The soberly dressed civilians in the compartment were avidly reading newsapers with huge headlines about the Dieppe Raid. 'Nine hour raid on Dieppe area; tanks and troops in heavy fighting: eighty-two enemy planes shot down and one hundred probably. RAF lose ninety-five; twenty-one pilots safe', Jack read in *The Times* over the shoulder of a man to his right. Opposite him, a woman sat reading the *Daily Mail*: 'Dieppe Victors come back singing; losses heavy on both sides: objects won; RAF gain major victory: 95/182.'

To them he must appear like a felon or deserter with the silent Canadian companion as his guard. What would they say if he told them that he had just come back from Dieppe? They would be amazed at first, because clearly he hadn't—otherwise how could he possibly be in the compartment with them? They would assume that he suffered from illusions and was probably a bit soft. If not, why was he dressed in what were clearly another man's cast-offs? And if he persisted, and told them about Smokey with his knife, and Frenchie in the orchard, or Charlie Sawden taking-out the pill-box, and Colonel Merritt rallying his men to cross the bridge over the River Scie—they would say he was mad, for these things were beyond the narrow spectrum of their experience, and there-fore, to the suburban English mind, suspect and dubious and to be treated with sceptical reserve. And if he still pushed his luck and gave them details of the unique conditions attached to his mission, then they would know he was mad beyond redemption—and probably prudently change compartments at the next station.

At Waterloo, Jack went downstairs into the underground lavatory and washed his face and hands, and his escort lent him a comb. Then they took the tube to Westminister, and walked along Whitehall, past Richmond Terrace, where only two days earlier he had reported to Combined Operations Headquarters. At the Air Ministry building, Jack gave his name to the sergeant on duty, and he and his companion were shown into the security office. Jack had hoped that the major who had remarked on his being Jewish would be on duty. But three officers he had never seen before were sitting behind the table. A telephone call, and despite his scruffy unshaven appearance, he was being shown upstairs on his own to Air Commodore Tait's office. They shook hands.

'I am very pleased indeed to have you back,' said Tait warmly. 'You were reported first as being captured, then as killed. I knew you could not have been captured, of course, so this report made me very unhappy.'

Tait listened with keen attention as Jack described how he had been forced to abandon the original intention of penetrating the RDF station because it had simply not been possible with the fire power at their disposal. Jack went on to say how and why he had cut the wires—and what he hoped would be learned as a result. Then it was the Air Commodore's turn to explain how monitoring stations along the south coast had intercepted these signals, and how at that moment, their recordings were being analysed. Jack knew instantly that the amount of information the Allies would now learn about German radar would be of the utmost importance.

'Thanks to you and all those Canadians who helped you to get up to the station we have learned a great deal,' Tait told him. 'We have, of course, gained much additional knowledge about the technical equipment the Germans are using. This all has great operational value. Now we know the capabilities of the Freya, and what happens when one Freya is put out of action. This will help us with planning air attacks, and especially when we come to jam German radar systems.

'We know so much more about the Freya now, that we can jam it and cause considerable interference. We'll also be able to use this information on Freya in our plans for future bombing operations and as a result our operational planning will be more efficient. You have also given our monitoring people the chance of a unique insight into the techniques the Germans use in operating the Freya.'

It was now apparent that if Britain could successfully jam or interfere with the operation of their Freya system, the Germans at that time had no alternative system they could bring into use.

If there had been such a secret standby system then, the moment Jack severed the landlines, the Freya operators would have immediately handed over to it. Instead, they had been forced to speak by radio telephone, and so give away details of their set's performance and capabilities.

From the number of their own aircraft involved in the raid, the British could now calculate how long the German operators took to process their plots, and the speed and precision with which the Freya was able to handle all the complicated details cascading into it. From these facts and figures, it was only a short step to assess the station's ultimate performance —and hence the efficiency of all others of similar type.

In due course Britain discovered that the modification— code named EMIL—that had improved the Freya was an electronic split. It was this split system, installed on the German radars by *Waffenwachtmeister* Christian Ganser (chief instructor at the main German radar school at Magdeburg) and his technicians, that had converted the earlier Freya into a precision radar. The secrets of this set that bore the name of a German goddess, whose guardian Heimdal could see for one hundred miles by day or night and in any direction, were secrets no more. The goddess's namesake could now be blinded at will—or, even more cunningly, could be made to see intruders who were not there, and with confidence that no other guardian station could take over the Freya's responsibilities.

Jack knew that it was impossible to set any price on such

knowledge, but in his view these discoveries were of equal value to the Allies as the strategic and logistic lessons that had made imperative such a rehearsal for invasion, which could be learned in no other way.

So it had all been worthwhile, perhaps immeasurably so—but how much more satisfying Jack felt, if only he could tell his Canadian companions what they had all helped to achieve! It might ease the shock and gloom of capture and the pain of wounds to realize that this knowledge could help to shorten the war and change the face of bombing strategy—as well as reducing casualties among bomber crews and future invaders of *Festung Europa*. This other side of the human equation might also give some comfort to widows and fatherless children and grieving parents of young men who would never come home again. Without this breakthrough, the long, tedious, sometimes inaccurate, always dangerous process of piecing together items of information from agents and regular aerial photographs would have been applied to the problems.

Operation Jubilee, the raid on Dieppe, had meant that this continuous process could be bypassed with instant results. But Jack, like everyone else involved with radar, had taken an oath of secrecy; he could speak to no one of these things.

The interview came to an end with an appointment being made for Jack to see Dr Jones, the Director of Air Intelligence, on the following morning around nine o'clock.

He rose to leave.

'Tell me, sir,' he said at the door. 'Did *you* think I'd get away with it?'

Tait smiled faintly. 'I did. That's why I was surprised when you were reported killed. I thought you were the sort of person who *would* be successful. I'd found out a great deal about you from Group, remember. Also, I felt sure the Canadians would look after you. I was very confident about that. I'm Canadian myself.'

They shook hands. Jack went out of the room, and down the stairs. The Canadian escort had disappeared, presumably satisfied at last that Jack was genuine, despite his extraordinary uniform, and Jack walked alone along Whitehall. The sun was shining. From the few shillings that the Canadian lieutenant had advanced him against future pay, he spent one penny on a *Daily Express*, and stood on the pavement, reading the front-page headlines: 'The Great Raid is Over; vital experience gained in nine hours of fighting: Commandos leave Dieppe in flames and RAF shoot up 182.'

That was a good score, Jack thought. And now this would only be a beginning. On the tube out to Ealing Broadway, Jack read the rest of the four-page paper. It contained little but news and comment on the raid. But one advertisement for Sylvan Flakes had a totally unexpected topicality. Jack read with amused astonishment: 'Beach coat from Dieppe . . . Wash it with gentle Sylvan Flakes . . . How could you have known when you bought it that sunny day before the war that such a flippant little coat would be so useful about the house in wartime?'

As he walked from Ealing Broadway Station to his mother's house at 27 Mattock Lane, the sun had never seemed brighter or warmer, nor the familiar shops and cinemas and stalls more welcome and attractive. He was nearly home, but when would the Canadians who had been captured see their homes? And would he ever see them again? He hoped so. And the old Frenchman on the hill near the church. Would he ever be able to thank him for an act of selfless courage that had undoubtedly saved his life?

Jack saw people looking at him in astonishment, thinking he was a tramp, dressed up in army cast-offs. And in a sense, they were right. After all, he wasn't really what he seemed. He was an airman wearing a soldier's uniform; but a soldier without a regiment; a man without a name. The idea amused him and he knocked a cheerful tattoo on his front door. His mother opened it, and stared at him in amazement, hardly recognizing her eldest son.

'Jack!' she gasped. 'What's happened to you?'

Had he been in an accident, or an air-raid? Why this odd uniform, which fitted only where it touched? And his face . . . it was all raw.

Jack handed her the *Daily Express*, and she read the main headline, and then gave it back to him.

'You've been there, Jack?' Nothing Jack did would ever surprise her; indeed, had ever surprised her.

Jack nodded. He felt too tired for any explanations—and, in any case, what could he tell her about his part in the raid? Nothing. Nothing at all.

'I just want to sleep,' he said.

'Your bed's made. Lucky you found me in. Another ten minutes, and I'd have been out at the shops.'

Jack walked upstairs, pulled off his clothes, had a bath and then crawled in between the crisp white sheets in his familiar bed in his familiar room. Within seconds, he was asleep.

All through the day, the waves washed up bodies for a distance of ten miles on either side of Dieppe. The German authorities had left floating corpses for the sea to bring in; their burial parties were already overwhelmed with work collecting dead from beaches, fields, and the streets of towns and villages along the coast. Within four days, the sea had washed up 475 corpses, rather more than half of the 907 Canadians who had been killed.

This figure caused understandable concern in Canada because it was the first time that any Canadian force had suffered casualties on this scale. Of the 4,963 Canadians who had sailed from Southampton to make the raid, nearly half —2,210—were back safely in England on the following day. About 1,840 had been taken prisoner and were released at the end of the war. Some died in captivity and a few others died from their wounds in England.

That about one in five should have died in Jubilee seemed a high percentage, but this had to be viewed in the context of casualties in air-raids, lost convoys, and troop ships; the dead on a dozen other Allied battle fronts, from Russia to the Far East.

Other Allied losses were relatively light. They included 14 British soldiers, and 31 Royal Marines and 75 sailors killed, with a total of 466 either missing or taken prisoner; a number of these died later. The RAF (including Allies) lost 69. The Navy reported 75 killed and 269 missing. Thirteen of the 50 US Rangers were casualties.

During the night of the 19th, a German officer took Dieppe's civil engineer, Monsieur Caseau, round the whole area, so that he could give his expert opinion on the best way of disposing of so many corpses as safely and speedily as possible. It was suggested that a communal grave might be the solution, and an immense trench was dug for this purpose in Janval cemetery. The bodies were taken there in carts and buried as quickly as possible, for August that year was a very warm month.

Later, the German Army Graves Commission decided that this was neither an honourable nor a fitting way to dispose of those who had died in battle. It was therefore agreed to exhume them and bury them in individual graves. An area of ground that the British Army Hospital had acquired outside Dieppe during the 1939–40 campaign for those who died of wounds or from illness, was proposed as a possible cemetery. This is near Vertus Wood, above the Scie Valley, in the commune of Hautot-sur-Mer. Five hundred German soldiers were detailed to exhume the bodies, which were moved to Vertus and placed in separate graves, with military honours.

The dead lie back to back, in the German way, and their headstones march in double rows with strips of lawn between them. Each is engraved with the Maple Leaf of Canada, and, where possible, the number, rank, name and regiment of the young Canadian who lies beneath it. Some graves have no identification beyond the simple inscription, 'A Canadian soldier'. The cemetery is ringed by a beech hedge, with Canadian maples on three sides, and a single row of thorn trees across the fourth. On an impressive stone of remembrance near the grounds are written five words: 'Their name liveth for evermore'.

When Colonel Merritt was an Army Cadet, he had been led to believe that a force which endured casualties of more than 15 per cent should consider itself defeated. But at Dieppe the Canadians had suffered up to 65 per cent casualties—

according to which beach they had attacked—and still the spirit of the survivors was undimmed and their eagerness to return for a second and decisive round in Europe remained unquenched. So who had won and who had lost?

Every man's death diminishes his fellows, but because these young men died, many, many more lived after them. Their sacrifice had exposed serious deficiencies in equipment and tactics that otherwise could have gone undetected until D-Day when it would be too late to know their weaknesses. It showed up the need for totally new types of amphibious vehicles, for differently designed landing craft, even a floating harbour, because the capture of an existing harbour had been shown to be too costly an operation.

Then there was the overwhelming necessity for full scale aerial bombardment before landing and supremacy in fire power from the sea; the development of better radios, the ability to blind the defender's radar system, the need for elaborate deception schemes which would lead the German forces to expect invasion in one area, whereas it would involve another.

The remarkably low casualty rate of the Normandy invasion less than two years later was in part due to the tactical and technical knowledge gained on the beaches around Dieppe. The raiders had fought at most for nine hours in a war lasting six years in all; never before in military history had the Allies learned so much in so short and savage a battle.

German working parties were detailed to clear the beaches almost as soon as firing stopped, and as a result suffered some unexpected casualties. Under a small pack on Pourville beach lay a primed grenade. When a German officer lifted the pack to look inside it, this grenade exploded and killed him. Afterwards, fatigue parties were more cautious. The Germans admitted to losing 600 men during the raid: there was no need for carelessness or folly to increase this total.

The Canadian prisoners were swiftly separated into two groups; Canadians who spoke French, and those who spoke English. The Fusiliers Mont-Royal were then given an issue of Red Cross food parcels in a crude attempt to divide their loyalties. But Major Sarto Marchand, their senior surviving officer, showed that Canadians—French- and English-speaking—were still primarily Canadians, by sharing these unsought gifts with their comrades-in-arms. This endeavour to divide Canadian allegiance failed. So did a later flight by a Luftwaffe plane over Canadian camps in Southern England, when the crew dropped parcels of photographs showing dead and wounded on the beaches and others being marched off to prisoner-of-war camps. Some of these photographs were valued as souvenirs. More were put to the same convenient use that Jack had found in Pourville for the leaflets addressed to the locals.

Jack woke up suddenly, feeling he was late for something—but what? He glanced at his bedside alarm; it was seven thirty in the morning, Friday morning. He had slept for a day and a night. Then he remembered; he had an appointment to see Dr Jones. He would have to rush. He had a quick bath, put on his No. 2 RAF uniform, which he kept in his wardrobe for use on leave, and with the promise to his mother that he would be home as soon as possible, he ran for the tube. He got out at St James's Park Station—across the road from 54 Broadway. A security officer in the entrance hall of the building made him fill out a form with his name and whom he wished to see. Then he was escorted to Dr Jones's office on the fourth floor. The walls were covered with large scale maps, stuck with coloured pins; some items were marked in different coloured crayons on celluloid sheets. Jones shook him warmly by the hand, and offered him a seat. Jack explained the details of the raid, and how finally the Canadians at Pourville had fired at the advancing enemy over pyramids of their own dead in the last desperate rearguard action.

'I understand from Air Commodore Tait that from a radar point of view the whole exercise had value, sir?'

'Indeed,' agreed Dr Jones. 'As a result of what you have done, we have been able to get an accurate idea of the handling capacity of the Freya station in an emergency. We can calculate *exactly* how many planes it can cope with—which makes a great contribution to our concentration tactics. We now know the upper limit of this particular Freya's handling capacity—and as a result we can saturate it.'

There was no doubt whatever now that the Freya was the keystone of the early warning system which alerted German night fighters. The Freya was now proved to have been upgraded and modified into a more sophisticated precision radar. No longer was it a relatively imprecise instrument that had in the past registered plots which could be between ten and twenty miles out under long-range conditions. It was a worthy stable-mate for the very accurate Würzburg and able to co-operate effectively with it in the task of seeking out RAF bombers.

Jack was later able to examine the radar plots that had come to light as a result of what he had done. He discovered that the Allies had also received a complete picture of the operational organization of German defences across Northern France. Before this, the Germans had cleverly concealed many of their inadequacies and weaknesses, for the bulk of their men and equipment—guns, tanks, planes—were in use on the Russian front. Skilful use of radio-telephone systems by Luftwaffe Ground Control had given the Allies a completely false impression of Germany's real air strength in Northern France and the Low Countries. The British monitoring stations had in the past intercepted these messages, but because the Germans used several different call signs for the same fighter squadron they had been able to deceive Allied Intelligence into assuming that their defensive strength must be far greater than it was.

Now all this was changed, for British monitoring stations had heard aircraft being alerted in the Low Countries and as far inland as Germany, to assist over the coast. It was also discovered that German aircraft plotting was extraordinarily accurate, even under the saturation conditions that had prevailed for hours on end during the raid. There was no room for doubt now that the long range early warning supplied by the Freya had given German defenders their great advantage when they intercepted bombers long before they approached their targets.

The problems that German bombers had faced in 1940 and 1941 from the RAF had by the first half of 1942 become the worries of British Bomber Command. But now the answer was clear: jam the German radar stations.

Immediately after the Dieppe raid, electrical jamming equipment, known as Mandrel, was rushed into production. Mandrel generated a constant 'radio noise' interference on Freya sets, producing much the same effect that a car with unsuppressed ignition has on a present-day TV receiver. By November 1942, three months after the raid, Mandrel was ready for action. First, it was used to jam the Freya early warning chain, then Freya stations built inland and employed for aligning narrow-beamed giant Würzburg radars on to their targets. In this way, a corridor 200 miles wide right through the German early warning system was cleared for the devastating RAF raid on Mannheim in that month.

Later, in 1943, Window—the dropping from aircraft of strips of aluminium foil to 'dazzle' enemy radars—was introduced for the mass raid on Hamburg by British and US bombers. So successful were these jamming techniques, which laid the target naked to the bombers, that the raid completely pulverized the city. Three quarters of Hamburg was destroyed —6,200 acres in all. A million people fled from blazing homes into the surrounding countryside, and Göring admitted that if such a raid hit Berlin, then Germany would have to sue for peace.

This was the measure of the jamming weapon that could blind an enemy's radar screens and leave them eyeless and exposed to aerial attack. And what gave Jack some personal satisfaction was that in cutting the land-lines from the radar station at Pourville, he felt he had also reduced some doubts and arguments regarding the feasibility of radar jamming. From then on until the end of the war, Mandrel, Window and other increasingly advanced jamming systems were used with mounting success in Europe and the Middle East and Far East. From Mandrel and Window grew the far more complex modern equipment calculated to deflect long range missiles and confuse the most sophisticated early warning system anywhere in the world.

—EPILOGUE—

Relatively few French civilians had actively helped the Canadians; they wisely followed the advice of the BBC and the leaflets that the troops distributed, specifically instructing them not to become involved. Two days after the raid, Colonel Bartelt, commanding the 571st Infantry Regiment, therefore asked the mayor of Dieppe to visit him in the office of the sub-prefect of police; he had some important news to impart.

The mayor arrived to find that a senior German civilian administrator was also present. He was then informed that because Dieppe had suffered casualties and damage and the citizens had, in the main, not helped the raiders, Hitler had instructed that ten million francs were to be distributed among them as a token of his appreciation. The mayor remained silent.

'Aren't you satisfied?' asked the German civilian sharply.

The mayor replied that the gift would be greatly appreciated, but even more welcome would be the release of 1,000 French prisoners of war whose homes were in Dieppe. Colonel Bartelt supported this unexpected request, and three days later Hitler gave his permission for these French servicemen to be released. The Führer, however, would not free any French POWs who had homes in Berneval or Varengeville, because he felt that local people there had deliberately helped the Canadians and British who landed.

The only qualification necessary for repatriation to Dieppe was that they should claim to have been living there when they were mobilized. The local French police were made responsible for checking addresses, and loyal to their countrymen, they listed every deserted or ruined house, and even holes in the ground in and around Dieppe as addresses from which soldiers had joined up. One modest house appeared to have contained nearly one hundred young men who left it simultaneously to join the French Army.

Hundreds of French prisoners of war who were set free and immediately went to their homes all over France, thus owed their release to the efforts of the Dieppe Police, and not least to *Brigadier Chef* Léon Michot.

Michot had been on duty during the night before the raid, tracing someone wanted for questioning in connection with a theft, and taking food to elderly people who could not fend for themselves. He thus saw the first Canadian prisoners being brought in.

The Canadians took rings from their fingers and watches from their wrists, and even French money from their pockets, to give to civilians in the streets as the Germans marched them off.

Some of the prisoners were marched out of Dieppe, across the flat inland fields that are not unlike parts of the prairies, towards Envermeu, the headquarters of the 302nd Infantry Division, about six miles to the south, along mainly flint roads which were hard on the feet. Canadians who had thrown away their boots in order to swim out to sea, hoping to find a landing craft, were wearing shoes crudely fashioned from rubber Mae West jackets; several marched barefoot. As they approached Envermeu in the heat of that August afternoon, a handful of French people at the roadside watched them pass through the little town under the shadow of the huge church.

One of these spectators was a grocer of forty-five, Paul Robillard, who had just finished his butter-round with his seven-year-old son, Jean-Claude. As the Canadians marched past, still surprisingly cheerful and in step, the boy saw a barefoot prisoner and said to his father: 'Give him *your* shoes, Papa!'

On the impulse, Robillard pulled off his shoes and threw them to the prisoner who, surprised and grateful, put them on. He waved his appreciation, but Robillard was already being manhandled by German soldiers, who marched him to Dieppe for interrogation. He was, of course, in his stockinged feet, and his escort made him walk on the flint road and not on the grass verge.

In Dieppe, Robillard stayed in prison for a week, and during that time none of his family had any idea where he was. Robillard's wife, Yvette, ran a café in Envermeu and the German authorities punished her and her family by putting this out of bounds to German troops for a month. Robillard was released from jail and returned to Envermeu, where he stayed until his death in a motor-cycle accident in 1945.

His family has prospered. They now own the leading supermarket in the town, but still run their original café. Madame Yvette Robillard keeps the sign she was forced to display in her café window: '*Für Wehrmacht verboten*'. She still displays it on occasion when Canadian tourists visit the town. A group of these, including several captured at Dieppe, recently presented her with an ornamental pair of shoes, carved from ivory, to show they still remember her husband's kindness to a stranger on a hot day, long ago when they all were young.

For the rest of that week, policemen and firemen were the only French citizens allowed to use the road behind the radar station. On the afternoon of the raid, one policeman, coming off night duty, cycled over the hill from Dieppe. He passed groups of German soldiers and lorries of reinforcements and carts of dead bodies. He also noticed that the familiar aerial on top of the concrete building was not rotating.

He waited with a group of other Frenchmen, hoping to learn more of the raid, about which they knew little. Several German soldiers were searching the short grass, working methodically, marking off the area they had covered with sharpened sticks.

'Something missing?' one of the policemen asked them conversationally.

'Greetings, Frenchman,' a soldier said affably. 'We're playing hunt the spanner. Why don't you join in?'

'Hunt the spanner?'

'The spanner, the pliers, even hunt the hacksaw. It's orders from above, you know.' The soldier looked knowingly at the policeman. 'Somebody dropped some tools recently. We want to find them.'

'*Eh bien*! Canadian tools, perhaps?'

The soldier shrugged; he did not want to say too much but he liked to appear important, in the know.

'Could be,' he admitted. 'Some of our lads found an RAF toolkit near here; half empty, it was. Our *Kommandant* wants the complete set to play with.'

The policeman nodded sympathetically, not wishing to appear too interested. He looked up towards the station compound and saw several wires trailing in the wind. Perhaps the soldiers were searching for the instrument that had cut those wires? Or had they been broken by a shell or shrapnel?

A group of young soldiers nearby were congratulating each other loudly on their survival, ridiculing the folly of the Canadians, the idiocy of the British. What a mad, ill-planned scheme it had been! They looked forward to the extra rations. A bit of leave would not be unwelcome, either.

The German soldiers went on searching diligently, paying no attention. The policeman cycled back slowly to Dieppe, feeling curiously, almost unreasonably elated. The Allies had perhaps not been such fools; somehow, something important had been achieved on that empty hill, something he believed that involved cut wires from the radio location station. One day, he would learn what it was.

The Germans had no prior warning of Jubilee; Canadian and British security had not been breached. On August 24, Major-General Konrad Haase, commanding the German 302nd Infantry Division, submitted a report to General Kuntzen, his corps commander:

Hq. 24th August, 1942

Department: Ic 713/42g. (I)
Subject: Monthly report for August 1942
Ref: Order No. 66/42g. I.c XXXIInd Army Corps (2)
Enclosures: I
Addressee: The officer commanding LXXXIst Army Corps.

1. *The state of mind and behaviour of the population in the divisional sector:*

The civilian population in the divisional sector manifested complete indifference at the scene of the British raid of August 19th, 1942. The great victories won by our troops in the east and in North Africa combined with our successes at sea — the annihilation of a convoy in the Western Mediterranean— dealt a fatal blow to the pretensions expressed by the British propaganda, that a Second Front was shortly to be opened. Except in a few isolated circles no one believed in the establishment of this Second Front in the West. They hoped for an attack at harvest time, as a prelude to an invasion. In certain places there was a rumour that the British would arrive on the night of the 20th/21st August, 1942.

Operation *Jubilee* carried out by the British on the 19th August, 1942, on Dieppe and the adjacent fortified positions of Berneval, Puys, Pourville and Quiberville is the sole topic of conversation among the French civil population. On the actual scenes of the combat the population was given complete liberty. There have been no records of sabotage. It has, however, been reported that the population did not disguise its satisfaction at the rapid conclusion of the conflict. Many people displayed some bitterness in noting that the British had carefully spared their own troops, at the expense of non-British forces.

It has been learnt in certain cases that the French were specially well-disposed to the German soldiers engaged in the battle, thus an ambulance reported to be French, carrying two French nuns immediately went to the aid of German wounded soldiers and drove them to the main first aid post. They were at pains to give first aid to the German soldiers. A few of the French, despite the enemy fire, gave information about the enemy. In the fighting sectors, the troops in the line received refreshments and cigarettes from the inhabitants. One unit reports that reinforcements en route were offered bicycles and motor cycles to reach their destination more rapidly. The Dieppe fire brigade, despite the cannon and machine-gun fire from aircraft, unremittingly fought the fires.

The outcome of the combat — the crushing defeat of the enemy — has filled the German troops with confidence and considerably reinforced our defences. During the day of the battle and during the following days the civil population did not conceal its admiration by its behaviour and by its friendly gestures. The anglophile section of the population, although the prospects of a British attack in force are evidently finished, and despite all outward reservations, has expressed its satisfaction at this event. The sympathizers assembled in small groups to await the liberators.

The German victory has been accepted unwillingly by these implacable anglophiles. They insist that if the British had not been restrained by their anxiety (!) to spare the civilian population and the town of Dieppe, the latter would rapidly have fallen into their hands.

The purely peasant section of the population remained quiet and absolutely indifferent, solely preoccupied with getting in the harvest. The only emotion shown was at places where their wains were requisitioned.

Three civilians, two men and a woman, were arrested at Envermeu, for openly expressing their sympathy for the British prisoners and for giving them presents and shoes. At Saint-Nicolas the bodies of two British fighter pilots, shot down at dawn of 18th August, were covered with flowers. By this behaviour and by the distribution of clothing, refreshments and provisions to the prisoners at the assembly camp of Saint-Nicolas, these civilians wanted to express their sympathy for the British. It needed energetic action on the part of the guards to control the civilians who flooded the camp to stop these manifestations.

After the battle, the civilian population helped to pick up and bury the fallen British, after having been invited to do so by the military authorities.

In two places, French peasants brought in carrier pigeons which had been dropped in cages by parachute. These passenger pigeons carried questionnaires apparently designed to be filled in by civilians before the birds were released. The division has been ordered by the competent authorities to reward these civilians. It is also reported that at Varengeville, near the battery, some civilians revealed the presence of a British soldier carrying a special apparatus. The *Feldgendarmerie* is checking this information.

2. *Relations with the Military Administration:* No difficulties.

3. *Relations with the French services of all kinds:* Further complaints that the system of ration cards for the workers is

far too cumbersome and causes hardships. (Cf. report Ic of the 27.4.42.)

4. *Absence without leave:* I.

5. *Cases of suicide:* (a) Attempts, nil.
   (b) Successful, nil.

Item from War Diary of South Saskatchewan Regiment:

18 Aug 42	Warning order came through for Exercise FORD I.
19 Aug 42	At Zero 0450 hrs SSaskR landed in France on raid.
20 Aug 42	First men reported back from raid on France at 0015 hrs. Muster parade at 1130 hrs.
21 Aug 42	Maj-Gen J. H. Roberts gave talk to unit on scheme FORD I, commenting on the good work carried out by the boys in the unit and told the new boys that they must buckle down and be ready for action in a short time. Coys fixing up kits of men missing and in hospital. Lt-Col. H. T. Kempton arrived as OC. SSR orchestra played for dance in Pulborough village hall.
23 Aug 42	Church parade at St Mary's Church, Pulborough. Memorial Funeral Service at Brookwood for 2 Cdn Div soldiers who died from wounds sustained while on active operations in France.

Dieppe has strong links with Canada that stretch back through the centuries. Samuel de Champlain first sailed from Normandy to Canada in 1603, and founded Quebec on his third visit five years afterwards, also becoming Canada's first French governor. A few years later, in 1639, Augustine nuns from Dieppe founded the Hotel Dieu Hospital in Quebec which still flourishes. Indeed, in 1910, when there was a shortage of nurses in Dieppe Hospital, Canadian nuns of this Order came to Dieppe to volunteer their services.

Such historical associations have been greatly strengthened since 1942. Every year, in August, the ancient port from which in 1066 the Normans had sailed to invade England, puts out flags and flowers to welcome contingents of Canadians who return to the beaches where they—or their fathers, their grandfathers, their brothers, husbands or sons—fought, and where hundreds of young Canadians honoured friendship to France with their blood.

Dieppe has been considerably redeveloped since 1942, for it suffered heavily in the bombardment, despite the fact that no preliminary bombing was carried out, but Pourville seems surprisingly unchanged. The same green wooden breakwaters rise from the shingle. The promenade still stands on top of the sea-wall, and old concrete gun emplacements still crouch menacingly on the cliff-tops, peering out to sea.

The casino has not been rebuilt, and grass grows where the building stood in which Jack and his colleagues discussed their dash across the beach to the sea. Behind the site of the casino, and closer to the cliffs, the Hans Andersen-style chalet which housed the casino generators, still stands with its red dormer roof, three small windows, two chimney pots and criss-cross imitation Tudor beams intact.

After the raid, the Germans requisitioned the Hôtel de la Terrasse. There was some discussion about destroying it, and also the church, because they had given cover to many soldiers and clearly could do so again. A local German commander, who had been a pastor in Germany before the war, heard of the proposal to demolish the church and prevailed against those who wished to do so. Thus, although the building was slightly damaged by a shell later in the war, it still stands and is filled for worship every Sunday.

Emile Sadé is dead, but his son, Michel, who was in Paris with his wife on the night of August 18/19, 1942, now keeps the keys of the church, and runs the hotel.

Part of the hotel was destroyed by the Germans to give a clearer area for defensive fire; and this has had the effect of also providing a far better view of the sea for Monsieur Sadé's summer guests. Shortly after the war, Monsieur Sadé and three friends made a wooden memorial to the Second Canadian Division. This they fixed to the wall facing the site of the casino. It has a blue background and a large 'C' with the Roman numeral 'II' and 'Canada' carved underneath. Later, an impressive granite memorial was set up on the flat land between the main street in Pourville and the beach, which specifically commemorates the landing of the South Saskatchewan Regiment.

The big houses set on the hillside above the road to Petit-Appeville remain beautiful, their lawns are well barbered, the hedges neatly manicured. Apples still grow in the orchard across the road, and geese loyally guard little farmhouses.

At the crossroads at Petit-Appeville a plaque is fixed on the wall of the *pâtisserie*: an outline of laurels and a steel helmet and the words: *'Ici carrefour des Canadiens en mémoire du 19 août 1942'*, for these pretty villages have their own memories of that August day.

The past indeed proves impossible to forget, even if anyone wished to do so, which the French in and around Dieppe emphatically do not.

Within weeks, the RDF station was further strengthened, and more earth piled up against the concrete walls of the blockhouse. Another, even more powerful radar installation was later constructed further inland on the edge of the golf course, with a heavily armoured underground operations room; but the secrets of the Würzburg and Freya were already known, and no amount of extra concrete laced with iron mesh could conceal them now. In the spring of 1944, before D-Day, the Freya 28 at Pourville was heavily bombed as part of a plan to destroy some German stations and leave others untouched so that they could be fed with false data.

This part of the French coast suffers from constant erosion, and slowly the cliff has been eaten away, until the concrete radar building was precariously suspended by wires and metal sinews at the edge. In the spring of 1974, after continuing falls of chalk, the whole building crashed down to the beach two or three hundred feet beneath. So well had the impressed workers of the Todt Organization carried out their task of construction that, although the concrete floor was cracked and split from the red brick concrete covered building, the three rooms that the station contained are intact. Their peeling, whitewashed walls are still scored with horizontal marks from the planks into which the liquid concrete had been poured. A rusting metal chimney points up at the sky, and six-inch nails on which the duty crew would hang steel helmets and greatcoats, sprout from one wall. On another, are the remains of the notice board where Hitler's congratulations were pinned after Dieppe, and beneath them two lines from Field-Marshal von Rundstedt's report which vindicated Willi Weber's faith in the equipment that had warned of the approaching ships, although the German Navy had refused to believe it: 'It is clear that a special unit of the Air Force correctly identified the approaching enemy ships in time'.

After the raid, when the copy of the Jubilee plan was found at Dieppe and it was discovered that a British radar specialist had been ordered to examine the Freya 28, prisoners and locals were interrogated, but none could throw any light on to who this had been or what had happened to him. Although Jack Nissen's bag was discovered and a report made to the *Feldgendarmerie* that a soldier had been carrying what locals called 'special apparatus' and a search was made for anything else the bag might contain, the importance of this discovery was not related to the fact that the wires had been cut and the radar station forced to use radio-telephone.

It was tacitly assumed that the breaks in the lines were due to the effect of bombardment, and there was indeed no reason why the repair squads should report otherwise. On that day enough shrapnel to sever a thousand cables had blasted Freya 28.

Two years to the day after Weber's arrival in Dieppe—on April 1, 1943—he was posted to the Eastern Front, where he commanded the group charged with radar coverage of Hitler's headquarters.

In 1944, he was promoted to command the radar unit which helped to ward off the British airborne landing at Arnhem.

'I knew about the operation of the British radar team at Dieppe,' he admitted later, 'though I was not aware of the particularly difficult conditions under which they had to work. It was therefore a considerable achievement on their part to have monitored our radar reports . . .'

Weber still visits Dieppe whenever he passes through northern France, and frequently eats in a little restaurant, La

Potinière Christophe, which takes its name from the patron, Christophe Larrite, whose wife is in charge of the kitchen.

The two men had first met during the war, and on a recent visit Larrite introduced Weber to another client, a Canadian. They got on extremely well. Only afterwards did Christophe Larrite explain to Willi Weber that the Canadian had also taken part in the Dieppe raid. 'What a difference if they had met *then*!' says the patron, shaking his head. Fittingly, the restaurant is in the Rue du 19 Août 1942.

The old gun emplacements that surrounded the radar station still stand on the cliff-top. On some of their inside walls, yellowed, faded pin-up pictures still survive. In several of the smaller, more waterproof emplacements, tramps sleep rough.

Outside, the concrete has mellowed with the sun and rain of more than three decades; lichen stains it yellow as spilled mustard. All around the area lie defence obstacles: lengths of railway line, strips of rusting barbed wire and weapon pits linked by trenches with concrete walls. The gorse grows thigh-high now, and the grass and the thistles and nettles wave gently in the wind that carries the laughter of children playing on the summer beaches far beneath. The children chase each other in an out of the doorway of the fallen radar building, and call to their parents through the narrow windows of what is possibly the most impressive memorial to courage and ingenuity on any beach.

Frenchmen cycle down the lane behind the houses where Jack ran so desperately for reinforcements, carrying nothing more lethal than long crusty loaves under their arms. Old man, perhaps old soldiers, too, stroll slowly in the sun near the church, showing a lot of watch chain. And when the tide is out young families enjoy their picnics beneath the break-water that sheltered Jack and Roy Hawkins a generation before they were born.

On the evening of the raid, Paul Brunet walked through the littered streets of Dieppe near the beach. Wounded were being helped or carried away for treatment.

As he stood, regarding the devastation of the day, two men came past him carrying an injured Canadian soldier on a stretcher. They walked under the eyes of an old German soldier of Brunet's generation. The man at the head of the stretcher incongruously wore what Brunet recalls were civilian clothes, and claimed to be an American doctor. Brunet walked a few steps with them. The injured man turned to him and said in French: 'There are thousands of us in Canada. The Canadians will come back.'

This prophecy was proved true two years later when the Second Canadian Division returned to Dieppe and liberated the city. Nowadays, too, few Canadian veterans return to Dieppe for the anniversary of the raid without calling on Paul Brunet in his splendid flower shop in the Rue de la Barre. They are as pleased to shake him by the hand as he is to meet them.

Some Canadians had remarkable escapes from death in 1942, and they do not forget them easily. One was Edward Mather, the younger brother of Major Jack Mather, whose broken leg had prevented him from taking part in the raid. Major Mather was helping to document the wounded as they reached hospital, when a soldier was carried past him on a stretcher, completely covered by a grey army blanket. Thinking that he must have died on the voyage, Mather pulled away the blanket from his face, and to his surprise saw his young brother Ted. He was not dead; the blanket had somehow been thrown over his face by mistake.

Half an hour later, Frank, the third brother, and 'B' Company's sergeant major, came to see Jack Mather. His face was grey and his eyes sunk deep in his head with weariness.

'How shall we tell mother?' he began.

'Tell her what?' Jack asked him.

'About Ted. He was killed as we both tried to get away from the beach. I saw him fall.'

He went on to explain that Ted had been hit when they were actually in the sea. He had dragged him back to the beach, but could not feel any heartbeat and so had most reluctantly left him on the shingle.

'He's not dead,' Jack assured him. 'I've just seen him. He's in the ward next door.'

Murray Osten, as a POW, became chief keeper of the illicit distillery in his prison camp, and was said by his colleagues to operate it efficiently. After the war, he met his old quartermaster-sergeant and reminded him of the bottle of rum he had given him aboard the *Princess Beatrix*. His debt was honoured. The former CQMS gave him a new bottle immediately. Murray Osten still keeps it—unopened.

Later, Osten studied at the University of British Columbia. One day, a professor, lecturing on the Napoleonic Wars, mentioned how scientists at that time had passed freely between England and France, and contrasted this civilized behaviour with an incident that had occurred during the 1939–45 war. He explained that a British scientist had crossed the Channel on a raid, and not only did he face danger of death from the Germans, but he knew so much that his guard had orders to shoot him if he was in any danger of being taken prisoner.

After the lecture, Osten approached the professor.

'I was the officer who was given those orders,' he said, to the other man's astonishment.

Osten was married by then, but he had not told his wife anything about his assignment until the professor's remarks unlocked his memory. Years later, he told Jack: 'I think the part I was asked to play was so repulsive to me that for twenty years afterwards I put it completely out of my mind, and forced myself to forget about it. I used to think sometimes, when I was a prisoner, "I wonder whether I had ever received these particular orders or whether it was all a figment of my imagination!"'

'*Would* you have shot me?' Jack asked him.

'Yes. Probably I would have.'

Les Thrussell returned to England convinced that Jack was dead—just as Jack was sure that Thrussell had been killed.

Thrussell was in fact awarded the Military Medal for gallantry at Pourville, and later received a bar to this decoration. On his return to Canada after the war he took an administrative job in a vast modern hospital complex concerned with the care of 700 retarded and mentally ill patients in Saskatchewan. His wife works there, too, and they have bought a fine house in a quiet street in Moose Jaw.

At weekends and holidays, Les Thrussell packs his guns into the back of his car and goes off to a small house he has in the country, for shooting remains his greatest interest, and the years have not dimmed his eye or diminished his aim.

Colonel Cecil Merritt had been a prisoner of war for some months when he was informed that he had been awarded the Victoria Cross, the supreme decoration for gallantry in British and Commonwealth services, in recognition of his inspiring leadership at Pourville.

Another officer, Captain Brian McCool, of Toronto, had just received from his wife in Canada a sample of a new chair cover she had made for their chesterfield. This resembled the colour of the VC ribbon, so the POWs made up a special ribbon and held their own investiture. When Merritt was released after nearly three years as a prisoner of war, he paid a visit to his regiment, then in Holland, before returning to Canada. An officer drove to meet him in a Jeep. He was delighted to see Leslie England, by then a major and recovered from his wounds. Back in Vancouver, Cecil Merritt returned to the practice of law; he became a Queen's Counsel, and is one of the most highly regarded advocates on the Canadian West Coast.

When Merritt was told later of the importance of Jack Nissen's mission, he was surprised at the lack of information he had been given about it.

'I didn't want them to tell me all about him,' he said. 'I am not suggesting they should have done that. But they did not give me any impression that the radar station was a primary objective of mine. My primary objective was to form a beach-head. If they had told me that one of my primary jobs was to get Jack into a position where he could find something out, then I would have made a plan for him. Maybe wiser heads than mine understand these things better. But if I had been told that this was of vital importance—they didn't even have to say radar—then I would have focused my eyes on him!'

Les England took a law degree at the University of British Columbia after the war, then returned to the Army. He served in Germany as Judge Advocate, then worked in Federal Government, then became a lawyer with the Privy Council in Canada. He is also married, and is the father of a very talented family.

Sergeant Blackwell, who had been wounded in the left arm and the right ankle at Dieppe, and who was evacuated in the landing craft that brought him ashore, remained in hospital for a long time. He was then posted as a signals instructor, and later attached to the Canadian Legion on Welfare duties, where his cheerfulness and his irrepressible good spirits were much appreciated.

Blackwell returned home to be demobilized in Regina, where he had enlisted. During his years overseas, his wife had joined her family in Vancouver, and when Blacky arrived at Regina, a blizzard was blowing and the prairie looked bleak and cold.

As Blacky tells it, his wife's first words to him were not, 'Hullo, dear,' but, 'I won't stay here.' She persuaded her husband to return with her to Vancouver. On arrival, Blacky went to the employment bureau and was offered a temporary job working at a local Army camp. It was expected that he would stay there for no more than a couple of months.

'When you've finished that job, you come right back here, and I'll give you another one,' the woman clerk assured him. But Blacky held that job for twenty years. When he retired, he returned to the employment bureau and saw the same woman clerk.

'Well, here I am,' he said.

'What do you mean, here I am?' she retorted, not recognizing him.

'You told me to come back here when I wanted another job,' Blacky explained. She asked him to wait while she checked his file, and when she returned, they both enjoyed the joke.

Now Amaranth Anthony James Blackwell, DCM, lives in retirement with his wife and her mother in a house on the outskirts of Vancouver. He is still bright-eyed and wears a haircut of military style; a warm-hearted old soldier whose cheerfulness and courage will never die.

When CSM Dunkerley was in hospital in England recovering from his wounds after the Dieppe raid, he wrote his own account of the operation. Being proud of the way in which the South Saskatchewan Regiment had conducted themselves in action, and wanting others to know about it, he sent this patriotic report to his local paper, the *Regina Leader Post*. His letter was, of course, intercepted by the censors and Ed Dunkerley was surprised to be threatened with a court martial for attempting to disclose uncensored and unauthorized military information to a newspaper. Dunkerley replied with spirit that if they wished to court martial him on this ludicrous charge, then they should get on with it. After some to-ing and fro-ing, the authorities decided not to accept this invitation, and the matter was quietly dropped.

Dunkerley's wounds were so severe that it was a year before he returned to Canada. When he left the Army, he decided to move west to British Columbia, and he bought as many acres as he could afford. Farmland was then relatively cheap, but the value has since increased dramatically, and the Dunkerleys are wealthy enough to enjoy trips to Europe and Australia —in considerably greater comfort than the trip across the Channel that Ed Dunkerley made in the *Princess Beatrix* on an August night in 1942.

Major John Green's hopes for Roy Hawkins' promotion were justified; he was commissioned. Rowena Henry accepted Roy's explanation for discarding her sweater, and they were married in 1943, and she returned with him to Canada. Life in Fort McMurray, one of the original Hudson Bay trading posts for trappers, on the banks of the Athabasca River, was totally unlike anything she had anticipated in Epsom, Surrey.

Fort McMurray is ringed by hundreds of miles of forest, and although now prosperity and expansion—because of an oil pipeline—have made it a busy, bustling place, in the mid-1940s it was still very quiet and a strange and total contrast to an English suburb. But she grew to appreciate the quietness and the kindness of Canadians, and the Hawkins had two sons and a daughter. Roy Hawkins became Supervisor of Operations at Fort McMurray Airport, and he is also the local Fire Chief, two positions that carry great responsibility.

Roy Hawkins is still as calm as when he followed Jack out from the casino along the beach and the breakwater to the sea. He is that rare person; a man at peace with himself, who has found lasting satisfaction in a life of genuine service to his community.

After the war, Captain George Buchanan stayed on in the Occupation Forces as CO of the Highland Light Infantry, and then returned to his pre-war career in fire protection, first as a fire fighter and a fire chief, then to the federal field as a Fire Protection Officer, specializing in fire equipment for Department of Transport airports across Canada.

From this he progressed to the office of Dominion Fire Commissioner working in the general field of technical fire protection.

He is married, with a nineteen-year-old son. His main interests have always been in sports and kindred activities of young people. He retired at the end of 1974, and like Roy Hawkins has given many years to the service of his fellow-men.

Of the fifty US Rangers who had sailed for Dieppe, some never even landed because their landing craft broke down, and so they were reluctantly forced to turn back to England.

Three of the US Rangers earned distinction of different kinds on the raid. In order of their seniority, Colonel Loren B. Hilsinger was the last man to be injured in the raid. He had gone on it as an official American observer at this first European landing of the war in which his countrymen would take part. With him was General Truscott, who had originally suggested forming the Rangers on the pattern of British Commandos.

Hilsinger was standing on the deck of *HMS Berkeley* heading home for England, when a low-flying Dornier unexpectedly jettisoned a bomb to gain more height to escape pursuing RAF planes. The bomb exploded near Hilsinger and blew off one of his feet. With great presence of mind, he ripped off his tie and bound this round his leg as a tourniquet.

Before Colonel Hilsinger had embarked, he had put on for the first time a new pair of boots, specially made for him in London. Now, from the heaving, blood-spattered deck of the stricken ship, he saw one of these boots, with his foot still inside it, floating alongside. With an involuntary action of rage and disgust, the colonel pulled off his other boot and threw it into the sea after the first.

Another officer, Lieutenant Edwin Loustalot, had the melancholy distinction of being the first American soldier to be killed by the Germans. And Corporal Frank Koons from Swea City, Iowa, became the first American soldier in the Second World War to kill a German in Europe, and also the first to win a British award—the Military Medal—for bravery in action. Captain Roy Mason, who had commanded the detachment, served on in the United States Army; he rose to command the battalion when it was stationed in West Berlin many years after the war.

For the priceless work that Dr Reginald Jones carried out analysing enemy advances in radar and other branches of science and neutralizing them, culminating in his discovery of the German plans for pilotless planes and rocket bombs, as well as for his earlier work in 'bending' the directional beams along which German bombers flew, Winston Churchill recommended that he should be made a Companion of the Bath. Churchill wrote enthusiastically of his 'magnificent prescience and comprehension, by which in 1940 he did far more to save us from disaster than many who are glittering with trinkets'.[1]

Sir Horace Wilson, the head of the Civil Service, and the *éminence grise* of Chamberlain during his appeasement days, opposed this proposal. His grounds were that Jones was still only technically a scientific officer at that time, a lowly Civil Service grade, and no one on that level could possibly have done work of such importance to merit a CB. The compromise of a CBE—Commander of the British Empire—was therefore reached, and Dr Jones had to wait until after the war before he became a CB.

Since the war, Reginald Jones, now Professor of Natural Philosophy at Aberdeen University, has reorganized Scientific Intelligence and is still consulted by Whitehall on specific Intelligence matters involving science.

He is a man of wide enthusiasms—which include a considerable knowledge of bagpipe music—and his interest in science remains as constant as ever. So does his regard for those who served with him during the war. After the raid, Jack Nissenthall sent a typescript of his account of his mission to Professor Jones, who wrote a foreword for it, in which he praised Jack as 'a man who willingly went into the "hard, savage clash" of Dieppe, spurred by patriotism and an enthusiasm for electronics, and knowing that if things went wrong —which they did—he had a peculiarly slim chance of returning . . . His own deeds speak for themselves . . . I only wish that I had such a tale as his to tell . . .'

One device Professor Jones has designed for his students at Aberdeen is a gravimeter, which measures changes in gravity so infinitesimal that they can be caused by the ebb and flow of the sea around the coast. The colossal debt owed by everyone in the British Isles to Professor Jones is far easier to assess.

* * *

[1] *The Second World War* by Winston S. Churchill.

In 1943, Lord Louis Mountbatten became Supreme Allied Commander, South-East Asia. Here he faced possibly his greatest challenge of the war—and achieved his greatest success. First, he had to overcome immense problems of strategy and logistics, involving vast distances and primitive conditions; then he had to raise the morale of the 14th Army, which, until his arrival, had bitterly claimed to be Britain's Forgotten Army.

Under his catalystic leadership, retreat was turned into attack, defeat into victory; and in 1945, in Singapore, Lord Mountbatten accepted the surrender of the Japanese forces.

On his return to England, he was appointed Viceroy of India, the last in a long line. Such was the esteem with which he was regarded, that when India became independent in August 1947 the new Indian Government paid him the honour of inviting him to stay on as their country's first governor general.

A few years later, when he had returned to his naval career, Lord Mountbatten received a further unique distinction. In addition to being British Commander-in-Chief in the Mediterranean, he was also appointed the first Commander-in-Chief of all Allied Forces, Mediterranean. He went on to become the British First Sea Lord, Chief of the UK Defence Staff, and Chairman of the Chiefs of Staff Committee—which he had first joined shortly before Dieppe.

With his unparalleled experience in devising the successful raids on St Nazaire, on Bruneval and half a dozen other vitally important targets before Dieppe, Lord Mountbatten in 1942 knew better than anyone else in high command how imperative it was to mount a large tri-service operation like Jubilee before the real Second Front was attempted. And he has always argued strongly and cogently that the battle of Normandy was won on the shingle beaches of Dieppe.

'It is impossible to over-estimate the value of the Dieppe Raid,' he has written. 'It was the turning point in the technique of invasion . . . For every one man who died at Dieppe in 1942, at least twelve or more must have been spared in Normandy in 1944.'

Lord Mountbatten appreciated the importance of the Freya as one of Jubilee's sixteen targets, but he had no idea of the incredible conditions which Jack Nissenthall willingly accepted when he agreed to try and learn its secrets. When I showed Lord Mountbatten the manuscript of this book, he commented: 'If I had been aware of the orders given to the escort to shoot him rather than let him be captured, I would immediately have cancelled them.'

While Lord Mountbatten had been responsible for the top level planning of Dieppe, and had approved the proposal to extract all possible information about the Freya, the detailed arrangements for this operation were left to the Army commander and the Air Force commander, while the Air Ministry produced the radar expert. Lord Mountbatten had therefore no idea—and there was no reason why he should—that Nissenthall was also to attempt to enter the radar station. Because the defences around all German radar stations had been heavily increased after Bruneval, this would have seemed to him an impossible task—as indeed it proved.

'It was my impression that he was going to cut the land line wires so as to force the station to go on the air, which worked well,' Lord Mountbatten recalled. 'I am horrified to learn that a man was chosen who knew about the cavity magnetron, and put in a position where he might have been tortured to the point of giving away this secret, and so it was arranged for ten men to shoot him so he would not be captured.'

What concerned Lord Mountbatten particularly was the fact that while Combined Operations maintained an organization for the purpose of providing former German Jews enlisted in the Commandos, and selected for particularly hazardous assignments with completely false identities, even to letters, backgrounds and relations, no use whatever was made of these sophisticated facilities on Jack Nisenthall's behalf. He could easily have been given a complete Canadian identity, but this was never requested.

'It is true,' Lord Mountbatten went on, 'that I have sent men off on tasks when I knew most would be killed. I remember ten Commandos from the Brigade of Guards who volunteered for a most dangerous attack on a vital hydroelectric plant at Glomfjord. I saw them all together, and I said: "You are Commandos. In theory, you've volunteered to go anywhere. In practice, you're now going to be sent on a mission where, in my own considered opinion, not more than two of you are likely to come out alive, and those will be interned in Sweden.

"Anybody can walk out now if they wish and there will be no hard feelings." But not a man withdrew. They all went. And eight of them were killed and two did reach Sweden.

'But never at any time have I heard of sending people out with instructions to kill one of their own men. Another failure of the machine below me was that nobody told me afterwards that Nissenthall had returned safely. If I had been told, he would most certainly have been decorated on the spot. To get him to do what he did and give him nothing is churlish.'

The German Field-Marshal von Rundstedt remained as Commander-in-Chief West until 1944, but suffered increasing irritation from Hitler's irrational refusal to accept his recommendations for defending France against invasion—while still holding him responsible for results. Hitler preferred the strategic advice of Erwin Rommel, with whom von Rundstedt came into running conflict.

In July 1944, Hitler informed von Rundstedt that he was going to replace him by Field-Marshal von Kluge, and the old field-marshal returned to his home in Bavaria. Within three months, events had forced Hitler to reinstate him, but by then there was little that Rundstedt—or any other German leader—could do in the face of overwhelming Allied military and air superiority.

Von Rundstedt was taken prisoner and brought to England where he stayed for three years. During this time, his only son, a Doctor of Philosophy who had joined his father's staff shortly after Dieppe, fell seriously ill. The field-marshal was grateful to the authorities, who largely at the instigation of Field-Marshal Montgomery, arranged for them to spend Christmas together shortly before he died. When von Rundstedt's former chief of staff wrote a memoir about him, he prefaced the book with words of Frederick the Great that appeared singularly apt in connection with the field-marshal's career: 'Military leaders are more to be pitied than is imagined. Without hearing them, the whole world sits in judgement upon them, the newspapers refer to them slightingly, and, of the thousands that condemn them, probably not one understands the leadership of even the smallest unit.'

Until 1943, General Hamilton Roberts had the distinction of being the only senior Allied military leader who had actually led a major sea-borne assault against occupied Europe. But this unique knowledge was not put to any further active use. Roberts was instead posted as commander of a camp in England occupied with training Canadian recruits and new reinforcements. When he retired in 1945, to live in Jersey in the Channel Islands, he still held the same rank of Major-General that had been his when he commanded the men of *Jubilee.* For five years from 1945, General Roberts was Chief Administrative Officer, Imperial War Graves Commission, North-West Europe. The words of Frederick the Great might also apply to him.

In 1943, Air Commodore Victor Tait was made a Companion of the Bath, and he was knighted in the following year, when he played a leading part in measures that rendered German radar largely ineffective during D-Day and the resulting campaign. After the war, Sir Victor became operations director of BOAC, chairman of International Aeradio Ltd., of Ultra Electronics, and the British Air Transport Electronic Council. For ten years from 1959, he was also director of the Flight Safety Foundation of America. Now retired, he lives quietly in Chelsea with his wife.

* * *

After the war, Colonel Douglas Catto, who returned to his practice as an architect in Toronto, renewed contact with the German Captain Schnösenberg and they were friends until the death of the Canadian colonel. The memory of their first meeting on top of the cliffs on the August morning is still vivid in Schnösenberg's mind.

'I think,' he says now, 'that this may have been one of the last chivalrous encounters of the war.'

According to Sir Stafford Cripps, when he was President of the Board of Trade in 1945, radar contributed more than any other scientific factor to victory over Germany. Marshal of the RAF Lord Tedder, a post-war Chief of the Air Staff, also subscribed to this view—and had even suggested that a statue should be erected to Robert Watson-Watt on the cliffs of Dover, such was the magnitude of the debt owned by his country to him. In 1949, the Treasury, which had asked that a Royal Commission on Awards to Inventors should look into the histories of people who had played an onerous and distinguished part in the prosecution of the war without thought or expectation of a pecuniary award, took a different view. They found that they could not agree that the invention of radar came into this category.

Sir Robert—who was knighted in 1942—and his colleagues, did not seek money, but only some official recognition of the value of their work. The fact that not one radar scientist had been invited to take any part in the Victory Parade in London in 1946 had deeply offended them. Sir Robert therefore decided to fight the Treasury's attitude, a battle that lasted for eighteen months, in which he spoke a third of a million words throughout the forty-four days during which he gave evidence before the Royal Commission.

The Crown had spent an estimated £100,000,000 developing radar. The Allies had, in addition, poured out between three and four times that amount on equipment and installations, and Sir Robert calculated that he and all the other nine claimants had probably only cost the country a *total* of around £6,500 in salary for each year of their work. Finally, after much argument, they were awarded £87,950 to divide between them. They had not sought money, but recognition; they received an insulting sum and grudging acknowledgement.

As a result, the team that had started at Bawdsey and ended at Malvern dispersed across the world. Australia, Canada, and the USA gained immeasurably through the short-sightedness and parsimony of the first post-war British Government and their creatures at the Treasury who were quite unable to comprehend what these brilliant men had accomplished.

In the 1950s, a curious legal footnote was written to the story of Jack's mission. Quentin Reynolds, the American journalist whose BBC broadcasts when America was still neutral had done so much to raise British morale, had been aboard *HMS Calpe* during the Dieppe raid. He had learned of Jack's involvement, but, of course, not knowing his name, he had given him a nickname, 'Professor Wendell'. In 1955, another American journalist, Westbrook Pegler, who wrote a column syndicated in 186 newspapers, branded Reynolds as a liar, a braggart, and a cowardly absentee war correspondent. Not surprisingly, Reynolds sued him.

The case dragged on inconclusively until Pegler's counsel asked about Professor Wendell. He demanded that Reynolds should admit that 'the story of the mad scientist who went on the Dieppe raid was a quirk of your mind, a falsification of your own vivid imagination ...

'If there was such a man, give the Court his name. If you can't give the name, admit that it was a story that you read in *Superman* Comics, *Space Cadet*, or *Mr Batman* . . . What person in his normal senses would invade enemy occupied territory with his body lined up in the sights of his friends behind, and the Germans before him, both with their fingers on their triggers? I demand that you now give the name of the man or admit here and now that you are a liar.'[1]

[1] *My Life in Court* by Louis Nizer (Heinemann).

Quentin Reynolds was confounded, for he did not know Jack's real name. Yet if he could not discover it, he could lose the whole case on this one point. A former member of Lord Mountbatten's staff, Colonel Jock Laurence, happened to be in New York, and he read a report of this case in a newspaper, and he willingly testified as to what Jack had done. Pegler's counsel demanded that he give Jack's name in open court. Laurence refused, although he knew it, because Combined Operations had never released the name. Instead, he wrote it down and handed it to the judge. As a result, Reynolds won his case and $175,000 punitive damage against Pegler and the newspapers that employed him. Jack read of this case and wrote to Quentin Reynolds, saying that if he had heard of this before, he would have flown to New York immediately to speak up for a man whose work he so much admired.

Quentin Reynolds wrote back to Jack: 'Even though you were several thousand miles away from the court room you did help me a great deal. . . .'

Jack was offered a commission in the RAF after Dieppe, but he declined it. A commission then would have meant accepting more administrative responsibilities and less technical ones, and this was unattractive to him. In 1943, he was posted to the Middle East in charge of the new radar installation protecting the Suez Canal. He returned home, and at the end of the war married Dell and was again offered a commission, this time a permanent one in the RAF. On the understanding that he could still be involved almost exclusively with radar, he accepted and went to the RAF College at Cranwell.

The memories of the mammoth Allied air-raids on Germany were still very clear, and while at Cranwell a senior officer suggested to him that should any German who had lost relatives or friends in these raids ever discover the identity of the man who had discovered the secrets of the Freya and so helped to bring nearer the jamming of German radar, he might possibly suffer personal hostility or other repercussions. It might thus be advisable for him to change his name—at least until time had softened the bitterness arising from these mass air-raids. So from the original German, Nüssenthall, which had in England become Nissenthall, Jack now shortened his surname to Nissen. He left Cranwell in 1946 without taking a commission, and instead joined the South African Air Force in a technical capacity. After serving for some years, advising on radar installations, equipment and techniques, he resigned from the service but stayed on in South Africa where he built up a considerable electronics business. His company introduced and built hi-fi sets, and then he started the first school for TV engineers in the Republic. This has prospered, and now he also owns and edits a TV and electronics magazine.

In August 1967, Jack was on holiday in Greece, when he read a newspaper report that Canadians who had landed at Dieppe in 1942 were gathering there for their 25th reunion. On the impulse, eager to discover how many of his former comrades would be present, he flew to Dieppe, arriving in time for a special commemorative service in the church at Pourville, outside which he and his comrades had sheltered a quarter of a century earlier.

Former soldiers of the South Saskatchewan Regiment were forming up in the street between the church and the Hôtel de la Terrasse. As he joined this column, Cecil Merritt recognized him; so did 'Hank' Forness and Murray Osten. Someone else already standing in line, medals glittering as they had glittered on the breast of that unknown French ex-soldier in 1942, shouted; 'My God, there's Jack! *There's the guy I should have killed!'*

Jack turned and shook hands with Les Thrussell. Both were astonished and delighted to find the other man alive. So were others in the regiment, who had assumed that Jack had been killed at Pourville, for there had been no contact between them during the intervening years. The Canadian Government later invited Jack to Ottawa where he met other former members of the South Saskatchewan Regiment.

Many who had served in the regiment had been decorated, either for what they had done on that August day, or for subsequent acts of valour later in the war. Cecil Merritt had the VC; Claude Orme, the DSO; Murray Osten, the MC; George Buchanan and Roger Strumm, the MBE. The former adjutant and the former RSM had also been awarded the French Croix de Guerre with silver star, as had 'Hank' Forness. Les Thrussell had been awarded the MM.

Jack considers his real reward came in Dieppe, on the evening of that 25th anniversary of a raid that cost so many lives, but which paradoxically also spared so many more lives. He was sitting in a café with three men who had been awarded the Victoria Cross for their courage during the raid, and some other friends. On one side of him sat Cecil Merritt. Across the table were Major Pat Porteous of the Commandos, and Major John Foote, the Presbyterian Chaplain of the Royal Hamilton Light Infantry, who had stayed behind voluntarily at Dieppe, feeling that his place was with the prisoners and not in a boat returning to England. The hour was late and the café was officially closed to any new customers.

'Now tell us, Jack, *why* couldn't you be captured? What *could* you have known so secret that you had to agree to be killed rather than taken prisoner?' he asked.

Jack put his hand into his pocket and brought out a circular piece of metal, painted black, and small enough to fit into his palm. Around the rim of the circle, four ridges had been cut to form cooling fins, and there was a hole bored in the middle, surrounded by eight smaller ones, all linked by narrow passages to the centre cavity.

'Here's why,' Jack said quietly. 'This is the cavity magnetron, the most valuable ally we had. This made possible radar sets of unbelievable accuracy. If the Germans had discovered this secret then the war could have been lost. When we gave this gadget to the Americans before they came in on our side, they admitted that it was the most valuable cargo that had *ever* been brought to their shores. And I knew all about it, and had been working with it. *That's* why I had to agree to be killed rather than captured.'

Before anyone could speak, the party was disturbed by a

loud banging on the front door. The proprietor reluctantly opened the door, and several young Canadian soldiers who were serving with NATO marched into the restaurant.

'Sorry, *messieurs*,' the proprietor told them. 'We're closed.'

'We don't want a meal,' the newcomers assured him. 'We have just heard that Jack Nissen is here. We want to shake him by the hand.'

'There I was,' recalled Jack afterwards, 'sitting with three holders of the Victoria Cross, and these young chaps wanted to shake *me* by the hand!'

Jack was astonished and moved to tears by this spontaneous tribute.

'*This* was my reward and the highlight of my life,' he says simply. And he means it.

FROM THE WRITER TO THE READER

The task of describing an event that happened more than thirty years ago presents the writer with totally different problems from recounting an incident that occurred, say, a century ago, or even last year.

If the action took place a hundred years ago, then all the participants are dead, and the writer relies wholly on written material, which may or may not be accurate, but which cannot be queried by survivors. If the events occurred last year, then written accounts are augmented by the sharp, clear recollections of people who were personally involved.

When it came to reconstructing some of the events of an August day in 1942, I discovered a mass of written evidence, and also was fortunate in being given great help by men who had been personally involved. But because so many years have passed since 1942, their recollections were sometimes slightly contradictory, for obviously what one man may remember clearly as being important, may not even be recalled by his companion. (Anyone wishing proof of this need only study the contradictory reports by witnesses of a motor accident!)

My debt is greatest to Jack Nissen, who wrote his own detailed account of his assignment at Pourville shortly after the raid. Where other later recollections have differed from his, I have therefore followed his narrative.

The Directorate of History of the Canadian Forces Headquarters in Ottawa kindly made available to me the War Diary of the South Saskatchewan Regiment, along with a number of personal reports written by soldiers in that regiment, on their return to England after the raid. Mr Edward

Dunkerley and Captain H. P. Forness have also generously allowed me to draw on their own accounts of events.

Lieutenant-Colonel G. B. Buchanan, MBE, whose regimental history, *The March of the Prairie Men*, has also proved extremely valuable, kindly lent to me other reports by soldiers of the South Saskatchewan Regiment, which brought the total of these accounts, written within hours of the events they described, up to 136. When subsequent interviews with some of these former soldiers differed from these earlier accounts, I have tended to disregard these differences.

Jack Nissen and I would also like to thank all who have so patiently helped us in our enquiries, which were conducted in Canada, in Scotland, in England, in Germany and in France.

Mrs Dorothy Bardock
Mr John Barratt
Mr A. J. Blackwell, DCM
Col. K. H. Böttger
Dr E. G. Bowen, CBE, FAA, DSc
Mr W. L. Brown
Monsieur Paul Brunet
Lt-Col. G. B. Buchanan, MBE
Mr David Burnett
Dr W. A. S. Butement, CBE
Mr Howard Cady
Mr Philip A. C. Chaplin, CD, BA, BLS, Senior Research Officer, Directorate of History, National Defence Headquarters, Ottawa
Mrs Jeannine Clapson
Monsieur and Madame Jacques Colle
Mrs Kathryn Court
Mrs Ruby Cox
Monsieur Marius David, President POW Associates, Dieppe
Mr W. A. B. Douglas, CD, PhD, Director, Directorate of History, National Defence Headquarters, Ottawa
Monsieur Charles Dubost
Monsieur Jacques Dubost
Frau Ursula Dülberg

Mr and Mrs E. A. Dunkerley
Mr Eric Emperingham
Lt-Col. Leslie England, CD
Mr Laurie Fellows
Capt. F. P. Forness, CD
Herr Christian Ganser
Mr Roland Gant
Mr John Gartshore, MC, Department of Veterans Affairs, Toronto
Mr Brian Gill
Monsieur Roger Guerville
Maj. Bob Hainault, MC
Maj. W. Hanke, Embassy Federal Republic of Germany, London
Mr E. B. Haslam, MA, FR Hist. S, Ministry of Defence, London
Mr Roy Hawkins
Mr Stan Hodge
Mr Richard Hough
Mr Lawrence Hughes
Mr Douglas Johnson, ED
Professor R. V. Jones, CB, CBE, FRS
Monsieur Pierre Jullien, Director of the Syndicat Initiative, Dieppe
Mr Fred Kerner
Mr. Kenneth Morgan King
Mr Bob Kohaly, QC, BA, LLB
Monsieur and Madame Christophe Larrite
Madame Elizabeth Lelong
The librarians at Amesbury, Wilton and Salisbury Public Libraries and the London Library
Mr George Mahon, B Com
Mr Lorne Manchester, Royal Canadian Legion: Editor, *The Legionary*
Maj.-Gen. C. Churchill Mann, CBE, DSO, CD
Mr Philip Mann
Col. Jack Mather, CD
Madame Germaine Maubert

Col. Cecil Merritt, VC, ED, OC
Herr Fritz Mezger
Monsieur Léon Michot
Brig.-Gen. L. C. Morrison, CD, Department of National Defence, Ottawa
Admiral of the Fleet, the Earl Mountbatten of Burma, KG, GCB, OM, PC, GCSI, GCIE, GCVO, DSO
Monsieur and Madame Valère Muyssen
Mr Ralph (Red) Neil
Mr Harold Nissenthall
Mr. John Northfield, Department of Veterans Affairs, Vancouver
Maj. Claude Orme, DSO
Capt. Murray Osten, MC
Mr Charles Pick
Monsieur Robert Poulhe
Mr D. H. Preist
Mr Denis Richards
Madame Yvette Robillard
Mr George Ronald
Monsieur Michel Sadé
Mrs Joan St George Saunders
Herr Richard Schnösenberg
Mrs Gladys Scott, Royal Canadian Legion
Capt. Marsha Scott, Department of National Defence, Ottawa
Mr Norman Shannon, Royal Canadian Legion
Mr Saul (Sandy) Shusterman
Mr Jeoffrey Spence
Mr Roger H. Strumm, MBE
Mr George Sylvester
Air V-M Sir Victor Hubert Tait, KBE, OBE, CB
Mr Les Thrussell, MM
Mr Percy Towgood
Mr Walt Tyler, Department of Veterans Affairs, Vancouver
Mr Gordon S. Way, CD, Director of Public Relations, Department of Veterans Affairs, Ottawa

Colonel Willi Weber
Mrs Jean Whitburn
Mr Gordon Wood
Mr Howard Wylie, Department of Veterans Affairs, Regina

I would like to acknowledge my indebtedness to the following books:

Abautret, René *Dieppe: Le sacrifice des Canadiens 19 août 1942* (Paris: R. Laffont, 1969)

Barker, Ralph *Aviator Extraordinary* (The Sidney Cotton Story as told to Ralph Barker) (London: Chatto & Windus, 1969)

Blore, Lieutenant-Commander Trevor, RNVR *Commissioned Bargees* (The Story of the Landing Craft) (London: Hutchinson, 1946)

Blumentritt, Guenther *Von Rundstedt, the Soldier and the Man* (London: Odhams Press, 1952)

Bonin, von *Wir waren dabei. Der Invasionversuch von Dieppe* in *Die Wehrmacht*, Vol. 3, 1942

Bryant, Sir Arthur *The Turn of the Tide, 1939–1943* (London: Collins, 1957)

Buchanan, G. B. *The March of the Prairie Men.* A History of the South Saskatchewan Regiment (The Regiment, 1957)

Buchner, Alex *Dieppe, das erste Invasionsunternehmen* in *Deutsche Soldatenzeitung*, November 8, 1957

Buckley, Christopher *Norway, the Commandos, Dieppe* (London: HMSO, 1951)

Canada, Parliament *Debates of the House of Commons*, 7 Geo VI, 1943, passim (Ottawa: King's Printer, 1943)

The Canadians at War 1939–1945 in *Reader's Digest* (Canada) Vol. 1 and 2, 1969

Churchill, Sir Winston *The Second World War* (6 vols) (London: Cassell, 1948–54)

Clark, Ronald W. *Tizard* (London: Methuen, 1968)

Clark, Ronald W. *The Rise of the Boffins* (London: Phoenix House, 1962)

Durnford-Slater, John *Commando* (London: William Kimber, 1953)

Fergusson, Bernard *The Watery Maze* (London: Collins, 1961)

Harris, Marshal of the RAF, Sir Arthur, GCB, OBE, AFC *Bomber Offensive* (London: Collins, 1947)

Harrison, Gordon A. *Cross-Channel Attack* (Washington: War Department. 1951)

Hartcup, Guy *The Challenge of War: Scientific and Engineering Contributions to World War Two* (Newton Abbot: David & Charles, 1970)

Higgins, Trumbull *Winston Churchill and the Second Front* (London: Oxford University Press, 1958)

History of the Combined Operations Organization, 1940–45

Hoffmann, Karl Otto *Das Unternehmen Jubilee.* Unpublished documents of the Luftnachrichtengruppe Munster, Westphalia

Hughes-Hallett, J. *The Dieppe Raid.* Supplement of the *London Gazette*, nr 380–45, August 14, 1947

Hughes-Hallett, J. *The Mounting of Raids* in *Journal of the United Service Institution*, November 1950

Iremonger, Lucille *The Ghosts of Versailles* (London: Faber & Faber, 1957)

Kennedy, General Sir John, ACMB, KCVO, KBE, CB, ML *The Business of War* (London: Hutchinson 1957)

Mann, C. Churchill *Dieppe was Necessary* in *The Beaver* Vol. 2, No. 19, August 25, 1967 (reprinted from *The Canadian Legionary*)

Mordal, Jacques *Les Canadiens à Dieppe* (Paris: Presses de la Cité, 1962; London: as *Dieppe. The Dawn of Decision*, Souvenir Press, 1963)

Nizer, Louis *My Life in Court* (London: Heinemann, 1962)

Price, Alfred *Instruments of Darkness* (London: William Kimber, 1967)

Reyburn, Wallace *Rehearsal for Invasion* (London: Harrap, 1943; Toronto: as *Glorious Chapter. The Canadians at Dieppe*, Oxford University Press, 1943)

Reynolds, Quentin *By Quentin Reynolds* (London: Heinemann, 1964)

Robertson, Terence *Dieppe, The Shame and the Glory* (London: Hutchinson, 1963)

Roskill, Capt. S. W. *The War at Sea*, Vol. 2 (London: HMSO, 1956)

Rowe, A. P. *One Story of Radar* (Cambridge: Cambridge University Press, 1948)

Saunders, Hilary St George *The Green Beret* (London: Michael Joseph, 1949)

Scott, Peter *The Battle of the Narrow Seas* (London: *Country Life*, 1945)

Shapiro, L. S. B. *Dieppe as the Enemy Saw It* in *Maclean's Magazine*

Shirer, William L. *The Rise and Fall of the Third Reich* (London: Secker & Warburg, 1960)

Smith, Waldo E. L. *Realism and War: Dieppe*, Chapter 3 of *What Time the Tempest, An Army Chaplain's Story* (Toronto: Ryerson, 1953)

Snyder, Louis L. *The War* (New York, Julian Messner, 1960; Dell, 1964)

Stacey, C. P. *Dieppe, 19 August 1942* in *Canadian Geographical Journal* Vol. 27, No. 2 August 1943, pp. 47–63

Stacey, Colonel C. P., OC, OBE, CD, BA, AM, PhD, LLD, D.LITT, FRSC *Six Years of War*. Official Story of the Canadian Army in the Second World War. Vol. 1 (Ottawa: Queen's Printer, 1955)

Taylor, A. J. P. *Beaverbrook* (London: Hamish Hamilton, 1972)

Thompson, R. W. *Dieppe at Dawn* (London: Hutchinson, 1956)

The Tools of War 1939–1945 in *Reader's Digest*, 1969

Trevor-Roper, H. R. *Hitler's War Directives, 1939–1945* (London: Sidgwick & Jackson, 1964)

War Cabinet *Report by Joint Intelligence Sub-Committee* (Bombing Policy 1942)

Watson-Watt, Sir Robert *Three Steps to Victory* (London: Odhams Press, 1957)

Whaley, Barton *Strategem: Deception and Surprise in War*
(Center for International Studies, Massachusetts Institute
of Technology)

I would also like to thank Earl Mountbatten for kindly letting
me make use of his speeches to Dieppe veterans in Canada
and for much other help; the Directorate of History,
Canadian Forces Headquarters, Ottawa, for making available
to me the German Intelligence reports on the Dieppe landing
and Field-Marshal von Rundstedt's personal report as
Commander-in-Chief, West, and other documents; and the
Public Records Office, London, for access to relevant British
War Cabinet papers.

When Jack Nissen and I first arrived in Ottawa, we went to
see Gordon S. Way, the Chief Public Relations Officer of the
Department for Veterans Affairs—a most efficient Canadian
Ministry that exists simply to safeguard the interests of all
who have served Canada in the Armed Forces.

We explained to Mr Way that we sought his assistance in
tracing some former members of the South Saskatchewan
Regiment who had landed at Pourville on August 19, 1942.
Mr Way replied that he had received a number of requests
for help from other writers who had reconstructed the story
of the Dieppe raid over the years, and he personally wondered
what new material could now be found after all this time.

'There is only one thing *I* would like to know about that
campaign,' he went on. 'A British scientist landed with the
Canadians under orders that he must be shot rather than
captured. Now, that would make an interesting story. I have
always wondered what happened to him.'

Some days later, we were in Regina, Saskatchewan, roughly
1,400 miles west of Ottawa, to meet SSR veterans, and Jack
and I hailed a taxi to take us to our first appointment. As we
climbed into the cab, the driver heard our accents and
asked whether we were English. We said we were, and he
gave us his name—Eric Emperingham—and explained that
he had landed with the South Saskatchewan Regiment at
Pourville.

'You know one thing?' he went on. 'There was an English guy there, too, a radar expert. Now some of our people were going to shoot him if there was any risk of him falling into German hands. I have often thought about that. I wonder what happened to him?'

To Gordon Way and Eric Emperingham—and all those others in Canada who have also asked us that question, for Jack's strange mission is something of a legend there—this book is your answer.